# Asperger Syndrome

## Strategies for Solving the Social Puzzle

- Oral and Written Communication
- Perceptions
- Executive Functions
- Nonverbal Communication
- Friendships
- Social Skills
- Perspective Taking

by Nancy J. Kaufman, PhD and Vicki Lord Larson, PhD

Thinking Publications® University
A Division of Super Duper® Inc.
Greenville, South Carolina

11   10   09   08   07   06   05                    8   7   6   5   4   3   2   1

*Library of Congress Cataloging-in-Publication Data*

Kaufman, Nancy J., date
     Asperger syndrome: strategies for solving the social puzzle/Nancy Kaufman, Vicki Lord Larson.
        p. cm.
     Includes bibliographical references and index.
     ISBN 1-932054-38-3 (pbk.)
        1. Asperger's syndrome. 2. Asperger's syndrome—Social aspects. 3. Asperger's syndrome—Patients—Education. I. Larson, Vicki Lord.  II. Title.

RJ506.A9K39 2005
362.196'858832—dc22

                                                              2005048594

*Printed in the United States of America*

*Cover redesign by Sharon Webber*

Thinking
Publications®
University
A Division of Super Duper® Inc.

Post Office Box 24997, Greenville, SC, 29616 USA
1-800-277-8737  •  Fax 1-800-978-7379
www.superduperinc.com
Email: custserv@superduperinc.com

To James R. Larson
Man of Integrity, Humanitarian,
Courageous Hero, and Loyal Supporter

and

To Nancy Lee McKinley
Friend and Colleague

# Contents

# Tables

# Preface

"What is Asperger Syndrome?" Education professionals, parents, students, medical personnel, and others are asking that question more and more these days. You might hear comments describing characteristics of Asperger Syndrome like these:

- I have a student in class that puzzles me.
- I have a nephew who has been "diagnosed."
- I have a grown son who is a financial whiz, but he cannot get a job because he has poor social skills.

So what is Asperger Syndrome (AS) all about? We have written this book to address this question and others like it:

- What are the characteristics of AS?
- Why does this intelligent student have no friends?
- What can I do about the student in my class who cannot stop talking about washing machines?
- What is the school's responsibility for meeting the needs of this child?
- How can I remediate language pragmatics?
- How can I teach this student with AS how to monitor his own behavior?

This text is geared toward teachers, speech-language pathologists, and other education personnel who want to know how to best teach students with AS and how to work with their parents. It has also been written for parents who want to know how to best help their child.

AS has only been on our "radar screen" since the mid-90s. We in the education profession are suddenly finding that we have students in our schools who meet the definition of AS, but we may be unsure about how to reach them. We certainly do not want to try, make a mistake, and make the situation "worse." So how can we make it better?

There are books available about AS—some are scholarly and research-based, while others are based on anecdotal experience. We performed an extensive review of the existing literature, seeking the best and most recent scholarly works and the best practices from education personnel. We then organized and have presented these findings in a practical arrangement of 7 chapters, 16 appendices (presented in a printable format on the CD-ROM), and a quick-reference glossary to help professionals easily locate the AS information they are seeking.

- Chapter 1 presents a basic overview of AS including history, definitions, prevalence statistics, and characteristic expectations and challenges associated with AS. Readers may wish to skip Chapter 1 if they feel knowledgeable about this basic information.

- Chapter 2 highlights assessment considerations using both formal/standardized tests and informal procedures.

- Chapter 3 reviews the general intervention strategies, clarifies a strategy approach to intervention, provides a continuum of service delivery models, presents issues in transition planning, and notes legal and public policy issues.

- Chapter 4 provides a discussion of what and how to intervene in areas such as friendship, social skills, oral communication, nonverbal communication, and perspective-taking.

- Chapter 5 provides intervention strategies for areas such as executive functions, reading, writing, and classroom routines and schedules.

- Chapter 6 contains information highlighting sensory and motor strategies.

- Chapter 7 presents behavior management strategies, that apply across social and academic areas, to increase or decrease behaviors.

All appendices are reproducible for your professional use (e.g., a case history form, an AS checklist, a learning style questionnaire, and a direct/dynamic assessment protocol). To save you a trip to the photocopier, all reproducibles in the book may be printed from the accompanying CD-ROM, which presents each item in a portable document format (PDF). PDFs can be printed with Adobe Acrobat Reader® 5.0 or higher, which can be downloaded for FREE at *www.adobe.com* if you don't already have it.

Although our backgrounds are different, they are related in ways that helped us pull the social intervention puzzle together. Vicki has expertise in speech-language pathology. She has co-authored six books about how best to assess and teach students with language disorders. She has been a public school speech-language pathologist as well as a university professor, teaching graduate and undergraduate students to become future speech-language pathologists. Nancy's expertise lies in special education—namely in the areas of emotional/behavioral disorders (E/BD) and learning disabilities (LD). She has taught students with disabilities in residential treatment centers and public schools, and has also taught university students who are future teachers of students with E/BD or LD. We both worked with students who had AS before we ever knew what AS was. We encountered such students in speech-language sessions; in classes for students with E/BD, LD, and cognitive disabilities (CD); and in general classrooms. Additionally, as university administrators, we each worked with faculty who were highly intelligent, but had severe social disabilities, and probably would have been diagnosed in today's world as having AS. Nancy currently substitute teaches in special education, at public schools where she frequently encounters students with AS and meets teachers who want to know more about AS.

Although our book addresses the history, assessment, and characteristics of AS, the main focus is on intervention. Entire chapters are devoted to intervention: in social competence (Chapter 4), in academics (Chapter 5), for sensory and motor disabilities (Chapter 6), and for behavior management (Chapter 7). We present a wide range of example strategies for teaching students with AS, and six of the seven chapters end with case studies of real students who have AS. (Their names have been changed to protect their identities.) Each case study is followed by analysis, sample individualized education program (IEP) goals, example interventions, and discussion points.

We have love in our hearts for students with AS. We want them to have the best possible education. We want them to have pleasurable and productive lives. We want them to have the same advantages as students who do not have AS. We hope this text is helpful to practitioners who work with students who have AS, as well as to university professors who instruct future teachers and speech-language pathologists.

There are a number of individuals who helped us throughout the process of writing this book about Asperger Syndrome and to whom we owe a debt of gratitude. A special thank you to the late Nancy McKinley, who contributed her knowledge, wisdom, and time in the initial stages. She was an inspiration to us and her help was invaluable. We have been very fortunate to have Linda Schreiber, who had the vision for this book, step in and guide us and our book through the final stages. She has been a tremendous asset to us. Other editors at Thinking Publications, including Sarah Thurs, Marietta Plummer, and Shannon Paulus, have offered their time and valuable suggestions. Four professionals in the field—Madge Bishop, Meg Farrington, Dan Mixer, and Barbara Pladziewicz—spent countless hours reading the manuscript and offering their suggestions based on their work with students who have AS and their professional experiences. The book is better because of them. We would also like to acknowledge the help of Sue Fellerer. In the very early stages of writing the book, she helped us gather materials about Asperger Syndrome.

Of course, we couldn't have done this at all if it weren't for the students with AS whom we have taught and observed, and their parents who shared their experiences, their laughter, and their tears with us. Thanks to all of you. We hope this book will help the students and educators who work with them now or will be working with them in the future as much as you have all helped us.

# An Overview of Asperger Syndrome

## Chapter 1

## Goals

- To provide a brief history of Asperger Syndrome
- To consider definitions of Asperger Syndrome as it relates to Pervasive Developmental Disorders, Autism Spectrum Disorders, and autism
- To present prevalence statistics
- To discuss possible causes of Asperger Syndrome
- To describe characteristic expectations of students with typical development and challenges for students with Asperger Syndrome

Asperger Syndrome (AS), a high-functioning form of autism, is currently one of the fastest growing disabilities in the United States, reaching epidemic proportions with projected continued rapid growth. The high rate of autism is estimated to cost the U.S. economy $90 billion annually for such expenses as loss of human resources and cost of intervention; it is projected to rise to a cost of $200 to $400 billion annually within 10 years. These incredible costs have brought more attention to autism, and specifically to AS.

The purpose of this book is to provide parents, professionals, and students with practical strategies for "solving the social puzzle," a task the student with AS often finds confusing and overwhelming. This first chapter provides a foundation for the chapters that follow by providing an historical perspective of AS, definitions of AS from several perspectives, and information regarding its relationship to pervasive developmental disorders (PDD) and autism spectrum disorders (ASD). Prevalence statistics are noted, particularly the rapid rise in autism and Asperger

Syndrome. Possible causes of AS are noted and hypothesized. A detailed overview of social and academic characteristics is presented in terms of expectations of students with typical development and the related challenges confronted by people with AS. Subsequent chapters focus on assessment methods and intervention strategies.

# History

A literature review (Attwood, 2001; Cumine, Leach, & Stevenson, 2001; Schopler, Mesibov, & Kunce, 1998; Tsai, 2002) revealed that Asperger Syndrome has been a recognized diagnostic category in the United States since 1994. Table 1.1 briefly highlights the major historical markers in the development of the term *Asperger Syndrome*.

**Table 1.1**      **History of the Definition of "Asperger Syndrome"**

| Researcher | Date | Contribution |
|---|---|---|
| Asperger | 1944 | First to describe the syndrome as "autistic psychopathy," emphasizing eight characteristics of students with AS. |
| Wing | 1981 | Suggested it be called "Asperger Syndrome," a mild variant of autism in which the main clinical features are lack of empathy; Naivete; inappropriate or one-sided interactions; little or no ability to form friendships; pedantic, repetitive speech; poor nonverbal communication; intense absorption in certain subjects; clumsy and ill-coordinated movements. |
| Tantam | 1988 | Purposed to use the term Asperger Syndrome to refer to people without delayed or deviant cognitive and language developments, but who have severely impaired social understanding and reciprocity, pragmatic difficulties, and unusual circumscribed interests. |
| Gillberg and Gillberg<br><br>Gillberg | 1989<br><br>1991 | Noted AS as having six diagnostic criteria: social impairment, narrow interest, repetitive routines, speech and language peculiarities, nonverbal communication problems, and motor clumsiness. |
| WHO-ICD–10, *DSM–IV–TR* | 1993<br>2000 | Adopted the definition highlighted by Tantam in 1988. WHO-ICD–10 and *DSM–IV–TR* (2000) note that AS is one of the distinct subtypes of Pervasive Developmental Disorders. |
| Attwood | 2002 | Emphasized that the WHO-ICD–10 and *DSM–IV–TR* (2000) definitions fail to consider that the person with Asperger Syndrome has a problem with the pragmatic elements of language. |

*Sources*: Attwood (2001, 2002); Schopler, Mesibov, & Kunce (1998); Tsai (2002)

In 1943, Leo Kanner, in Boston, MA, described the behaviors of people who totally withdrew from the social world, and who later became known as autistic (Kanner, 1943). In 1944, Hans Asperger, in Vienna, described a set of behaviors he called "autistic psychopathies," which later became known as Asperger Syndrome. Independently of one another, Kanner and Asperger were each concerned about people that did not seem to relate well to others and were unable to fit into the typical social world, though those whom they described were different in terms of severity and overall defining characteristics. Both Kanner and Asperger contributed enormously to our understanding of those who are socially challenged and thus have provided educators with insight on how to help those with autism and/or Asperger Syndrome function more appropriately in the social world (or at least better than if left to their own devices).

Asperger noted that the group of boys he was studying had difficulty fitting in socially, made their parents' lives miserable, and drove their teachers' to despair. To Hans Asperger, these students were failing to assimilate the automatic routines of everyday life (e.g., motor skills, academic skills, and social conventions). Asperger (1944; as cited in Wing, 1998) emphasized the following eight points as characteristic of students with AS:

1. Socially odd, naive, and inappropriately emotionally detached from others

2. Markedly egocentric and highly sensitive to others' criticism, but simultaneously oblivious to other's feelings

3. Extremely good grammar and vocabularies with fluent speech, but often literal and pedantic and engaging in monologues but not in dialogues or reciprocal conversations

4. Remarkably poor nonverbal communication and vocal intonation

5. Intensely interested in specific or personal subjects

6. Although borderline to having a gifted IQ, and possibly producing original ideas and exceptional skills connected with their special interests, have difficulty with conventional schoolwork

7. Poorly coordinated

8. Conspicuously lacking in common sense

These are usually lifelong traits, but as adults, individuals may be able to achieve success by finding a niche with their special interests and talents (Wing, 1998). In fact, Ozonoff, Dawson, and McPartland (2002) noted tremendous variability in people with AS as they get older, most likely due to different interests, world experiences, and knowledge. Some individuals with AS go on to college and have highly successful careers, while others do not graduate from high school, live with their families for life, and are underemployed or unemployed.

## Asperger Syndrome

Asperger's 1944 paper was written in German. As a result, his findings reached only a limited readership. It wasn't until Wing's (1981) English translation of Asperger's 1944 paper during her own research that the set of behaviors described by Hans Asperger achieved a wider readership in the United States. It was Wing who first suggested the term *Asperger Syndrome* and presented a set of behaviors that described a milder form of autism:

- Lack of empathy
- Naivete
- Inappropriate or one-sided interactions
- Little or no ability to form friendships
- Pedantic, repetitive speech
- Poor nonverbal communication
- Intense absorption in certain subjects
- Clumsy and ill-coordinated movements

In 1988, Tantam extended the concept of Asperger Syndrome into adolescence and adulthood, also noting that such individuals do not have delayed or deviant language but are severely socially impaired. Gillberg and Gillberg (1989) and Gillberg (1991) later presented a list of characteristics, delineated in Table 1.2, that included the following:

- Social impairment
- Narrow interest
- Repetitive routines
- Speech and language peculiarities
- Nonverbal communication problems
- Motor clumsiness

However, the American Psychiatric Association, in the *Diagnostic and Statistical Manual of Mental Disorders* (4th edition, Text Revision; *DSM–IV–TR;* 2000) and the World Health Organization in *The ICD–10 Classification of Mental and Behavioural Disorders* (WHO, 1993) adopted definitions based on the description presented by Tantam, thus deleting the notion of a language delay or deviancy as a problem. Attwood (2002) questioned this omission. He maintained that although language structure or form may be intact, the person's pragmatic ability (i.e., the ability to use language across and within a variety of social situations) is problematic.

These historical and chronological data provide a perspective on the evolving definition and defining characteristics of Asperger Syndrome. These data highlight why, even today, controversy exists around the defining characteristics of AS.

Controversy also exists as to the causes of Asperger Syndrome. A wide array of causes have been hypothesized in AS literature (Gillberg & Ehlers, 1998), resulting in additional confusion. It is not clear what causes AS, but there appears to be a general consensus that the condition is

## Gillberg and Gillberg's (1989)
Table 1.2      ## Diagnostic Criteria of Asperger Syndrome

### Social Impairment (extreme egocentricity; at least two of the following)

- Inability to interact with peers
- Lack of desire to interact with peers
- Lack of appreciation of social cues
- Socially and emotionally inappropriate behavior

### Narrow Interest (at least one of the following)

- Exclusion of other activities
- Repetitive adherence
- More rote than meaning

### Repetitive Routines (at least one of the following)

- On self, in aspects of life
- On others

### Speech and Language Peculiarities (at least three of the following)

- Delayed development
- Superficially perfect expressive language
- Formal pedantic language
- Odd prosody, peculiar voice characteristics
- Impairment of comprehension including misinterpretations of literal/implied meanings

### Nonverbal Communication Problems (at least one of the following)

- Limited use of gestures
- Clumsy/gauche body language
- Limited facial expression
- Inappropriate expression
- Peculiar, stiff gaze

### Motor Clumsiness

- Poor performance on neurodevelopmental examination

From *Asperger's Syndrome or High Functioning Autism?* (p. 82), by G. Gillberg and S. Ehlers, 1998, New York: Plenum Press. © 1998 by Plenum Press. Reprinted with permission.

caused by a brain dysfunction or variation, thus a neurological or neurobiological disorder. Many times, frontal lobe dysfunction is noted in neuropsychological studies, demonstrating executive function deficits. Genetic predispositions toward AS have been noted, since AS tends to run in families. Cumine, Leach, and Stevenson (2001) emphasized that there is probably no single cause of Asperger Syndrome, but rather a set of triggers which may occur at certain times. Thus, the brain dysfunction may be biological, neurochemical, neurological, and/or occurring during pregnancy or birth. There have been myths surrounding the causes of AS—including the possibilities of a nutritional cause, parenting inadequacy, and reaction to immunizations—that have been mostly dispelled in AS literature.

# Definitions

To understand Asperger Syndrome, it is important to discuss it within the context of the range of conditions identified as Autism Spectrum Disorders (ASD) and Pervasive Developmental Disorders (PDD). The umbrella term *Autism Spectrum Disorder* suggests that there is a range of related qualities that overlap, but that are clinically distinct and separately diagnosed. Core characteristics differ in how they are manifested in terms of number and severity of the characteristics. The term ASD usually includes:

- PDD
- PDD-NOS
- Autism
- Atypical autism
- Asperger Syndrome
- High-functioning autism

The umbrella term *Pervasive Developmental Disorders* describes a broad classification of disorders that are *pervasive* (affecting many areas of development), *developmental* (occurring during early development and expected to continue during development), and *disordered* (areas of learning are affected but learning can occur). The following five disorders are included within the PDD category:

- Autistic disorder
- Rett's disorder
- Childhood disintegration disorder (CDD)
- Asperger's disorder
- Pervasive developmental disorder not otherwise specified (PDD-NOS)

The terms Autism Spectrum Disorder and Pervasive Developmental Disorder overlap and are used interchangeably at times. Whether discussing ASD or PDD, educators and parents are usually thinking of autism and thus autism is more specifically defined here. Individuals with autism have a neurological disorder that usually appears in the first three years of life and has these characteristics (Autism Society of America, 2003):

- Interacts with other children inappropriately
- Laughs or giggles inappropriately
- Uses minimal to no eye contact
- Has diminished sensitivity to pain
- Prefers being alone rather than being with others
- Spins or manipulates objects over and over
- Fixates and inappropriately attaches to objects
- Prefers sameness and resists change
- Does not perceive or fear danger
- Sustains or perseverates on play routines
- Uses echolalia in place of normal language
- Responds to cuddling inappropriately
- Does not respond readily to verbal cues
- Uses gestures more often than words
- Uses extreme amounts of physical activity (either too much or too little)
- Does not respond well to typical teaching methods
- Has tantrums for no apparent reason
- Uses inconsistent gross and fine motor skills

Each of the PDD disorders has specific diagnostic criteria, which are listed by the American Psychiatric Association in the *DSM–IV–TR* (2000). In addition, some professionals refer to the criteria of the World Health Organization—the *ICD–10* criteria (see Sidebar 1.1 on page 8). It should be noted that, in general, the *ICD–10* and the *DSM–IV–TR* diagnostic criteria for Asperger Syndrome are based on the following: (1) impairment in social interaction, social communication, social imagination, flexible thinking, and imaginative play; (2) absence of a significant delay in cognitive development; and (3) a general delay in language development. Sidebar 1.2 on pages 9–11 presents the *DSM–IV–TR* diagnostic criteria for PDD and each of the five disorders in the PDD category.

Typically, these symptoms occur across situations and are notably inappropriate for the individual's age. According to Attwood (2000, 2001, 2002, 2003), AS is usually diagnosed later in life (i.e., around school-age) than classic autism, and may be a milder form of autism. Sometimes, AS is referred to as high-functioning autism (HFA), noting that AS is not characterized by cognitive disabilities, but frequently by higher intellectual abilities.

# Asperger Syndrome

**Sidebar 1.1**  *ICD–10* **Research Criteria for Asperger Syndrome**

A. There is no clinically significant general delay in spoken or receptive language or cognitive development. Diagnosis requires that single words should have developed by 2 years of age or earlier and that communicative phrases be used by 3 years of age or earlier. Self-help skills, adaptive behavior, and curiosity about the environment during the first 3 years should be at a level consistent with normal intellectual development. However, motor milestones may be somewhat delayed and motor clumsiness is usual (although not a necessary diagnostic feature). Isolated special skills, often related to abnormal preoccupations, are common, but are not required for diagnosis.

B. There are qualitative abnormalities in reciprocal social interaction in at least two of the following areas (criteria as for autism):

   a. Failure to adequately use eye-to-eye gaze, facial expression, body posture, and gesture to regulate social interaction;

   b. Failure to develop (in a manner appropriate to mental age, and despite ample opportunities) peer relationships that involve a mutual sharing of interest, activities, and emotions;

   c. Lack of social-emotional reciprocity as shown by an impaired or deviant response to other people's emotions, or lack of modulation of behavior according to social context; or a weak integration of social, emotional, and communicative behaviors;

   d. Lack of spontaneous seeking to share enjoyment, interests, or achievements with other people (e.g., a lack of showing, bringing, or pointing out to other people objects of interests to the individual).

C. The individual exhibits an unusually intense, circumscribed interest or restricted, repetitive, and stereotyped patterns of behavior, interests, and activities in at least one of the following areas (criteria as for autism; however it would be less usual for these to include either motor mannerisms or preoccupations with part-objects or nonfunctional elements of play materials).

   a. An encompassing preoccupation with one or more stereotyped and restricted patterns of interest that are abnormal in content or focus; or one or more interests that are abnormal in intensity and circumscribed nature though not in their content or focus;

   b. Apparently compulsive adherence to specific, nonfunctional routines or rituals;

   c. Stereotyped and repetitive motor mannerisms that involve either hand or finger flapping or twisting, or complex whole-body movements;

   d. Preoccupations with part-objects or nonfunctional elements of play materials (such as their odor, the feel of their surface, or the noise or vibration that they generate).

   e. Distress over changes in small, non-functional, details of the environment.

D. The disorder is not attributable to the other varieties of pervasive developmental disorder; schizotypal disorder (F21); simple schizophrenia (F20.6); reactive and disinhibited attachment disorder of childhood (F94.1 and .2); obsessional personality disorder (F60.5); obsessive-compulsive disorder (F42).

From *The ICD–10 Classification of Mental and Behavioural Disorders: Diagnostic Criteria for Research* (pp. 180–181, 186–187), by the World Health Organization, 1993, Geneva, Switzerland: Author. © 1993 by the World Health Organization. Reprinted with permission.

# Diagnostic Criteria for the Pervasive
**Sidebar 1.2**   ## Developmental Disorders as Stated in the *DSM–IV–TR*

**Autistic Disorder**

A.  A total of six (or more) items from (1), (2), and (3), with at least two from (1), and one each from (2) and (3):

    (1)  qualitative impairment in social interaction, as manifested by at least two of the following:

        (a)  marked impairment in the use of multiple nonverbal behaviors such as eye-to-eye gaze, facial expression, body postures, and gestures to regulate social interaction

        (b)  failure to develop peer relationships appropriate to developmental level

        (c)  a lack of spontaneous seeking to share enjoyment, interests, or achievements with other people (e.g., by a lack of showing, bringing, or pointing out objects of interest)

        (d)  lack of social or emotional reciprocity

    (2)  qualitative impairments in communication as manifested by at least one of the following:

        (a)  delay in, or total lack of, the development of spoken language (not accompanied by an attempt to compensate through alternative modes of communication such as gesture or mime)

        (b)  in individuals with adequate speech, marked impairment in the ability to initiate or sustain a conversation with others

        (c)  stereotyped and repetitive use of language or idiosyncratic language

        (d)  lack of varied, spontaneous make-believe play or social imitative play appropriate to developmental level

    (3)  restricted, repetitive, and stereotyped patterns of behavior, interests, and activities, as manifested by at least one of the following:

        (a)  encompassing preoccupation with one or more stereotyped and restricted patterns of interest that is abnormal either in intensity or focus

        (b)  apparently inflexible adherence to specific, nonfunctional routines or rituals

        (c)  stereotyped and repetitive motor mannerisms (e.g., hand or finger flapping or twisting, or complex whole-body movements)

        (d)  persistent preoccupation with parts of objects

B.  Delays or abnormal functioning in at least one of the following areas, with onset prior to age 3 years: (1) social interaction, (2) language as used in social communication, or (3) symbolic or imaginative play

C.  The disturbance is not better accounted for by Rett's Disorder or Childhood Disintegrative Disorder

*Continued on next page*

## Rett's Disorder

A. All of the following:

  (1) apparently normal prenatal and perinatal development

  (2) apparently normal psychomotor development through the first 5 months after birth

  (3) normal head circumference at birth

B. Onset of all of the following after the period of normal development:

  (1) deceleration of head growth between ages 5 and 48 months

  (2) loss of previously acquired purposeful hand skills between ages 5 and 30 months with the subsequent development of stereotyped hand movements (e.g., hand-wringing or hand washing)

  (3) loss of social engagement early in the course (although often social interaction develops later)

  (4) appearance of poorly coordinated gait or trunk movements

  (5) severely impaired expressive and receptive language development with severe psychomotor retardation

## Childhood Disintegrative Disorder

A. Apparently normal development for at least the first 2 years after birth as manifested by the presence of age-appropriate verbal and nonverbal communication, social relationships, play, and adaptive behavior.

B. Clinically significant loss of previously acquired skills (before age 10 years) in at least two of the following areas:

  (1) expressive or receptive language

  (2) social skills or adaptive behavior

  (3) bowel or bladder control

  (4) play

  (5) motor skills

C. Abnormalities of functioning in at least two of the following areas:

  (1) qualitative impairment in social interaction (e.g., impairment in nonverbal behaviors, failure to develop peer relationships, lack of social or emotional reciprocity).

  (2) qualitative impairments in communication (e.g., delay or lack of spoken language, inability to initiate or sustain a conversation, stereotyped and repetitive use of language, lack of varied make-believe play)

  (3) restricted, repetitive, and stereotyped patterns of behavior, interests, and activities, including motor stereotypes and mannerisms

D. The disturbance is not better accounted for by another specific Persuasive Developmental Disorder or by Schizophrenia.

## Asperger's Disorder

A. Qualitative impairment in social interaction, as manifested by at least two of the following:

    (1) marked impairment in the use of multiple nonverbal behaviors such as eye-to-eye gaze, facial expression, body postures, and gestures to regulate social interaction

    (2) failure to develop peer relationships appropriate to developmental level

    (3) a lack of spontaneous seeking to share enjoyment, interests, or achievements with other people (e.g., by a lack of showing, bringing, or pointing out objects of interest to other people)

    (4) a lack of social or emotional reciprocity

B. Restricted repetitive and stereotyped patterns of behavior, interests, and activities as manifested by at least one of the following:

    (1) encompassing preoccupation with one or more stereotyped and restricted patterns of interest that is abnormal either in intensity or focus

    (2) apparently inflexible adherence to specific, nonfunctional routines or rituals

    (3) stereotyped and repetitive motor mannerisms (e.g., hand or finger flapping and twisting, or complex whole-body movements)

    (4) persistent preoccupation with parts of objects

C. The disturbance causes clinically significant impairment in social, occupational, or other important areas of functioning.

D. There is no clinically significant general delay in language (e.g., single words used by age 2 years, communicative phrases used by age 3 years).

E. There is no clinically significant delay in cognitive development or in the development of age-appropriate self-help skills, adaptive behavior (other than in social interaction), and curiosity about the environment in childhood.

F. Criteria are not met for another specific Persuasive Developmental Disorder or Schizophrenia.

## Pervasive Developmental Disorder Not Otherwise Specified (Including Atypical Autism)

This category should be used when there is a severe and pervasive impairment in the development of reciprocal social interaction associated with impairment in either verbal or nonverbal communication skills or with the presence of stereotyped behavior, interests, and activities, but the criteria are not met for a specific Pervasive Developmental Disorder, Schizophrenia, Schizotypal Personality Disorder, or Avoidant Personality Disorder. For example, this category includes "atypical autism"–presentations that do not meet the criteria for Autistic Disorder because of late age at onset, a typical symptomatology, or subthreshold symptomatology, or all of these.

From the *Diagnostic and Statistical Manual of Mental Disorders* (4th ed., text revision; pp. 75, 77, 79, 84), by the American Psychiatric Association, 2000, Washington, DC: Author. © 2000 by the American Psychiatric Association. Reprinted with permission.

# Asperger Syndrome

As Attwood (2002) noted, the definition of Asperger Syndrome is still evolving. Onset is later than for autism, or perhaps it is merely recognized later. A large number of students are diagnosed between the ages of 5 and 9 years of age or when they begin school. Children may exhibit a variety of characteristics (Attwood, 2002; Susman, 1996), such as:

- Social communication or pragmatic language problems (social skills)
- Difficulties with transitions or change
- Preference for sameness
- Obsessive routines
- Preoccupation with and possession of in-depth knowledge of a particular subject of interest
- Difficulties reading nonverbal cues such as facial expressions, gestures, body language, and proxemics
- Oversensitivity to sounds, tastes, smells, and sights
- Motor clumsiness

People with AS perceive the world differently and have a difficult time taking the perspective of others. They have few friends and have trouble interpreting others. People with AS also have problems developing a sense of who they are in respect to others. Behaviors the neurotypicals may perceive to be odd, unusual, rude, or bad are not perceived as such by the person with Asperger Syndrome.

Many people with AS have normal to high IQs (Manjiviona & Prior, 1999); have exceptional skills or talents (e.g., computer knowledge); or have what appears to be normal language development but with deficits in language pragmatics (i.e., the use of language) and prosody (i.e., the tone, inflection, rhythm of language). Some people have a rich vocabulary that makes them sound like a "little professor" with very precise speech that sounds pedantic. People with AS may be naive and therefore become victims of teasing and bullying. Their use of language may be very literal and, therefore, they may have difficulty with comprehending and using language in a more figurative, ambiguous sense; in a social context; or in an abstract sense in academic assignments.

Of all these diagnostic criteria, Attwood (2001) preferred Gillberg and Gillberg's (1989) criteria (see Table 1.2 on page 5) believing it to be clear, concise, and comprehensive. Leekam, Libby, Wing, Gould, and Gillberg (2000) researched using Gillberg and Gillberg's criteria in comparison to the *ICD–10* (WHO, 1993) criteria and noted a slightly higher number of people were diagnosed using Gillberg and Gillberg's criteria. It should be noted, however, that Gillberg and Gillberg's definition encompasses more criteria, includes more specific criteria for current behaviors, and is closer to Asperger's original definition. However, the criteria to be used are often left up to the discretion of each diagnostician who is applying the diagnosis. This may become problematic, as will be illustrated in the next chapter on assessment. It is hopeful that future and better diagnostics may help define AS and thus reflect the prevalence of the disability more accurately.

# Prevalence Statistics

Statistics readily demonstrate the increased number of autism spectrum disorders (of which AS is a subset) over the 1990's. As indicated in Figure 1.1, an alarming rise in autism has occurred and indicates an increase of 1,354% in the entire United States (Autism Society of America, 2004). An approximate increase of 10 to 17% per year is reported nationwide. Prevalence statistics also indicate that autism is more common in males than in females (Cowley, 2003).

As illustrated in Figure 1.2 on page 14, this high rate of autism has been estimated to have cost the U.S. economy $90 billion annually in 2003, with an annual projected cost of $200 to $400 billion by 2010 (Autism Society of America, 2003). This alarming rise in autism prevalence, and in its costs to the nation, has brought about increased national attention to autism spectrum disorders.

These overall trends in autism appear to be occurring with Asperger Syndrome as well. According to Safran, Safran, and Ellis (2003), the number of children with AS is rapidly rising throughout the world. Wing and Potter (2002) attributed this rise in AS to two reasons: (1) a greater recognition in the wider scope of ASD, and (2) changes in the diagnostic criteria for AS since 1994.

**Figure 1.1**  **Autism Growth Comparison Chart**

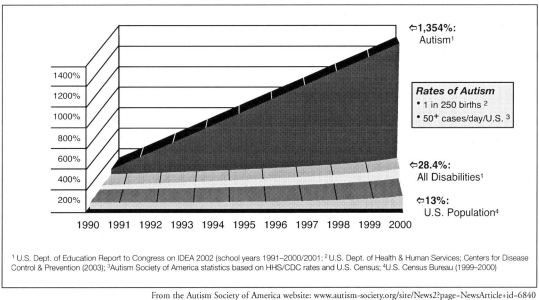

[1] U.S. Dept. of Education Report to Congress on IDEA 2002 (school years 1991–2000/2001; [2] U.S. Dept. of Health & Human Services; Centers for Disease Control & Prevention (2003); [3] Autism Society of America statistics based on HHS/CDC rates and U.S. Census; [4] U.S. Census Bureau (1999–2000)

Figure 1.2      **Annual Cost of Autism on U.S. Economy**

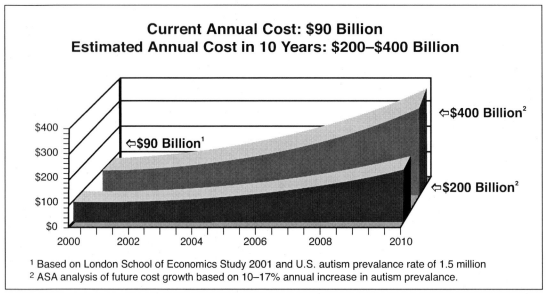

¹ Based on London School of Economics Study 2001 and U.S. autism prevalance rate of 1.5 million
² ASA analysis of future cost growth based on 10–17% annual increase in autism prevalance.

From the Autism Society of America website: www.autism-society.org/site/News2?page=NewsArticle+id=5828
Retrieved 8/31/05. © 2003 by the Autism Society of America. Reprinted with permission.

Gillberg and Ehlers (1998) noted the prevalence rate of AS to be at least 3.6, and as high as 7.1, per 1,000 students 7–16 years of age. Kadesjo, Gillberg, and Hagberg (1999) noted that AS has been diagnosed as high as 1 in every 200–250 seven-year-olds. Clinical studies also suggest a male-to-female ratio of 4:1 (Ehlers & Gillberg, 1993). Ramanowski-Bashe and Kirby (2001) noted that AS is more difficult to diagnose in girls than in boys and is more likely to be misdiagnosed as a nonverbal learning disability, depression, or an anxiety disorder. Thus, it is debatable if the male-to-female ratio will hold over time as assessment procedures become more sensitive to signs of AS.

# Characteristic Expectations and Challenges for Students with Asperger Syndrome

A review of the literature revealed a number of characteristic expectations and challenges in social competence and academic achievement. Under the area of social competence are issues of friendship/relationship development, perspective-taking/theory of mind, social skills, nonverbal communication, and language features of syntax and semantics. Under the area of academic achievement are issues of executive functions, self-management, reading to learn, writing, sensory perception, and gross and fine motor control—skills pertinent for the student with AS to succeed in today's society. Table 1.3 lists the two umbrella categories of Social Competence and Academic

Table 1.3

# Characteristic Expectations and Challenges
# of Students with Asperger Syndrome

| Social Competence | | |
|---|---|---|
| | **Expectations** | **Challenges** |
| **Friendship or Relationship Development** | • To make friends and know how to keep them<br>• To recognize when and how to join in with a group of peers<br>• To respond to a friend's compliments appropriately<br>• To incorporate the ideas of others into play activities<br><br>• To use reciprocity and sharing during a conversation, or while playing<br>• To manage disagreement with compromise and accept the opinions of others<br>• To take the perspective of others while playing or conversing<br><br><br><br>• To deal appropriately with being left out<br><br>• To respond appropriately to peer pressure<br><br>• To play appropriately by the rules of the game<br>• To interact appropriately with peers<br><br><br>• To understand humor<br>• To recognize when they are being teased | • They often do not know how to make and keep friends.<br>• They often do not know when and how to join in with a group of peers.<br>• They may not respond or respond inappropriately to the compliment.<br>• They may play alone or use only their own ideas as to how to play the game. They may fail to engage others in the enjoyment and interest of an activity.<br>• They do not take into account the idea of sharing or reciprocity in play or conversations.<br>• They tend to not want to compromise and may disregard the opinions of others.<br>• They tend not to take the perspective of others during a game and often do not know how to take another's point of view and incorporate it into the play or conversation.<br>• They respond as if being left out is good, or they are sad and confused as to why they were left out.<br>• They do not realize when they are being pressured to do something inappropriate.<br>• They may not want to play by the game rules, but prefer to make up their own rules.<br>• They may bother others with teasing, touching, laughing, or interrupting. They may fail to establish appropriate peer relationships.<br>• They may not understand humor<br>• They may not realize that they are being teased or bullied. |
| **Theory of Mind/Perspective-Taking** | • To take another's perspective on a topic<br>• To seek comfort from others<br><br>• To offer comfort or affection to others<br>• To assess communication breakdowns and revise them<br><br>• To identify and take on the emotions of others (i.e., to have empathy)<br>• To understand the thoughts and feelings of others<br>• To respect differences in others (e.g., point of view and physical looks) | • They have difficulty taking the perspective of another person on any subject.<br>• They often do not seek comfort or affection from others.<br>• They often do not offer comfort or affection to others.<br>• They do not have awareness of breakdowns; if they do, they lack repair strategies because they cannot take the perspective of the listener.<br>• They do not take on the emotions of others as if they were their own. They lack empathy.<br>• They do not understand the thoughts and feelings of others.<br>• They do not value differences in others and assume others share their point of view. |

15

Table 1.3—*Continued*

| Social Competence | | |
|---|---|---|
| | **Expectations** | **Challenges** |
| **Social Communication/Pragmatics/Language Use** | • To produce language that is organized, coherent, and intelligible to listeners<br>• To follow adult conversational rules for speakers (e.g., initiating, maintaining, or terminating a topic)<br>• To be effective listeners during conversation without displaying incorrect listening habits<br>• To demonstrate reciprocity (balance) between participants in a conversation (e.g., turn taking)<br>• To analyze critically other speakers<br>• To express their own attitudes, moods, and feelings and to disagree appropriately<br><br>• To use appropriately the code of social conduct (e.g., knowing when and how to interrupt the speaker)<br>• To use appropriate comments and stay on track or topic when conversing<br><br>• To recognize that communication is a dialogue between two or more speakers<br><br>• To recognize and accept different points of view while communicating | • They use formal, pedantic speech and disregard whether the listener is interested or listening.<br>• They may consistently violate conversational rules for initiating, maintaining, and ending topics.<br><br>• They often do not listen if they are not interested in the topic.<br>• They lack the ability to have reciprocity between participants in a conversation and to take turns.<br>• Their judgments are arbitrary, illogical, and impulsive.<br>• They may use what others perceive as blunt, abrasive, and insensitive conversational speech even though they perceive themselves as just being honest.<br>• They interrupt inappropriately both in terms of when and how to do the interruption.<br><br>• They may use inappropriate comments and often may not stay on topic when conversing if the topic does not interest them.<br>• They communicate as if carrying on a monologue or script and primarily converse on a single topic (i.e., the one that interests them).<br>• They often have a single point of view and do not readily change their mind. They may dominate a conversation with their statistics, cataloging, and detailed knowledge of a special topic of interest. |
| **Social Skills** | • To engage in a wide variety of appropriate behaviors, interests, and activities<br><br>• To manage anger appropriately<br><br>• To resolve conflicts appropriately<br>• To disagree appropriately<br><br>• To understand that contradictions are typical<br><br>• To deal appropriately with criticism, disappointment, embarrassment, fear, anxiety, accusations<br>• To deal with hurt feelings<br><br>• To manage teasing and bullying effectively<br><br>• To give and receive a compliment<br><br>• To share and cooperate with others on a project | • They typically engage in restricted to stereotypical patterns of behavior, interests, and activities. They tend to display ritualistic behavior.<br>• They often do not manage their anger and strike out in inappropriate ways.<br>• They often have difficulty resolving conflicts.<br>• They often bluntly and rudely disagree with statements or concepts.<br>• They often do not like contradictions because they appear illogical and irrational and disturb their desire for sameness or consistency.<br>• They do not like to be criticized and cannot often take the perspective of the person providing the constructive criticism.<br>• They tend to either not feel hurt or be oblivious to what is being said, or they overreact and take things far too personally.<br>• They often do not respond appropriately to teasing and bullying and either are hurt by it or oblivious to it.<br>• They often do not know how to give or receive a socially acceptable compliment.<br>• They often do not select to share and cooperate or simply do not know how to share and cooperate on a project. |

Table 1.3—*Continued*

| Social Competence | | |
|---|---|---|
| | **Expectations** | **Challenges** |
| Nonverbal Communication | • To understand nonverbal rules for reading facial expressions, eye contact, gestures, and body language<br>• To use facial expressions, gestures, and body language to complement verbal communication and to express thoughts<br>• To understand and use nonverbal rules for proxemics (e.g., standing at an appropriate distance or using good posture) | • They misinterpret facial expressions, gestures, and body language.<br><br>• They do not use facial expressions, gestures, or body language appropriately to complement their verbal communication or to express their thoughts.<br>• They violate the rules for proxemics or social distance, standing too close or too far away, depending on the situation. |
| Language Features of Syntax and Semantics | • To change pitch, volume, and rhythm to indicate emotions, to stress key words and ideas, and to provide vocal variation<br><br>• To understand the relevance of change in pitch, volume, rhythm, or emphasis of certain words when listening to the speech of others<br>• To know when to code-switch between formal and informal speaking styles<br><br><br>• To use grammar correctly and with variability in terms of complexity and length of sentences<br>• To use a variety of words with different meanings to fit the situation<br>• To use ambiguous language appropriately (e.g., figurative and humorous language)<br>• To understand and use both literal and abstract language appropriately<br>• To make or give a report, tell or retell a story, and explain a process in detail<br><br><br>• To listen to lectures and to select main ideas and supporting details | • They do not change their pitch, volume, and rhythm when indicating emotions, stressing key words and ideas, and providing vocal variation. They may speak in a monotone or in their own unique vocal manner.<br>• They do not understand the speech characteristics of others.<br><br>• They do not code-switch and often use overly formal speech, excessive technical detail, and precise intonation and may sound pedantic in their communication style.<br>• They tend to use overly formal, sophisticated grammar or phrases, sounding very adultlike or like a "little professor."<br>• They may use only the literal meaning of words and not understand the more abstract meaning of words.<br>• They tend to not understand or to not use figurative and humorous language appropriately.<br>• They tend not to be able to move from literal to abstract language readily.<br>• They may not be able to give a report, tell a story, or explain a process unless it is in their area of interest. They may be indifferent to assignments they do not want to do.<br>• They often do not grasp the essential message of a lecture. |
| **Academic Achievement** | | |
| Executive Functions | • To organize and categorize information and materials<br><br>• To complete tasks in an efficient manner<br><br>• To produce step-by-step plans to achieve goals<br>• To remember a sequence of events<br><br>• To remain focused on a topic, issue, or problem until it is resolved | • They may not organize and categorize information and materials (e.g., not bringing the correct materials to class).<br>• They may complete tasks in an inefficient, random, chaotic manner.<br>• They may not produce a step-by-step plan to achieve goals or take action on goals.<br>• They may use limited strategies for remembering a sequence of events if it does not interest them.<br>• They are often distracted and unable to resolve an issue or make a decision. |

*Continued on next page*

Table 1.3—*Continued*

| Academic Achievement | | |
|---|---|---|
| | **Expectations** | **Challenges** |
| **Executive Functions—continued** | • To be flexible in their thinking | • They often have a one-track mind or stay on a single topic beyond its usefulness, and they find it hard to change a routine. They feel more comfortable by sameness. |
| | • To put limits on their own behaviors (self-monitoring) | • They have difficulty putting limits on their own behaviors and tend to be impulsive. |
| | • To concentrate on academic tasks | • They may have difficulty concentrating on academic tasks unless the academic subject is one of interest to them. |
| | • To become more advanced in academic problem-solving tasks as concepts become more abstract | • They have difficulty with word problems, estimations in math, etc. |
| **Self-Management** | • To comply with classroom and school rules and expectations | • They are sometimes noncompliant in the classroom or in other areas of the school and playground because they do not know the school rules and routines or because they think they are silly. |
| | • To participate appropriately in group discussions | • They do not know when it is appropriate to speak in class discussions and may interpret and blurt out answers. |
| | • To know how to ask the teacher for help | • They do not know how to ask appropriately for help from authority figures. |
| | • To think and learn silently about their thoughts | • They tend to think aloud about their thoughts when they are learning. |
| | • To monitor their own intellectual understanding of a situation | • They often do not know that they misunderstand or misread a situation. |
| **Reading to Learn** | • To comprehend printed symbols in various academic, social, and vocational situations | • They may not consistently and/or efficiently decode and comprehend words, sentences, and discourse in a meaningful way. |
| | • To read fluently across a variety of genres (e.g., narratives and expository text) and across a variety of disciplines (e.g., literature, science, math, English) | • They may not alter their reading strategies across genres and disciplines. |
| | • To read fluently for a variety of purposes (e.g., to be informed, to be persuaded, to be entertained) and to change reading strategies (e.g., skimming, analyzing), depending on the outcome | • They may not adjust their reading strategies to accommodate the writer's purpose or the instructional requirements. |
| **Writing** | • To produce cohesive written language required in various academic, social, and vocational situations by organizing, planning, composing, and editing | • They do not consistently and/or efficiently generate written language that conveys their messages. They tend not to plan or edit their writing. They may become far too specific in areas that are of special interest and not detailed enough in areas that do not interest them. |
| | • To write on a wide array of topics and not just one or two preselected topics of interest | • They tend to be extremely good at selected topics, but once out of their range of interest, they struggle to write on a topic. |

**Table 1.3—*Continued***

| Academic Achievement | | |
|---|---|---|
| | **Expectations** | **Challenges** |
| **Sensory Perception** | • To be aware of sights, sounds, touch, taste, and smell<br><br>• To be aware of pain and temperature within a typical range<br>• To be able to tolerate tactile sensations in school<br>• To be able to accept visual sensory experiences in school<br><br>• To be able to accept the range of sounds and noises in the school routine<br><br>• To accept typical food tastes<br><br>• To have typical sensitivity to smells that are associated with school | • They are frequently overly sensitive to sights, sounds, touch, tastes, and smells to the extent that it gets in their way of learning or functioning in the environment.<br>• They may be either stoic in response to pain or temperature or overly sensitive.<br>• They are often hyper- or hyposensitive to normal tactile experiences.<br>• About 50% of students with AS respond appropriately to normal visual input. The other 50% may have oversensitivity to visual sensations (e.g., florescent lights).<br>• They are often hyper- or hyposensitive to noise (e.g., fire drills, bells, material rubbing against itself, forks on a plate, chalk on a blackboard).<br>• They frequently avoid many tastes that are typical in students' diets and are often picky eaters.<br>• They often cannot tolerate typical school smells (e.g., cleaners, glue, paste, paint, cafeteria food, locker rooms, others' perfume or aftershave). |
| **Motor/Balance** | • To demonstrate typical gross motor skills (e.g., walking, skipping, jumping)<br><br>• To demonstrate appropriate fine motor skills (e.g., writing)<br>• To tolerate activities in school that involve movement<br><br>• To perform typical activities that require body awareness | • They may appear clumsy in walking, skipping, jumping, and playing in sports or physical education classes that require gross motor coordination.<br>• They may have difficulty writing legibly and cutting accurately with scissors.<br>• They may have difficulty changing direction or speed and fear having their feet leave the ground, or they rock or swing for stimulation.<br>• They appear clumsy and have difficulty with large and small motor activities. They do not automatically learn body awareness skills and are often off balance, have poor posture, and get confused about left and right. |

*Sources:* Attwood (2001, 2002); Connor (1999); Cumine, Leach, & Stevenson (2001); Grandin (2001); Jackel (1996); Larson & McKinley (2003); Myles, Cook, Miller, Rinner, & Robbins (2000); Myles & Southwick (1999); Willey (1999); Williams (1995); Winter (2003)

Achievement, with subcategories describing expectations that might be had of any student with typical neurological development age six or older, and the types of challenges likely to be observed in people with AS. Obviously, no single problem would result in difficulty for the student. It is when a series of these social and academic concerns occur within the same person that problems arise, resulting in the person being socially challenged and academically under-utilized.

People with AS also have a number of strengths, such as honesty, creativity, excellent memory for details, reliability, dedication, and determination. If properly cultivated, an area of special interest can become a productive means of employment or a major contribution to society (Winter, 2003). Ozonoff, Dawson, and McPartland (2002) summarized a mother's hopes and fears for her child with AS, saying, "I bet he'll become a rocket scientist, but I'll probably have to dress him and drive him to work" (p. 18).

Attwood (2002) noted that people with AS tend to approach life differently, with an emphasis on the pursuit of knowledge and truth. Winter (2003) emphasized that people with AS often do not understand why other people lie, because they do not lie themselves, but are extremely honest (some say too blunt). As Gerland (2001) noted, "Being different is just as good as being like everyone else" (p. 46).

Table 1.3 (beginning on page 15) was generated by doing an extensive review of literature as to the typical expectations, and then challenges, facing students with Asperger Syndrome. It is important to realize that the areas of social competence and academic achievement are not necessarily mutually exclusive categories, but entail significant overlap. The characteristics needed to succeed socially may also be needed to succeed academically, and vice versa.

Table 1.3 can be used as a reference point for assessment (see Appendix A on the CD-ROM, which is a checklist based on Table 1.3) and for intervention goals. The selection of a specific assessment procedure and intervention goals and objectives or benchmarks is contingent upon the student's specific needs.

## Discussion Points

1. How has the overall history of Asperger Syndrome lead to the current problems in attempting to define AS?

2. How does Asperger Syndrome relate to Autism Spectrum Disorders and Pervasive Developmental Disorders?

3. Why has the prevalence of Asperger Syndrome grown so rapidly in the past decade in the United States?

4. What are the speculative causes of Asperger Syndrome?

5. Based upon the expectations and challenges listed in Table 1.3, what are the characteristics of Asperger Syndrome?

# Identification and Assessment

## Chapter 2

## Goals

- To present what behaviors should be assessed
- To describe how to assess these behaviors using formal and informal procedures

Asperger Syndrome (AS) is not always easily recognized or diagnosed. Oftentimes, AS is first noted by parents or teachers who recognize that the child is different from other children, especially in terms of social abilities—both specific social skills and social communication—and in having special interests or talents and repetitive behaviors. It is not uncommon for students to be misdiagnosed or to warrant dual diagnosis and treatment.

Many students are misdiagnosed with other neurological disorders, such as Tourette Syndrome or autism. It is not uncommon for students to be misdiagnosed with attention-deficit/hyperactivity disorder (AD/HD), oppositional defiant disorder (ODD), or obsessive-compulsive disorder (OCD). Obviously, misdiagnosis can lead to the following:

- Absence of or delay in proper treatment
- Inappropriate placement in school programs
- Confusion on the part of parents
- Bewilderment on the part of educators
- Frustration for the students

Regardless of the type of misdiagnosis, it is evident that individuals with Asperger Syndrome experience serious consequences because of inappropriate diagnosis.

At other times, dual diagnosis is warranted (e.g., the person may have both Asperger Syndrome and attention-deficit/hyperactivity disorder). It is critical that the duality of the person's disability be recognized so that proper services for both types of problems are provided. It is not uncommon for the following disabilities to be associated with AS: learning disability, attention-deficit/hyperactivity disorder, obsessive-compulsive disorder, anxiety disorder, Tourette Syndrome, Fragile X Syndrome, and visual and/or hearing impairments.

Differential diagnosis is the process of deciding what AS is and is not. According to Myles and Adreon (2001), in many states, the diagnosis of AS must be made by a physician using the criteria from the *DSM–IV–TR* (2000; see Sidebar 1.2, on pages 9–11) or the criteria of the *ICD–10* (1993; see Sidebar 1.1 on page 8). In summary, these criteria note that an individual must demonstrate a social impairment and exhibit restrictive, repetitive patterns and/or stereotypical behaviors, interests, and activities.

Powers and Poland (2002) noted that any evaluation should indicate the extent to which the child's behaviors meet the criteria described in the *DSM–IV–TR* (2000); how the child demonstrates impaired social interaction; impaired communication; and circumscribed, unusual, or repetitive interests and behaviors. The evaluation should include a thorough developmental history; observe actions of the child in structured and unstructured situations; include a review of records; and include standardized testing for cognitive development, social communication, and motor skills.

According to Powers and Poland (2002), it is critical that other diagnoses be ruled in or out by carefully considering three elements to a good evaluation. The evaluation should be (1) holistic; (2) a team effort consisting of such professionals as a psychologist, a physician, a speech-language pathologist, special and general education teachers, and an occupational therapist; and (3) prescriptive (i.e., it does not just identify and describe deficits, but it also tells you what to do about them).

It is critical that each professional participating on the team be mindful of stated diagnostic criteria, characteristics, or ways to gather informed observations, use informal procedures (e.g., checklists, questionnaires, observations, and interviews), and use formal/standardized tests in systematic and constructive ways to gather the most pertinent information. According to Cumine, Leach, and Stevenson (2001), no single test can definitely confirm AS, since AS is inferred on the basis of interpretation of the patterns of evidence of specific behaviors. These behaviors are the ones noted in Table 1.3 on pages 15–19.

According to Attwood (2001), the diagnosis of AS is a two-stage process. First and foremost, the parents and teachers who are the closest to the student should complete a questionnaire, checklist, or rating scale that identifies the behaviors and abilities most indicative of AS (see Table 2.1 for examples). With older students (i.e., age 10 and above) and adults, the individual with AS may be the one to complete the questionnaire, checklist, or rating scale.

Table 2.1        # Example Scales for Asperger Syndrome

| Rating Scale | Authors | Publication Year | Description |
|---|---|---|---|
| The Australian Scale for Asperger Syndrome (ASAS) | Garnett & Attwood | 1995 | This questionnaire and rating scale examines six categories: social and emotional abilities, communication skills, cognitive skills, specific interests, movement skills, and other characteristics. |
| Asperger Syndrome Diagnostic Scale (ASDS) | Myles, Block, & Simpson | 2000 | This scale has 50 items and can be completed in 15 minutes by an individual who knows the person with AS. The ASDS examines five areas: language, social competence, maladaptions, cognition, and sensory motor skills. |

In addition, using a checklist such as the one provided as Appendix A on the CD-ROM (and shown in Figure 2.1) will help to identify specific behaviors. The checklist provided is based on the list of characteristic expectations and challenges facing students with Asperger Syndrome listed

Figure 2.1        **Social and Academic Competence Checklist**

**Directions:** State whether the student "Always," "Sometimes," or "Never" exhibits the behavior in question. Note that "Always" equals 5 points, "Sometimes" equals 3 points, and "Never" equals 1 point. The rankings will help program planning (e.g., if a majority of the items in the category entitled "Friendship or Relationship Development" are ranked at the "Never" to "Sometimes" levels on the scale, a social skills program might be initiated to address the special needs of the student).

**Social Competence**

**Friendship/Relationship Development**

| Does the student: | Unsure | Never | Sometimes | Always |
|---|---|---|---|---|
| 1. Make and keep friends? | 0 | 1 | 3 | 5 |
| 2. Recognize when and how to join in a group of peers? | 0 | 1 | 3 | 5 |
| 3. Respond appropriately to a friend's compliment? | 0 | 1 | 3 | 5 |
| 4. Incorporate the ideas of others into play activities? | 0 | 1 | 3 | 5 |
| 5. Use reciprocity and sharing during conversations, or while playing? | 0 | 1 | 3 | 5 |
| 6. Manage disagreement with compromise and accept others' opinions? | 0 | 1 | 3 | 5 |
| 7. Take the perspective of others during conversation and play? | 0 | 1 | 3 | 5 |
| 8. Appropriately handle being left out? | 0 | 1 | 3 | 5 |
| 9. Respond appropriately to peer pressure? | 0 | 1 | 3 | 5 |
| 10. Play by the rules of the game? | 0 | 1 | 3 | 5 |
| 11. Interact appropriately with peers? | 0 | 1 | 3 | 5 |
| 12. Understand humor? | 0 | 1 | 3 | 5 |
| 13. Recognize when being teased? | 0 | 1 | 3 | 5 |

**Printable from the CD-ROM**

in Table 1.3 (beginning on page 15). After a student has been diagnosed as having AS using the diagnostic criteria stated in *DSM–IV–TR* (2000), the checklist can be used by professionals to determine the strengths of and challenges faced by students with AS. The outcomes of the checklist should be used as a guide for selecting a service delivery model and for generating an intervention program (e.g., an Individualized Education Program [IEP]) that best meets the student's needs.

Attwood (2001) noted that the second stage of the diagnostic process should be done by clinicians and professionals who use a variety of assessment tools and established criteria to clearly describe the individual's behavioral characteristics as they pertain to AS. Thus, once a student has been identified with AS using the appropriate diagnostic criteria, it is critical to determine the nature and severity of the problem, as well as to establish what specific behaviors are of concern and how best to assess them. Table 2.2 illustrates what behaviors need to be assessed and how to do so using informal procedures and formal/standardized tests. The information in this table is explained in detail in the sections that follow.

**Table 2.2**    **Direct Assessment of Students with AS**

| What to Assess | How to Assess |
|---|---|
| **History**<br>　Developmental<br>　Environmental<br>　Educational<br>　Medical | **Informal Procedures**<br>　Interviews<br>　Questionnaires<br>　Checklists<br>　Observations at home, at school, in the community<br>　Oral and written language samples<br>　　(conversations, narrations, writing samples)<br>　Rubrics<br>　Portfolios<br>　Directed tasks<br>　Functional behavior assessment |
| **Social Competence**<br>　Friendship/Relationship building<br>　Social skills<br>　Communication skills (speech/voice characteristics,<br>　　language features, and discourse [conversations<br>　　and narrations])<br>　Perspective-Taking/Theory of Mind/Meta-Abilities<br>　Nonverbal communication | |
| **Academic Dimensions**<br>　Learning style<br>　Cognitive abilities<br>　Executive functions<br>　Written communication (reading and writing)<br>　Sensory integration<br>　Motor skills<br>　Curriculum-based tasks/textbook analysis<br>　Classroom schedules, rules, and routines | **Formal/Standardized Tests** |

# What Behaviors Need to Be Assessed?

## History

The student with AS (or his or her parent[s]) needs to be engaged in a dialogue about the student's history, including developmental, environmental, educational, and medical factors. The **developmental** data will help determine when the problem was first recognized and what has been done thus far to determine the existence and degree of the problem. The **environmental** history should document how, over time, the student with AS has interacted with family members and immediate peers. The **educational** history should document how the student has performed in various academic subjects, in extracurricular activities, and in interactions with classmates and teachers. If he or she is an older student (i.e., age 10 and above), you should document what type of interests the student has that might ultimately lead to success in school and to postsecondary school or vocational goals being reached. Since it has been hypothesized that causes of AS may be genetic or neurobiological, the student's **medical** family history should be obtained. That is, it should be determined if there are other members of the family who have Asperger Syndrome characteristics—whether diagnosed or undiagnosed.

## Social Competence

For the purpose of this book, *social competence* is defined as the ability to accommodate or adapt to ongoing social situations. Although every society has a set of social norms or rules, social rules and routines are constantly changing. Social interactions demand moment-to-moment integration of multiple contextual, social, emotional and language cues. Social interactions demand that the person be able to adjust and read the social cues within the situation on a continual basis and to adjust one's own behaviors within milliseconds of the behaviors occurring. This multitasking and reading of diverse social cues and simultaneously understanding the perspective of the persons within the social situation is very difficult for the person with AS. Many of the social norms are not taught but are assimilated by people with typical neurological development by integrating, monitoring, and adjusting to the behaviors of others as they interact within social situations. These social behaviors, typically learned automatically or incidentally, usually need to be taught deliberately to the individual with AS.

Our definition of social competence includes friendship/relationship building; social skills (e.g., giving and getting compliments, anger management); communication skills, including speech and voice characteristics, language features of syntax, semantics, and pragmatics, as well as discourse of conversations and narrations; perspective-taking or meta-abilities; and nonverbal communication skills. Each of these areas will be discussed as to what should be assessed, and how to assess the behaviors to determine the extent of the problems. Later chapters will present how best to establish intervention goals, objectives, or benchmarks in these areas.

## Friendship/Relationship Building

As the student advances through the grades, the need to make friends and to develop personal relationships increases. During the elementary years, most students' environment consists of one teacher, a single classroom, and one set of classmates. During the middle and high school years, the student must interact with a more diverse and larger student body and multiple classes and teachers (Myles & Adreon, 2001). The student's friendship/relationship building skills should be evaluated by assessing competency in the following areas:

- Initiating play activities or games with a peer
- Remaining flexible and sharing in play routines and games
- Initiating a friendly interaction with a peer
- Maintaining a friendly interaction with a peer
- Responding appropriately to a peer's initiation of play
- Responding appropriately to peer pressure
- Enjoying play with others rather than preferring to always play alone
- Showing interest in playing with others and having friends

## Social Skills

Social skills are critical to the student being successful in and across the settings of school, home, and community. According to Walker, Schwarz, Nippold, Irvin, and Noell (1994), competent social skills allow students to develop positive relationships; cope with the demands of various settings; and communicate one's desires, needs, and preferences effectively. Gajewski, Hirn, and Mayo (1998a, 1998b) noted a number of social skills that need to be taught directly to people who lack the social competence which students with typical development appear to learn incidentally. The following areas might be examined to determine the student's ability to understand and use social skills, rules, and routines:

- Managing anger appropriately
- Using manners appropriately
- Offering and asking for help
- Giving and receiving compliments
- Resolving conflict appropriately
- Understanding contradictions
- Sharing and cooperating on a project
- Dealing with hurt feelings appropriately
- Understanding friendly teasing and responding appropriately
- Understanding the hidden or unspoken social rules and routines across and within various social situations

- Dealing with criticism constructively
- Disagreeing appropriately

## Communication Skills

Communication competence is the ability to know what to say; who to say it to; where, when, why, and how to say it across and within a variety of social situations. It is the ability to use appropriate speech and voice characteristics; select the appropriate syntax, semantics, or discourse parameters; and then use these appropriately within social situations. To use communication appropriately within social situations, one needs to know about the speaker, the listener, and the social and physical setting, as well as the social and cultural norms that apply within a given situation.

### Speech/Voice Characteristics

Shriberg, Paul, McSweeny, Klin, and Cohen (2001) noted that unusual prosody (e.g., hypernasality and the placement of stress) have been a problem for students with AS. Thus it is important that the following characteristics be assessed in the student:

- Appropriate stress placement within words, sentences, etc.
- Appropriate rhythm placement on the overall fluency and melody of speech
- Demonstration of clear voice characteristics

### Language Features

Students with AS tend to have appropriate but restrictive use of syntactic (word order or grammar), semantic (word meaning and figurative language), and pragmatic (language use) features. They tend to struggle with using the appropriate sentences or word meanings at the appropriate time. They tend not to be very flexible in their use of language. Literal language appears to be easier for them than abstract language. Therefore, the following areas might be assessed when evaluating the student's flexibility with language features of syntax and semantics:

- Use of variation in syntax and semantics
- Use of a variety of simple and complex sentences while speaking or writing
- Use and comprehension of figurative language
- Use of various complex sentences in terms of types of clauses, conjunctions, and length
- Recognition of when nonspecific words are being used and their clarification when necessary
- Variation of word order and word meaning given the situation (i.e., formal or informal)
- Use of different word order and word meaning when speaking versus when writing

In addition to the speech/voice characteristics and the language features of syntax and semantics, the pragmatics of language (i.e., the ability to use language appropriately across and within various situations) must be considered. Two aspects to be considered are conversations and narrations, both of which may be difficult for the person with AS.

# Asperger Syndrome

### Discourse/Conversations

A conversation is a rule-governed dialogue between two or more people in which one person initiates a topic that is maintained until a topic shift is initiated and ultimately a topic is terminated. Also, the conversational partner or listener engages in such behaviors as maintaining eye contact and head nodding. The two conversational partners take turns, use appropriate topic shifts, and attempt to mutually understand how to engage in the topic at hand. These "rules" may prove difficult to follow for students with AS, and the following areas may be assessed when evaluating a student's skill in initiating, maintaining, and ending a conversation (Larson & McKinley, 1995, 2003):

- Knowledge and adherence to the rules of conversation
- Conversation initiation in a variety of situations
- Appropriate topic selection
- Ability to maintain a topic for a sufficient length of time and number of exchanges
- Sensitivity to listener's interest (does not maintain a special topic of interest for too long)
- Ability to switch topics in an appropriate and orderly fashion
- Ability to terminate the conversation in an appropriate manner
- Awareness of when to switch registers or code switch (i.e., formal versus informal language) given the social situation
- Knowledge of the functions of communication and when to use them such as,
  - ▲ Giving information
  - ▲ Getting information (i.e., when and where to ask a question appropriately)
  - ▲ Describing an ongoing event
  - ▲ Getting the listener to do something (i.e., persuade)
  - ▲ Expressing one's own intentions, beliefs, and feelings (i.e., self-disclosure)
  - ▲ Indicating a readiness for further communication
  - ▲ Using language to solve problems
  - ▲ Using language to entertain

### Discourse/Narrations

A narration is a real or imaginary time-ordered sequence of events in which the events are interrelated in some way. Narrations can be analyzed using a story grammar approach or using a developmental sequence, as well as using the student's ability to generalize, analyze, and summarize stories to glean pertinent information. Oftentimes, students with AS do not decipher the abstract meanings within stories, but rather take a more literal interpretation. Also, according to Paul and Sutherland (2003), students with AS may have difficulty understanding the motives and feelings of characters in a story. Thus, it is important to determine if students understand the elements of a story, so they can then analyze, generalize, and summarize the various story types or genre. To accomplish this, ask how well the student:

- Uses story grammar elements to determine:
  - ▲ The setting
  - ▲ The identification and description of the characters
  - ▲ The characters' motives and feelings regarding each other and the events of the story
  - ▲ The events in the story both initiated and causal relationships between and among events
  - ▲ Whether or not there is a goal present and an attempt to attain the goal
  - ▲ Whether or not there is a consequence to attaining the goal and, if so, what it is

- Summarizes the story in a sentence or two

- Provides a good title for the story

- Determines the type of story (i.e., drama, mystery, comedy)

- Generalizes what was learned in this story to new experiences

## Perspective-Taking/Theory of Mind/Meta-Abilities

Cumine, Leach, and Stevenson (2001) define *theory of mind* (i.e., perspective-taking) as "the ability to think about other people's thinking, and further, to think about what they think about our thinking, and, even further, to think about what they think we think about their thinking and so on" (p. 19). Another term for this is *meta-abilities* (i.e., the ability to know that we know). Meta-abilities can be specified into the abilities of meta-linguistic (talking about talking); metacognitive (thinking about thinking); metapragmatic (being aware of cultural rules for using language appropriately within and across various social contexts); and metanarrative (being aware of story elements and how to intentionally manipulate them).

The following areas might be assessed to determine a student's skill in engaging in meta-abilities. How well does the student:

- Demonstrate the ability to talk about talking—for example in terms of the following:
  - ▲ Grammatical rules
  - ▲ Word definitions
  - ▲ Literal versus figurative language

- Demonstrate the ability to think about thinking

- Demonstrate the ability to apply cultural/social rules for using language appropriately within and across various social contexts

- Demonstrate the ability to determine the elements and structure of a story and to intentionally manipulate them to create new stories

- Recognize when the listener does not understand, and then uses repair strategies to clarify communication

- Understand the feelings of another person as one's own feelings

## Nonverbal Communication

Nonverbal communication is the ability to both produce and to read nonverbal stimuli that occur in communication situations. It has been noted that as much as 90% of the social intent of a message is transmitted nonverbally (Samovar & Porter, 1991).

> Nonverbal communication serves the basic functions: to repeat, complement, or contradict what one said; to substitute for a verbal action; to regulate a communication event; and to accentuate a message. Nonverbal messages are communicated by various means: body movements (kinesics and posture), proxemics (space and distance), dress, facial expressions, eye contact, touch, smell, and paralanguage. (Larson & McKinley, 2003, p. 232)

When assessing students with AS as to their skill in engaging in appropriate nonverbal behavior, the following areas might be examined. How well does the student:

- Use appropriate facial expressions
- Understand others' facial expressions
- Use appropriate eye contact when speaking and listening
- Understand others' appropriate eye contact when speaking and listening
- Stand at an appropriate distance, given the culture of and familiarity with the person
- Understand others' proxemics or distance, given the cultural and social rules of the situation
- Use gestures that enhance communication and do not detract from it
- Understand others' gestures
- Use an appropriate rate of speech for the social situation
- Understand others' use of rate of speech in the social situation
- Use an appropriate tone of voice for the social situation
- Understand others' appropriate tone of voice for the social situation
- Use a variety of vocal inflections to accommodate different speaking situations
- Understand a variety of vocal inflections to accommodate the situation
- Use appropriate pauses given the social situation
- Understand the use of others' pauses given the situation
- Match verbal and nonverbal communication characteristics to enhance overall communication

# Academic Dimensions

The academic dimensions of learning style; cognitive abilities; executive functions; written communication (i.e., reading and writing); sensory integration; motor skills; curriculum-based tasks or textbook analysis; and classroom schedules, rules, and routines need to be assessed to determine where the problems interfering with academic success are. The student with Asperger Syndrome may not have problems with all of these academic dimensions, but rather with isolated areas that may present academic difficulties.

## Learning Style

The reason for assessing the student's learning style is to provide information needed to determine how, what, where, and when the student learns best. This provides you with knowledge of the student's strengths, as well as areas of concern. The following types of assessment questions might be asked about the learning style of a student with AS:

- What is the best time of day to learn a task?
- What level of noise is OK while the student is learning?
- What level of light is needed to learn?
- What should the temperature in the room be to feel comfortable to learn?
- Where is the best place to learn (e.g., at school, at home, at the library)?
- Where is the best location to learn (e.g., sitting at a desk, on the floor, on a bed, on a chair)?
- Does the student prefer to work with others or alone?
- Why does the student want to learn the topic?
- Does the student prefer to work visually or auditorially?

## Cognitive Abilities

According to Tsatsahis, Fuerst, and Rourke (1997), "Cognitive abilities comprise the mental processes involved in knowing, thinking, learning, and judging" (p. 5). The authors go on to note that these cognitive domains include such areas as attention and memory, conceptual thinking, problem solving, verbal and nonverbal reasoning, and acquired knowledge. The following areas may be examined when assessing the student's skill in undertaking cognitive tasks. How well does the student:

- Recall information from short- and long-term memory
- Engage in problem solving such as calculating, analyzing, and synthesizing information
- Demonstrate the ability to think critically about various subject areas
- Demonstrate the ability to learn independently
- Demonstrate the ability to understand and use a range of knowledge
- Demonstrate the ability to know how to learn to learn

## Executive Functions

Executive function abilities are to plan, organize, shift attention, and do multitasking successfully. Many students with AS do not do well at executive function tasks and therefore need assistance in planning, organizing, attending, and multitasking. The following areas should be examined when assessing the student's performance of executive function tasks. How well does the student:

- Plan events or tasks
- Organize events or tasks

- Logically sequence events and tasks
- Appropriately prioritize events and tasks
- Attend to tasks until completion
- Engage successfully in multitasking abilities

## Written Communication

### Reading

Reading to learn as opposed to learning to read (which is done in the early grades) may have challenging aspects for students with AS, especially if the individual is literal in his or her comprehension of reading material, or prefers to learn only about a special topic of interest (as opposed to a wide variety of topics and those required by the teacher or curriculum). Assuming the student knows how to read, but now needs to read to learn, the following areas might be assessed. How well does the student:

- Read differently depending on the text structure and genre (e.g., narrative versus expository text)
- Read differently depending on the purpose of the text (e.g., persuade, negotiate, inform, entertain)
- Know how and when to use different styles of reading (e.g., skimming, overview, analytic, critical)
- Know how to use various reading strategies to facilitate comprehension of reading (e.g., headings, subheadings, table of contents, summaries, end-of-chapter questions, glossary)
- Recognize his or her lack of understanding of the author's intent

### Writing

Students with AS may or may not have problems with writing. To determine whether this area is a challenge or a strength, the following areas should be assessed. How well does the student:

- Gather or research information about a topic
- Organize the information gathered
- Take the readers into account at the beginning of the writing process
- Consider the purpose for writing (e.g., narrative, expository text, giving directions)
- Outline before writing a first draft
- Use appropriate syntax, semantics, and mechanical skills
- Edit the written draft for content, clarity, and brevity
- Edit the written draft for spelling and grammatical errors

## Sensory Integration

Sensory integration (SI) is the process by which incoming sensations are interpreted, connected, and organized. SI abilities are necessary for a child to feel safe and comfortable in the environment and to function effectively within the environment (Ozonoff, Dawson, & McPartland, 2002). The following areas should be considered when assessing sensory integration. How well does the student:

- Tolerate typical tactile sensations when touched or rubbed up against
- Tolerate typical tactile sensations when touching certain substances (e.g., paste, finger paints, glue)
- Tolerate typical pain and injury sensations
- Tolerate typical visual sensations (e.g., fluorescent lights and sunlight)
- Tolerate typical distractions from visual stimuli
- Tolerate a range of sounds (e.g., school bells and fire alarms)
- Tolerate a range of tastes (e.g., sweet, salty, sour)
- Tolerate a range of smells (e.g., food, cleaners, glue, paste, paints)

## Motor Skills

The student typically has a range of fine and gross motor abilities that are needed to be successful at school, at home, and in the community. The following should be considered when assessing the area of motor abilities. Does the student:

- Have difficulty with gross motor abilities (e.g., walking, running, skipping, jumping)?
- Have difficulty with fine motor abilities (e.g., writing, painting, drawing, keyboarding)?
- Have difficulty changing direction or speed?
- Have a fear of heights or of his or her feet leaving the ground?

## Curriculum-Based Tasks or Textbook Analysis

Although students with AS may be highly competent in the areas of their special interest, other curriculum-based tasks and special-subject textbooks may be problematic. Therefore, it is important that the following questions be addressed. How well does the student:

- List those subject areas that are strengths and/or challenges in the curriculum
- Understand sequentially organized (little interaction among units [e.g., one unit is weather and the next is electricity]) versus spirally organized (i.e., major interaction among units [e.g., parts of speech, then sentence diagramming]) curricula
- Accommodate diverse requirements (i.e., excessive reading, lengthy term papers, detailed experiments, or public speaking)
- Accommodate to the textbooks' readability levels
- Adapt to certain types of tests (e.g., essay questions, multiple choice, true or false, short answer)

- Accommodate certain aspects of teachers' language (e.g., instructional mode [explanations, directions and questions]; syntactical and semantic mode [sentence variability and complexity; vocabulary] and speaking mode [length, rate, and intonation]; Gruenewald & Pollack, 1984; Larson & McKinley, 2003)

## Classroom Schedules, Rules, and Routines

A set of schedules, rules, and routines exists in every classroom. This is sometimes referred to as the "hidden curriculum." The hidden curriculum involves knowledge of the rules and the routines of the classroom that are not taught explicitly, yet students are expected and assumed to know (Myles and Adreon, 2001; Paul and Sutherland, 2003). This is very difficult for students with AS to understand. Explore the following areas when assessing knowledge of the hidden curriculum. How well does the student:

- Understand what to do at the beginning of a class
- Know what the teacher does to signal it is time to begin or end the lesson
- Know when it is OK to ask a question in class and when it is not
- Know what the most important thing that he or she should always or never do in class is
- Know how to read teachers' verbal and nonverbal cues that something is important
- Know what to do at the end of the day
- Know where students hang out during lunch
- Know rules about special community events (e.g., where to sit during a sporting event)
- Know hidden rules and routines surrounding school (e.g., where to hang out in the halls or where to hang out at a school dance)

# How Should Behaviors Be Assessed?

The lists of questions in the previous section addressed the type of information that should be gathered to determine and, in turn, to remediate the student's social competence and academic achievement issues. Equally important is the ability to determine how to best assess the student's behavior. The following is a synopsis of how to effectively assess a student with Asperger Syndrome.

# Informal Procedures

There are a variety of informal procedures that should be considered as part of the evaluation process. These procedures include, but are not limited to: interviews; questionnaires; checklists;

and observations at home, at school, and in the community; oral and written language samples; rubrics; portfolios; directed tasks; and functional behavioral assessments. Each contributes in different ways to a better understanding of the student with Asperger Syndrome.

## Interviews

Interviews play a critical role as an informal assessment procedure. An interview is a face-to-face interaction between two or more people (usually an interviewer and the interviewee), in which responses to specific questions or statements are recorded. It is recommended that parents, teachers, other professionals, and the student him- or herself be interviewed to gain as wide a perspective as possible on how the problem is being perceived. According to Pierangelo (2003), an interview can be either structured or unstructured. In a structured interview, questions and comments are predetermined, and there is control over the interview session by the interviewee. In an unstructured interview, questions and statements are not predetermined, and open-ended discussion is pursued.

In addition to interviewing the parents or students using a general case history form, a supplemental case history form might be used to gather data on the students' perspective of how well they think, listen, speak, read, and write in various academic situations. Also, the supplemental case history form gathers data on the students' perspective of their ability to plan and organize, to initiate and maintain friendships, to take the perspective of others, and to understand and use nonverbal communication. A Supplemental Case History Form (shown in Figure 2.2 on page 36) is provided as Appendix B on the CD-ROM.

## Questionnaires

A Learning Style Questionnaire (shown in Figure 2.3 on page 36) is provided as Appendix C on the CD-ROM. A learning style questionnaire can provide insight into when, where, what, and how the students learn best. The questionnaire can be used either by the examiner with the student, or by the student him- or herself, to provide insight into how learning best occurs. This questionnaire has been designed to accommodate the needs of students with AS to determine their specific learning styles.

## Checklists

Gajewski et al. (1998a, 1998b) noted that there are a number of methods for assessing social skills, such as observations, sociometric devices (students identify peers who are most acceptable or unacceptable), hypothetical situations, and behavioral checklists. Social-Emotional Skills Rating Scales (developed by Gajewski et al. and shown in Figure 2.4 on page 37 and Figure 2.5 on page 38), are provided as Appendices D and E on the CD-ROM. The adult form is filled out by the adults in the students' lives (e.g., parents, teachers, coaches); the student form is completed by the

**Figure 2.2**

# Supplemental Case History Interview Form

Student: _____  Age: _____

Interviewer: _____  Date: _____

### Feelings and Attitudes

**Planning and Organizing**

1. What is planning and organizing? _____

_____

_____

2. How important is planning and organizing in your life? Use this scale: 1 = Not at all important, 3 = Sometimes important, 5 = Extremely important

| 1 | 2 | 3 | 4 | 5 |

3. Whom do you know that you consider to be a good planner or organizer? _____

What makes you think that he or she is a good planner or organizer? _____

_____

4. Have you ever felt you would like to plan better? _____ No _____ Yes

If "Yes," when? _____

Have you ever felt you would like to be better organized? _____ No _____ Yes

If "Yes," when? _____

5. What interferes with your ability to plan? _____

_____

**Figure 2.3**

# Learning Style Questionnaire

Name: _____

Date: _____  Gender: M  F  Grade: _____

Birthdate: _____  School: _____

**Directions:** This is NOT a test. There are no right or wrong answers. The following items are simply
a way to find out how you learn best. If an item is unclear, feel free to ask questions.

The purpose of this questionnaire is to determine how you learn best, not how much
you like to learn a subject. For example, you might like to have the TV on while you
are studying, but you study best when it is quiet. Also, you might like to study at night,
but you are more productive if you study in the morning. *Learn best* means how you
remember information the longest, pay attention to a task the most, and recall details
and main ideas easiest. Knowing how you learn best will allow your teachers to help
you be more successful in school.

Before you begin to answer the questions, write your name, the date, and other identification information requested in the spaces provided above. Then answer the following
statements honestly about when, how, where, why, and with whom you learn best.

My most difficult subject is: _____

**I learn my most difficult subject best: When?**

1. Time (✓ only 1 box)  ☐ Morning  ☐ Afternoon  ☐ Night

Other (explain): _____

2. Timing (✓ only 1 box)  ☐ Before meals  ☐ After meals

**I learn my most difficult subject best: How?**

1. Sound (✓ only 1 box)  ☐ When quiet  ☐ Radio on  ☐ When talking
☐ TV on  ☐ Music on  ☐ When noisy

Other (explain): _____

students themselves to provide insight into the students' social-emotional behaviors. (NOTE: For some students, it may be advantageous to read the checklist to them.) The checklists identify problematic skills (these would be *items rated 1),* and those needing more practice or intervention (these would be *items rated 2).* In addition, you can compare and contrast the student's responses to those of the adults to determine if there is agreement on which skills are problematic. Another checklist, The Children's Communication Checklist (CCC; see Bishop, 1998), investigates children's pragmatic aspects of communication by asking parents or professionals to report on 70 items in nine broad categories (speech, syntax, inappropriate initiation, coherence, stereotypical language, use of context, rapport, social relationships, interests). Additionally, recall that a checklist based on Table 1.3 (on pages 15–19) is provided as Appendix A on the CD-ROM and will determine where the student is on a 1 to 5 rating scale in the areas of social competence and academic achievement.

## Observations at Home, at School, and in the Community

Observations provide valuable insights into students' behaviors. A thorough observation should include the following situations (Pierangelo, 2003):

**Figure 2.4** **Social-Emotional Skills Rating Scale–Adult Form**

Name of Student: ______

Grade: ______ Age: ______ Date: ______

Name of Person Completing Rating Scale: ______

Relationship to Student (e.g., parent, teacher, coach): ______

**Directions:** Rate this student on his or her use of the following social-emotional skills.

Circle:
1—if the skill is SELDOM used appropriately.
2—if the skill is SOMETIMES used appropriately.
3—if the skill is ALMOST ALWAYS used appropriately.

For example, if a student usually complains and begs when he or she is told "No" by an authority figure, rate the student as follows:

ACCEPTING "NO"—Responds appropriately when told "No" by an authority figure. (1) 2 3

Write examples and comments in the margin areas when appropriate (e.g., if you give a SELDOM rating for ACCEPTING "NO," you might explain that the student argues with you when he or she is told "No").

| Social-Emotional Skills | SELDOM | SOMETIMES | ALMOST ALWAYS |
|---|---|---|---|
| 1. USING BODY LANGUAGE—Uses body language (components of the body that communicate messages) that is appropriate to the situation. | 1 | 2 | 3 |
| 2. USING MANNERS—Speaks and acts politely in social situations. | 1 | 2 | 3 |
| 3. CHOOSING THE RIGHT TIME AND PLACE—Chooses an appropriate time and place before beginning a conversation with another person. | 1 | 2 | 3 |

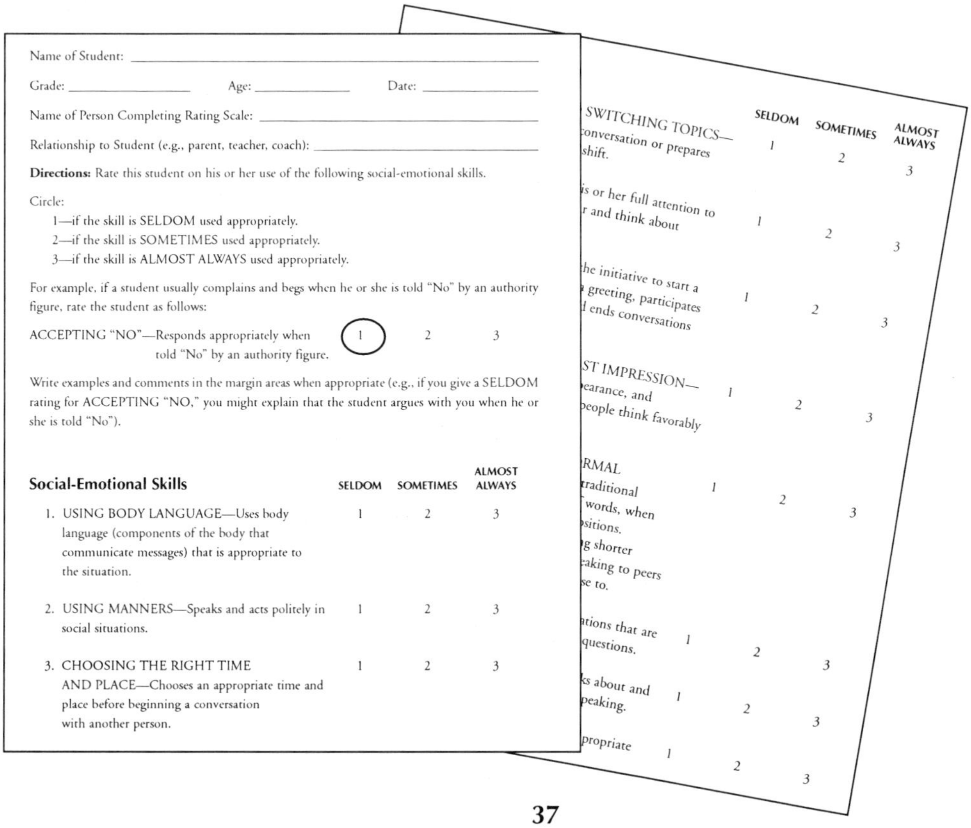

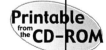

Printable from the CD-ROM

Figure 2.5        **Social-Emotional Skills Rating Scale–Student Form**

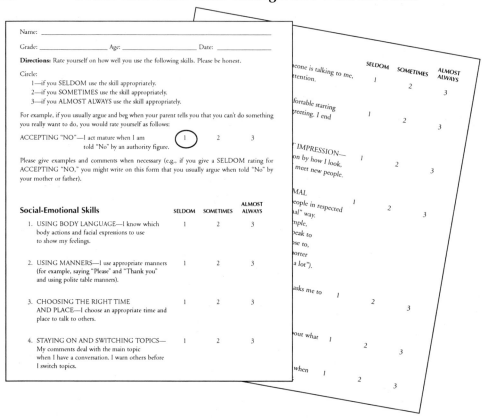

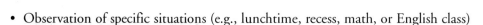

- Observation of specific situations (e.g., lunchtime, recess, math, or English class)
- Observation in various settings (e.g., classroom, playground, sports activities, band practice)
- Observation at different times of the day (e.g., morning, afternoon, evening)

Also, a complete observation method should include various types of recording (Pierangelo, 2003), such as the following:

- **Anecdotal recording**—All behaviors are recorded within a given time frame (e.g., from 2:00 to 3:00 pm)

- **Event recording or frequency recording**—One targeted behavior is recorded within a specified timeframe (e.g., the number of times a student puts his hands over his eyes)

- **Latency recording**—The amount of time between a stimulus and a response (e.g., the teacher asks a question and the student answers)

- **Duration recording**—The amount of time a targeted behavior occurs (e.g., the number of minutes the student reads silently during an hour session)

Observations are valuable tools to determine the student's most frequently occurring positive or negative behaviors, baseline information against which progress can be measured, and data for program development or the individualized education program (IEP) planning and implementation.

## Oral and Written Language Samples

Some of the most valuable types of information that can be obtained are representative oral and written language samples. Oral conversations and narrations, as well as writing samples are important.

### Conversations

Assessment of conversational abilities of students with AS is critical to determine if they engage in turn-taking and know how to initiate, maintain, and terminate a topic. Because students with AS can be verbose about their topics of special interest, it is important that the student with AS not always select the topic. Therefore, you should select some topics and the student should select other topics to determine if the conversational sample changes depending on the topic and who selects it. Also, it is important that at least one of the language samples be done with a peer and not just with you as examiner. You should not dominate the conversation, but should use open-ended questions or comments to facilitate student responses. Also, it is recommended that at least

Figure 2.6                    **Conversational Analysis Form**

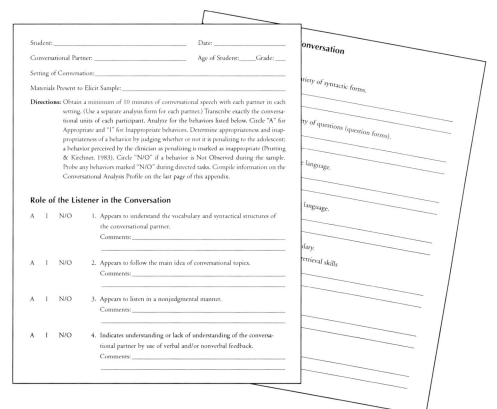

two 10-minute conversational samples be collected with different listeners, settings, and topics. Once the samples are obtained, it is recommended that they be transcribed and then analyzed using a conversational analysis form. One such form (shown in Figure 2.6 on page 39) is provided on the CD-ROM as Appendix F.

## Narrations

How you obtain a narrative sample may result in different outcomes. For example, if asked to relate a personal experience, students will produce a narrative or story that is more like an oral sample. If asked to tell a story about a TV program or movie that they have just seen, they will produce a more literal or structured story. If asked to tell a story like it was written in a book, they will use the most literary structured story style. Thus, what you ask the student to do to produce a story may alter the type of story outcome received. Also, the narrative sample changes whether it is a storytelling (i.e., story generation) or story retelling task. Therefore, it is recommended that both a storytelling and retelling sample be obtained. Once the stories have been obtained, they

Figure 2.7

# Narrative Analysis Form

Student:_____     Examiner:_____

Age:_____     Grade: _____     Date: _____

**Directions:** Check to reflect the highest level of narrative development for formulated and reformulated tasks.

| Cognitive Period | Approximate Age of Emergence | Narrative Stage | Tasks | |
|---|---|---|---|---|
| | | | Formulated | Reformulated |
| Preoperational | 2 years | Heap Stories | | |
| | 2 to 3 years | Sequence Stories | | |
| | 3 to 4 years | Primitive Narratives | | |
| | 4 to 5 years | Chain Narratives | | |
| | 5 to 7 years | True Narratives | | |
| Concrete | 7 to 11 years | Narrative Summaries | | |
| | 11 to 12 years | Complex Narratives | | |
| Formal | 13 to 15 years | Analysis | | |
| | 16 to Adulthood | Generalization | | |

Description of Formulated Task: _____

Description of Reformulated Task: _____

Comments: _____

_____

_____

should be analyzed using either a developmental hierarchy (such as the one provided on the CD-ROM as Appendix G and shown in Figure 2.7) or a story grammar approach, as indicated earlier in this chapter, on pages 28–29.

## Writing Samples

The way in which a writing sample is obtained will determine how formal or informal the sample will be. For example, a writing sample will be more informal if students are told to write their autobiography than if told to write a story like it might be written in a book. Expository text writing will vary if the writing sample is a book report versus a scientific lab report. When gathering a written sample, give specific directions as to time limit, whether it should be handwritten or word-processed, the type of topic, and so on. As with oral language samples, the extent of the sample for students with AS may be contingent on who chooses the topic and whether it is an area of special interest to the student with AS. Once the sample has been obtained, it should be analyzed for writing-process characteristics, as well as mechanical features. An analysis form (shown in Figure 2.8) is provided as Appendix H on the CD-ROM.

Figure 2.8

# Writing Analysis Profile

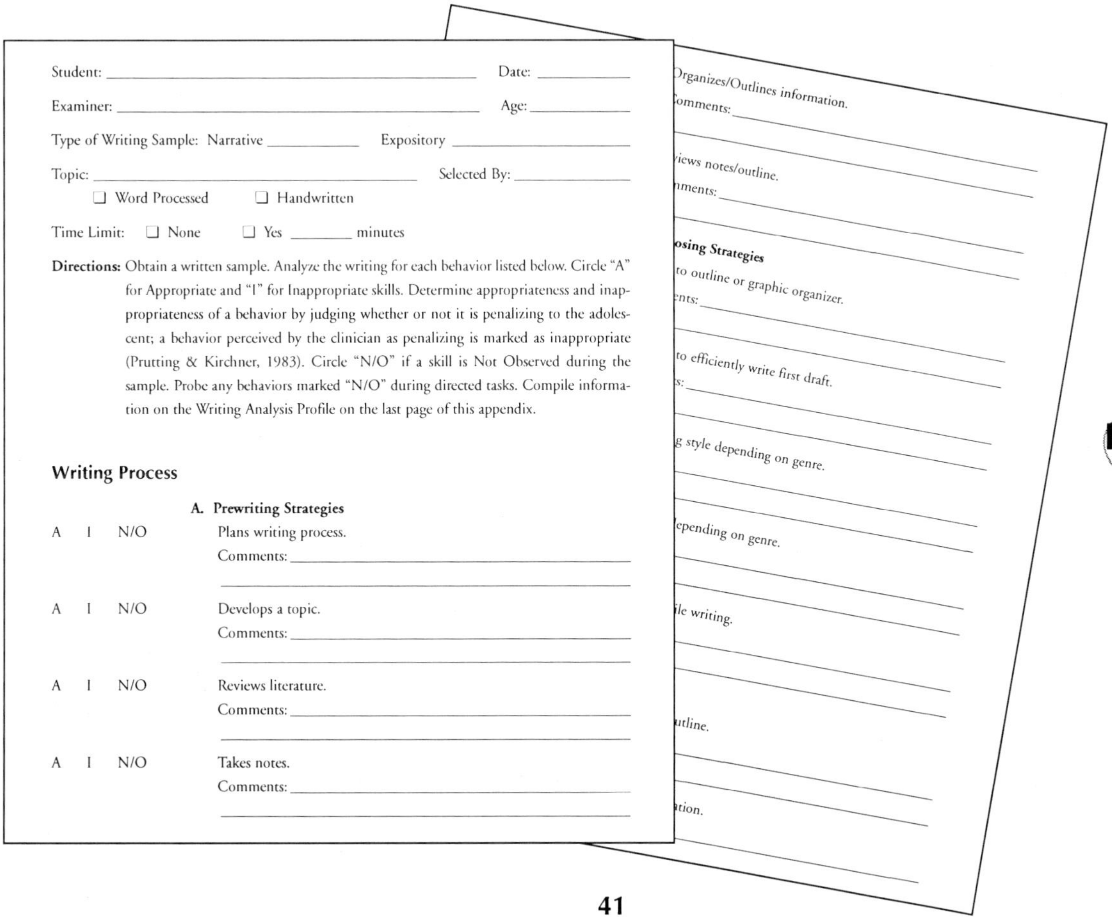

Student: _____  Date: _____

Examiner: _____  Age: _____

Type of Writing Sample: Narrative _____  Expository _____

Topic: _____  Selected By: _____

☐ Word Processed     ☐ Handwritten

Time Limit:  ☐ None     ☐ Yes _____ minutes

**Directions:** Obtain a written sample. Analyze the writing for each behavior listed below. Circle "A" for Appropriate and "I" for Inappropriate skills. Determine appropriateness and inappropriateness of a behavior by judging whether or not it is penalizing to the adolescent; a behavior perceived by the clinician as penalizing is marked as inappropriate (Prutting & Kirchner, 1983). Circle "N/O" if a skill is Not Observed during the sample. Probe any behaviors marked "N/O" during directed tasks. Compile information on the Writing Analysis Profile on the last page of this appendix.

**Writing Process**

**A. Prewriting Strategies**

A   I   N/O   Plans writing process.
Comments: _____

A   I   N/O   Develops a topic.
Comments: _____

A   I   N/O   Reviews literature.
Comments: _____

A   I   N/O   Takes notes.
Comments: _____

Organizes/Outlines information.
Comments: _____

...views notes/outline.
...nments: _____

...osing Strategies
...to outline or graphic organizer.
...nts: _____

...to efficiently write first draft.
...s: _____

...g style depending on genre.
_____

...epending on genre.
_____

...le writing.
_____

...utline.
_____

...tion.
_____

Printable from the CD-ROM

**41**

## Rubrics

According to Benjamin (2000), rubrics are scoring guides. Wiig, Larson, and Olson (2004) have developed a rubric assessment tool called *S-MAPs (Structured-Multidimensional Assessment Profiles)* for both students and professionals to use to assess areas such as basic and advanced communication skills; literacy and discourse development; and thinking and creativity. The rubric or S-MAP is provided as a 4" × 4" grid in which four skill dimensions for a topical area are listed across the top of the grid, and four performance levels or criteria are listed down the side. Appendix I on the CD-ROM contains several S-MAPs that would be appropriate for use with students who have AS. Figure 2.9 provides an example of an S-MAP. For a full array of S-MAPs, see Wiig, Larson, and Olson (2004).

## Portfolios

According to Paulson, Paulson, and Meyer (1991):

> A portfolio is a purposeful collection of student work that exhibits the student's efforts, progress, and achievements in one or more areas. The collection must

**Figure 2.9**                                         **S-MAP**

**Nonverbal Communication**

**Grades K–12**

This S-MAP addresses the understanding and expression of meaning conveyed through means other than oral language. It focuses on the use of gestures, body language, facial expression, and distance to support the meanings of verbally stated intents and responses to verbal and nonverbal messages from others. Nonverbal communication varies significantly between cultures, so examiners must be familiar with their students' cultural norms.

**Purpose**
- To assess the student's interpretation and expression of meanings and intents conveyed by gestures, body language, facial expression, and use of distance (proxemics)

**Uses**
- Nonverbal communication is used across social interactions with peers and authority figures in natural contexts. Tasks may include greetings and introductions, play, asking or answering questions, or interacting with store clerks.
- Nonverbal communication is used across classroom activities. Tasks may include participating in cooperative learning groups, role-playing, game playing, performance of skits and plays in staged contexts, and participating in instructional activities.

**Skill Dimensions**
**Gestures**
- Use gestures to express consistent meanings without accompanying oral communication (e.g., head nods, holding nose, shaking hands).
- Use gestures appropriately to enhance accompanying oral communication (e.g., Say, "Come here," and motion with hand).
- Understand and respond to the meaning of gestures used by others with and without accompanying oral communication.
- Use gestures flexibly to express the various purposes of nonverbal communication (e.g., repeat, contribute, substitute, elaborate, encourage, accent, and regulate communication).

nguage and posture appropriately to context (e.g., slouching versus sitting
ay from versus facing a speaker).
ge and posture to express a variety of meanings with and without accom-
munication (e.g., folding arms across chest or shrugging shoulders and
ow").

spond appropriately to body language and posture of others.
nd posture flexibly to express various purposes of nonverbal communica-
ontribute, substitute, elaborate, accent, and regulate oral communication).

expressions to express consistent meanings (e.g., smiling, frowning,
lips, making eye contact).
ressions that match and enhance accompanying oral communication
ying, "I'm mad," or a frustrated expression and saying, "I give up").
to a variety of facial expressions by others with and without
unication.

ly to express various purposes of nonverbal communication (e.g.,
tute, elaborate, encourage, or regulate oral communication).

ween speakers, taking context into account, when initiating
reen speakers when initiating, speaking, and responding in
en speakers when initiating, speaking, and responding in
ly, depending on context and familiarity of others present.

ific Grade Level

verify their grade-level expectations.
culum documents and texts for samples of the content
ce, and adjust expectations accordingly.
al expectations when judging typical versus disordered
pical developmental expectations for taking others'
munication skills.

include student participation in selecting contents, the criteria for selection, the criteria for judging merit, and evidence of the student self-reflection. (p. 60)

In portfolio assessment, the student, teacher, speech-language pathologist, or all of the above may place samples of students' work in a portfolio. Work samples in the portfolio allow for the comparison of past with present performance and allow for the student's authentic work done in the classroom or centered on the curriculum to be shown. The use of portfolios not only supports authentic assessment (i.e., performance-based assessment that demonstrates the application of knowledge to real-life activities, real-world settings, or simulation of such settings using real-life and real-world activities [Pierangelo, 2003]), but also provides for the student to become an active participant in the assessment process.

## Directed Tasks

Directed task assessment is what Larson and McKinley (2003) describe as informal procedures designed to assess a specific skill. The focus is on the process that the student goes through and not on the product that the student generates. Directed task assessment is another name for dynamic assessment in that the focus is on determining how the student is learning and on identifying some teaching or scaffolding that helps the student learn the task at hand. Several approaches to directed tasks have been devised by Larson and McKinley (2003) and are presented in Appendix J on the CD-ROM (Figure 2.10 on page 44 presents an example). One directed task is on problem solving, another is on giving and getting directions, and the third is on curriculum analysis. Additional directed tasks of organization, topic management, informational listening, critical listening, question asking and answering, and word retrieval are described in *Communication Solutions for Older Students* (Larson & McKinley, 2003).

## Functional Behavioral Assessment

The purpose of a functional behavioral assessment (FBA) is to determine and alter the factors that account for a student's misconduct in school (Hallahan & Kauffman, 2003). Behavior is maintained by antecedents (events that happen before the behavior is exhibited), consequences (events that happen after the behavior), or setting events (the context in which the behavior occurs). If the inappropriate behavior seems to be preceded or followed by an event in the environment, educators should try eliminating the event before they try to eliminate the behavior. For example, if students with AS have random outbursts in the classroom, educators should observe these students over time to see if there are events that take place in the environment before or after the behavior (e.g., a certain loud noise always precedes the outburst). If, for instance, it is determined by talking to the parents that these students have a very low threshold to auditory stimuli, it might be easier to eliminate the noise rather than try to eliminate the behavioral outbursts. In another case, the behavior might be followed by attention from the teacher or other peers. Eliminating the

Figure 2.10

# Directed Tasks

## Problem Solving

### Areas Assessed

The following informal assessment task for problem solving provides information primarily on cognition, but it also provides data on conversational abilities when the problem-solving task involves dialogue.

### Administrative Steps

1. Say to the student, **"Let's talk about how you would handle some problem situations. Here's the first one. You try to turn on your TV with the remote control and nothing happens. You're surprised because the TV was on just a few minutes ago. Tell me about the problem."** Pause and wait at least five seconds for a response. If the student does not generate an appropriate response, repeat the situation and cue the student. If necessary, model a correct response (e.g., the TV won't turn on). Once the student has satisfactorily answered or you have modeled a response, say, **"Okay. Now tell me about the problem by asking me a question."** Pause and wait for a response. Prompt for the question form. If the student appears not to understand, model the question (e.g., "Why doesn't the TV start?"). Write the question to be answered on a piece of paper and place it in front of the student.

2. Ask the student, **"What are the ways you could answer that question?"** Pause and wait for a response. If the student says nothing, ask the question written on the paper, shrug your shoulders, and ask, **"Why?"** Usually students will say at least a generic answer like, "It's broken." That is one answer, but prompt for additional options such as "The TV is unplugged" or "The batteries in the remote control are dead." If necessary, provide these answers yourself and write them on the piece of paper below the question.

3. Ask, **"What is the best answer?"** Review the list of answers and have the student pick one. Ask, **"Why did you choose that one?"** Record the rationale.

4. Say, **"Let's make a plan to check out your best answer. What would you do next?"** (e.g., "The remote control batteries are dead"—Change the batteries and see if the TV can be switched back on). Prompt for the student's best answer.

5. Ask ...

ur answer is the best one?" Pause and wait for a response. e that the TV will turn on. Ask, **"If the TV doesn't turn** Vait for the student to choose another answer. Say, **"Let's** ur second best answer. What would you do next?" er. Then ask, **"How will you know if that answer** se like "The TV will turn on." Prompt as needed. As a

oblem situation: **"You just popped a movie into your** ntrol's Play button, but nothing happened. What is itional problem situations, or create your own based student (e.g., **"You have a 10-page paper due for** tarted the assignment. What is the problem?"). and content to fit the new problem.

prompts; 5 = dependent on prompts), rate how of the problem-solving steps for situations a form such as the attached *Problem-Solving*

pendence as additional problem situations were ith Problem #1, since Problem #2 was a slight mance improved toward more independence. ative Step #3. Analyze the strength of the

em to be solved, focus intervention on e answered.

(answers) and fails to generate more vergent thinking skills. In addition, perspectives.

r to generate a logical rationale for ntrasting features of alternative solu- gical reasoning skills.

attention may reduce or eliminate the behavior. For example, a behavior might only occur in physical education class. Through the process of FBA, it might be determined that students have gross motor problems and cannot meet the teacher's expectations. Students might be exhibiting inappropriate behavior, so they are being removed from class. Having this kind of information will help determine how to best change the behavior. If nothing can be found in the environment that affects the behavior (e.g., eliminating an aversive noise) the educator can try, at this point, to use a behavior management technique.

If the behavior is odd or eccentric (e.g., lining up all the pencils in his desk before each class), but does not affect the students with AS, their peers, or the educator, there is no reason to try to change the behavior. If the environment can be changed to better accommodate or to reduce the behavior (e.g., the elimination of a loud noise that causes a "melt down"), it would be better to change the environment. A good rule of thumb is to use the least invasive approach possible to change the behavior. A good FBA will give the educator this kind of information.

Sidebar 2.1 delineates the steps for completing a functional behavioral assessment, and Appendix K on the CD-ROM provides a recording form for listing the behavior, the antecedent, and the consequence. See pages 168–171 for a detailed explanation of each step listed in Sidebar 2.1.

# Formal/Standardized Tests

At this point, the focus has been on informal procedures, but a variety of standardized tests also exist to assess isolated communication, language, cognitive, and academic variables. Formal tests that are pertinent to the assessment of students with AS will be highlighted. Most standardized tests are discrete point testing (e.g., they test isolated aspects of language—such as syntax or semantics—through a cloze procedure, or by asking a specific question that requires a single-word or simple-sentence response). Thus, a caveat for the professional is that these standardized tests should be used cautiously and should never supplant—but only supplement—informal procedures. Standardized tests are usually not a good indicator of current performance or an accurate predictor of future potential for students with AS, because of the narrow way in which they test behaviors.

There are two basic types of standardized tests: (1) norm-referenced tests, in which large numbers of children are sampled on a given item and then students who take the test can be compared to this sample to determine how well they performed; and (2) criterion-referenced tests, for which a predetermined criterion has been established in which most children are successful, and the student being assessed must pass this criterion before being able to move forward developmentally. There are several areas of assessment that might warrant the use of standardized tests:

**Sidebar 2.1**                    **Steps for Completing an FBA**

1. Identify and describe the behavior to be observed.

2. Determine how the behavior will be counted.

3. Determine how the behavior will be recorded.

4. Decide when the observations will take place.

5. Do the assessment by observing the behavior, the antecedent (what triggers the behavior), and the consequence (what purpose the behavior serves).

6. Analyze the results.

7. Develop a behavior management plan.

- Cognitive abilities
- Language and communication skills
- Sensory processing

Cognitive abilities are frequently evaluated by psychologists using norm-referenced intelligence tests, such as the Wechsler Intelligence Scale for Children (WISC–IV; Wechsler, 2003) and the Stanford-Binet Intelligence Scale (SB5; Roid, 2003). Although not an intelligence test, the Woodcock-Johnson Tests of Cognitive Ability (WJ–III; Woodcock, McGrew, & Mather, 2001) might also be used to determine cognitive functioning.

In the area of language and communication skills, speech-language pathologists might use a variety of norm-referenced tests, such as the Clinical Evaluation of Language Functions–4th Edition (CELF–4; Semel, Wiig, & Secord, 2003); the Peabody Picture Vocabulary Test–III (PPVT–III; Dunn & Dunn, 1997); the Test of Language Competence–Expanded Edition (TLC–E; Wiig & Secord, 1995); the Test of Problem Solving Adolescent (TOPS–Adolescent; Zachman, Barrett, Huisingh, Orman, & Blagden, 1991); the Test of Problem Solving–Elementary, Revised (Bowers, Huisingh, Barrett, Orman, & LoGiudice, 1994); the Comprehensive Assessment of Spoken Language (CASL; Carrow-Woolfolk, 1998); and the Test of Pragmatic Language (TOPL; Phelps-Terasaki & Phelps-Gunn, 1992).

In the area of sensory processing, an occupational therapist might administer some of the following tests: The Sensory Profile (Dunn, 1999); The Short Sensory Profile (McIntosh, Miller, Shyu, & Dunn, 1999), and the Sensory Integration Inventory–Revised (Reisman & Hanschu, 1992). According to Paul and Sutherland (2003), students with AS frequently score within the normal range on many, if not all, of the formal measures of language. Thus, it is critical that informal procedures be used in conjunction with standardized tests.

# Case Study: Maria

This last section provides an opportunity to apply the skills for assessment that have been addressed thus far in this chapter. The case study focuses on a third-grade student named Maria, who has not been referred to or diagnosed as needing special education, but has consistently exhibited some unusual and inappropriate behaviors since kindergarten.

Following the case study is a guide to help the reader analyze the kind of assessment protocol that should be used to determine if Maria needs the services offered in special education. Following the analysis is an assessment plan that will help the professionals consider how to best plan services for Maria.

## Assessment of Maria

Maria is in third grade at Lincoln Elementary. She is a small girl with dark hair and dark eyes who is almost invisible in school. No one notices Maria and she does not seem to notice anyone else. She comes into the classroom every day, goes to her seat, and does not get up from her desk unless she has to. She works at her desk with her head down most of the time. When she is called on by the educator to answer a question or make a comment, Maria will tilt her head to one side, keeping her eyes on her desk or lap and quietly answer the question. She almost always knows the answer. If students address her with a "Hi, Maria," she will very quietly respond or ignore the approach. On the playground, she does not play with the other students. She usually stands next to the building looking at the ground. She stays there until the bell rings, and then she walks toward the door and stands in line. She always stays at the back of the line away from the other students.

The only time Maria makes her presence known is if she gets crowded in line or in groups; if she has to touch certain substances, like paste, paper wmaché, or silly putty; or if she is forced to play games that use balls. In instances when she is asked to stand anywhere except at the end of the line, be in a crowd, touch substances she does not like, or play games with balls, she adamantly refuses to comply with the request of the teacher. She will try to flee the situation, which is out of character for her. A few times in previous grades, an educator has forced her to into one of the situations that she clearly disliked. As an example, her first-grade teacher tried to force Maria to do finger painting and Maria quietly said no. When the teacher touched Maria's hand and moved it into the paint, Maria cried out and ran from the room into the bathroom and hid in a toilet stall. She stayed there until her mother came to school and picked her up. Educators do not force her anymore as long as her behavior does not interfere with the other students, the curriculum, or her learning. None of the educators understand why she has these strong feelings or reacts as she does.

Until third grade, in spite of an occasional outburst, Maria has always finished her assignments and has been compliant in school. She loves to read and, when she has any free time, she stays at her desk and reads about or draws pictures of horses. She is very interested in and extremely knowledgeable about horses. Mrs. Washington, Maria's third-grade teacher, has taken an interest in Maria. She thinks she might be depressed because she looks so sad and shows so little affect. She also has heard from other teachers about Maria's "over-reaction" to certain things, which has Mrs. Washington baffled.

*Continued on next page*

*Maria—Continued*

Mrs. Washington has asked Maria to stay after school a couple of times to try to engage her in a conversation to find out more about what Maria is like when there are no other students around. She has opened up a little with Mrs. Washington. When asked about why she ran away from certain situations, Maria merely said she was scared and she didn't like to come to school, but she did not elaborate beyond that. Mrs. Washington has also noticed that Maria is starting to have trouble comprehending some of the things she reads.

In a conference that Mrs. Washington had with Maria's mother, she found out several interesting things. She learned that Maria will only wear certain clothes and refuses all others; likes clothes that are tight fitting; hates to have her hair washed; follows a very rigid routine at home; does not have any neighborhood friends; and has never liked being touched, held, or snuggled. Maria has a large collection of horses and books about horses. She wants a horse of her own, but she does not want to take horseback riding lessons. Maria's mother is very frustrated and anxious about her daughter's behavior. She has asked the family doctor if something is wrong with Maria, but she has been told that Maria will outgrow "this." She has tried to take Maria to a counselor because she is so worried about her apathy and depression, but Maria has refused to go.

Mrs. Washington is worried, too. She knows that Maria has a problem, but she cannot pinpoint it. In her 15 years of teaching, she has never had a student quite like Maria. She has decided to have a meeting with the school psychologist, the speech-language pathologist, and Maria's mother to talk about some possible ways to help Maria. Mrs. Washington is tempted to refer her for an evaluation to see if she might need special education services.

# Analysis

Answering the analysis questions will help school professionals develop an understanding of the students in their classrooms that might need special education and related services, even though they seemingly do not fit into any program that is already in place.

- Is the teacher right about referring Maria for a special education evaluation? Why or why not?
- What would you say are the presenting problems?
- Do you think these problems might be symptoms of AS? If so, why?
- What services do you think Maria needs, based on her problems?
- Does Maria belong in regular education? Is she getting the kind of help she needs?

- What informal procedures listed in Table 2.2 would you use to evaluate Maria?
- What formal/standardized tests would you use to evaluate Maria?

# Assessment Plan

Using a disciplinary approach, a team of professionals from various disciplines participated in developing an assessment plan for Maria. The team members included the school psychologist, the general educator, the speech-language pathologist, and the occupational therapist. Depending on the team members' expertise, they selected and administered the following informal procedures and formal/standardized tests.

In the first stage of diagnosis, the parents and teachers closest to Maria participated in informal procedures, answering questions like those presented in the beginning of this chapter and completing questionnaires and checklists (i.e., The Australian Scale for Asperger Syndrome; Garnett & Attwood, 1995). Maria was not old enough to complete a questionnaire. In addition to interviews, questionnaires, and checklists, the examiners also observed Maria's school, home, and community interactions. Oral and written language samples were obtained. Rubrics and portfolio assessment were also undertaken, as well as an FBA.

In the second stage of diagnosis and evaluation, professionals administered formal instruments including the following: an intelligence test (i.e., WISC–IV; Wechsler, 2003); a language test (i.e., TLC–E; Wiig & Secord, 1995); a sensory integration test (i.e., The Sensory Profile [Dunn, 1999]); a social skills scale (i.e., the Social Skills Rating Scale–Adult Form; Gajewski, Hirn, & Mayo, 1998a, 1998b); and an Asperger scale (i.e., Gilliam Asperger's Disorder Scale (GADS; Gilliam, 2001).

After the evaluation was completed, the team of professionals and the parents analyzed the data to determine what services Maria needed to be successful in school. They also discussed whether or not she should be placed in special education.

## Discussion Points

1. Why does misdiagnosis of Asperger Syndrome occur, and what are the most frequent types of misdiagnosis?

2. How can one most effectively engage in a differential diagnosis?

3. What types of behaviors need to be assessed to determine the students' social competence and their academic success?

4. What types of informal procedures should be used to provide the most comprehensive description of Asperger Syndrome?

5. What types of formal or standardized tests are most widely used to assess students with Asperger Syndrome?

# General
# Intervention Strategies

## Goals

- To explain general intervention guidelines

- To discuss a strategy approach to intervention

- To present a continuum of service delivery options

- To highlight transition planning for students with AS

- To discuss the public policy and legal issues surrounding special education and AS

The purpose of this chapter is to discuss general intervention guidelines to consider using with students who have AS, regardless of their age or specific areas of concern (e.g., social competence, academic, sensory/motor skills). Also, a discussion of the relevance and importance of using a strategy approach to intervention is presented. According to Bernstein and Polirstok (2003), research has not identified that one specific intervention method is better than another. It appears "most effective interventions are eclectic or multimodal and require a collaborative approach by speech-language pathologists, teachers, parents, and other key school personnel" (p. 72).

A continuum of service delivery models, from inclusion in the general education classroom to provision of services in resource rooms with special educators, to an individualized program delivered by a specialist are options. Transition planning required under the 1997 Individuals with Disabilities Education Act (IDEA, 1997) and supported by the Individuals with Disabilities Improvement Act (IDEA 2004), is highlighted as it applies to the student with AS. In addition, public policy and legal issues relevant to students with AS receiving special education services are presented.

# General Intervention Guidelines

Regardless of the student's age, strengths, challenges, or grade level, certain guidelines should be followed during intervention sessions:

- Explain the purpose of intervention to the student with AS.
- Move from literal to ambiguous concepts and from concrete to more abstract strategies.
- Adapt materials, methods, and procedures to the student's developmental levels.
- Establish ground rules for intervention sessions.
- Be prepared to counsel.
- Open the class period with class meeting routines geared to each student's development levels.

Each of the intervention guidelines listed above is discussed more completely in the section that follows.

## Purpose of Intervention

Once an assessment has determined a student's strengths and challenges and the need for intervention, the purpose of intervention should be explained. This encompasses telling the student what the issues are and how best to intervene and change behaviors that are getting in the way of being successful at school, at home, and in the community. Older students (preadolescents and adolescents) should be a part of the evaluation team's deliberations about establishing goals, objectives, or benchmarks. The more the student is included in the assessment decision-making process, the more likely the student will be willing to participate in the intervention decision-making process. Educators need to communicate openly to the student with AS what needs to be accomplished and why it is important to achieve the goals set forth. Keep in mind that many of these students have above-average IQs, and students with AS do not like surprises or rapid change. By making them part of the process, they are aware of the routines, challenges, and procedures that await them.

## Concrete to Abstract

Students with AS struggle with abstract and ambiguous concepts and, therefore, it is desirable to work from a concrete and a literal level to a more abstract level. This can be accomplished through the use of social stories (see page 86), and moving from role-playing, modeling, and prompting activities to real-world situations. Overall, students with AS benefit from rules and routines being explained first in a very literal sense and then, eventually in a more abstract way, to help ground them in the school's rules and routines.

# Materials and Procedures at
# Cognitive Level or Slightly Above

Students with AS may have above-average IQs; thus, the materials and procedures used should be at the student's cognitive level or slightly above and not at their chronological age. Also, students who have lower IQs than their chronological age should have materials that are appealing to someone of their chronological age, but with the difficulty of the content at their mental age or slightly above so that they are required to stretch and challenge their intellectual and social skills. Typically, intervention should be designed with some of the following principles in mind (Larson & McKinley, 2003):

- Design curricula to stimulate students to reach toward the next level of cognitive development.

- Structure activities to emphasize application of communication and social skills (e.g., role-playing activities, rather than worksheet completion).

- Conduct activities within social groups. Including peers who have the appropriate communication and social skills is highly desirable because the student with AS will observe first-hand how to engage in successful communication and social situations by observing peers. The student with typical development serves as a role model for the student with AS, and over time may become a friend or at least an advocate for the student with AS.

- Structure activities to be sensitive to peer pressure as the student becomes older. It is also desirable when learning new behaviors that it is done in a place where the student with AS is most comfortable (e.g., for some it will be one-on-one and for others it may be within the classroom surrounded by their peers).

- Design activities to allow the student with AS to practice taking the perspective of others in a communication situation or social situation.

# Ground Rules for Intervention Sessions

Students with AS like to have clear, concise, consistent rules to follow since they do not enjoy change and many times even fear it. Oftentimes the student with AS does not understand the rules of the classroom or the school, because they are implied. The rules of the classroom, which are readily assimilated by a student with typical development, may need to be taught explicitly to the student with AS, who may be oblivious to implied rules. (Often professionals refer to these rules as the "hidden curriculum" [Myles & Adreon, 2001; Paul & Sutherland, 2003]). Therefore, rules of the general education classroom, small-group, or individualized sessions should be noted and consistently applied. One of the ways to accomplish this is to post the rules clearly on the wall for everyone to see. Also, it may be desirable to start each class session with a review and reminder of the rules.

# Be Prepared to Counsel

The reason for including counseling as one of the intervention guidelines is that many times students with AS have difficulty academically, in personal-social relationships, and reaching vocational potential because their social communication and other social skills get in the way of them being successful in various interpersonal situations. Counseling should be specific to the communication problems or social skills issues. General and special educators should not become counselors for critical problems; professionally trained counselors should undertake that task. Some specific procedures for educators to use to communicate understanding when the student with AS wants to discuss a problem (e.g., lack of friends because of communication and social skill problems) are as follows:

- Listen to the issues.

- Listen to the student's perspective of the problem, and take the time the student needs to resolve the issue.

- Ask open-ended questions, and do not be judgmental or jump to conclusions.

- Keep focused on the issue at hand, and do not change the topic too soon or remain on a given issue too long.

- Try to find ways to reasonably provide solutions to the problem or issues at hand.

Try to objectify the issues or problems so that the student can leave the session with a strategy as to how to approach the problem (e.g., use social stories or do a social autopsy; see pages 86–88).

# Class Meeting Routines

As noted above, students with AS have a strong preference and seem to thrive on having established routines to rely on in situations in which they feel unsure of themselves. According to Larson & McKinley (2003), one of the methods for accomplishing this, for students who are developmentally ready, is to use the first few minutes of any class to conduct a class meeting for routines. They recommend the following three parts to this discussion time:

1. Self-reports allow students with AS to discuss how well they have transferred their newly learned behaviors into new situations. The self-report should be limited to reporting on two or three behaviors that have been successfully incorporated into new situations. If peer buddies are part of the session, they might report their observations of the student with AS to determine if they all have the same perspective of how well new behaviors are being transferred to new situations.

2. Time should be set aside to discuss issues or problems that are of primary concern to the students. It is important to help the student focus on the problem and not use the whole time covering one student's problem. Again, because students with AS prefer having an established routine or structure, it may be highly desirable to have a problem-solving chart posted, like that found in *Daily Communication: Strategies for Adolescents with Language Disorders* (Schreiber & McKinley, 1995; see Figure 3.1 and Appendix L on the CD-ROM).

**Figure 3.1**                          **Problem-Solving Chart**

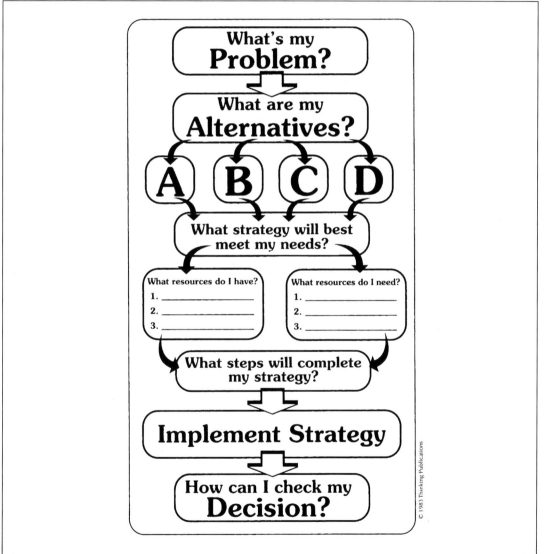

From *Daily Communication: Strategies for Adolescents with Language Disorders* (p. 38), by L. Schreiber and N. McKinley, 1995, Eau Claire, WI: Thinking Publications. © 1995 by Thinking Publications. Reprinted with permission.

3. Reinforcement or complimenting each other is not an easy task for many students with AS, since they tend to be blunt and assume that giving compliments is not necessary. Therefore, the third part of the class meeting time is to give the students an opportunity to practice giving compliments to each other that are meaningful, such as actions demonstrated, rather than physical attributes (e.g., saying "I like the way you included me in the conversation" rather than saying "I like your sweatshirt").

In summary, generally the class meeting should not take more than 5–10 minutes of the entire class session. Given the issues, it may at times go longer, but be careful that the student does not try to take up the whole session with issues and not get to the lessons at hand.

# Strategy-Based Approach

For nearly 25 years, professionals have discussed and researched a strategy-based approach to intervention for students with special needs (Alley & Deshler, 1979). This strategy-based approach has been proven to be successful with a wide variety of students with disabilities. A strategy is a tool, plan, or method for accomplishing a given task (Beckman, 2002). According to Beckman, a variety of strategies comprise a strategy-based approach to instruction:

- **A cognitive strategy**—One or more strategies used to perform an academic or social skills task (e.g., visualization, verbalization, making associations, chunking, questioning, scanning, underlining, accessing cues, using mnemonics, sounding out words, and self-checking and monitoring).

- **A cuing strategy**—Either a visual or verbal prompt that reminds the student to learn something or reminds the student what he or she has already learned (e.g., an educator may say "manners" to remind the student to give a compliment to a peer).

- **A learning strategy**—A set of steps needed to accomplish a particular task (e.g., taking a test, writing a story, giving an oral presentation, or listening to a lecture).

- **A metacognitive strategy (also referred to as *self-regulation*)**—A tactic that aids students' comprehension of how well they understand their own learning process. This would include how to use strategies to accomplish tasks, and the process by which learners oversee, monitor, and even critique their use of strategies. An independent strategic learner is one who knows how to use cues and strategies to learn new material. These strategies may include asking questions, listening, checking and monitoring one's own work or one's own behavior, and setting personal learning goals. The strategic learner knows the value of using strategies and is eager to learn them so that he or she can learn new material.

Regardless of the type of strategy used, the underlying premise is that a strategy-based approach is most conducive to learning. With a strategy-based approach, the student learns *how* to learn, not just *what* to learn.

# Outcomes to a Strategy-Based Approach to Intervention

Beckman (2002) provides an excellent list of outcomes that can be expected when students use strategies to learn and grow, both academically and socially. These outcomes are as follows:

- "Students trust their minds
- Students know there is more than one right way to do things
- They acknowledge their mistakes and try to rectify them
- They evaluate their products and behavior
- Memories are enhanced
- Learning increases
- Self-esteem increases
- Students feel a sense of power
- Students become more responsible
- Work completion and accuracy improve
- Students develop and use a personal study process
- They know how to try
- On-task time increases; students are more engaged" (p. 2)

Thus, a strategy-based approach to intervention has many benefits for students with AS. Learning strategies can help them become independent learners.

# Basic Steps in Teaching a Strategy-Based Approach

A five-step approach is recommended when teaching students how to use a strategy (Beckman, 2002). They are presented in order as follows:

1. **Describe the strategy**. It is critical to discuss with the students the value of the strategy. To accomplish this, discuss with the students why the strategy is important, when the strategy can be used, and how to use the strategy.

2. **Model its use.** Model using the strategy while also explaining how to use the strategy.

3. **Provide ample practice time**. Monitor, provide cues, and give feedback as the students practice using the strategy, so that the strategy becomes more automatic to the students and they do not have to think about it, but simply use it.

4. **Promote student self-monitoring and evaluation of the strategy**. Teach students to monitor and evaluate their use of a strategy so that they perfect their use of it.

5. **Encourage students to use the strategies in new and different situations**. Using a strategy across and within multiple situations will help in solidifying when, how, and why to use a strategy and in integrative strategy use within the students' repertoire.

If these five steps are followed, the student is more likely to learn a strategy approach and thus learn how to learn. (See Chapter 5 for more detailed information about learning and using strategies.)

# Continuum of Service Delivery Options

One of the most controversial issues in special education today is full-inclusion verses a continuum of service delivery options or alternative placements. A continuum of service delivery options is defined as a broad range of services available for students who have been diagnosed with a disability and are in need of special programming. According to Hallahan and Kaufman, (2003) these services include the following.

- **Regular class only**—The regular educator meets all the students' needs, and there is no special educator involvement. In this case, the student has not yet been identified as having special needs. Students are fully integrated.

- **Special educator consultation**—The students spend all of their day in the general classroom, and the educator gets some support from a special education consultant. The consultant may suggest curricular or environmental modifications or behavioral management plans. The students are fully integrated.

- **Itinerant special educator**—Specially trained educators, who may travel from school-to-school, meet with the students intermittently for short periods of time. Itinerant teachers may also provide consultative services to the classroom educator. Students spend most of the school day in the general classroom.

- **Resource teacher**—Students spend some time with the special educator almost every day in their special education or resource classrooms. Primary responsibility for the students is with the resource teacher.

- **Diagnostic-prescriptive center**—Students spend most or all of their time in a center for a designated period of time, where a special educator observes, works with, and evaluates students to determine their needs. Subsequently, special educators will develop a plan for the student. This plan might be implemented in a general or special education class or both.

- **Hospital or homebound instruction**—Students receive all of their education outside of school (e.g., in the hospital or at home) until they are ready to return to school. General or special educators or both provide the educational program.

- **Self-contained class**—Students spend all or a vast majority of their school time in a special education class with a special educator.

- **Special day school**—Students are segregated in a day school where only students with similar disabilities are taught.

- **Residential school**—Students live and receive an education in a special school for students with similar disabilities. They spend most or all of the time away from home.

A major provision of IDEA (1997, 2004) is that students are educated in the least restrictive environment (LRE) consistent with their educational needs and, whenever possible, with students who do not have disabilities. Justification for a student not to participate with nondisabled peers must be made for every subject area, extracurricular activities, and transportation (Gartner & Lipsky, 2002). Educational programming for students with disabilities is based on the assumption that there are a variety of services available in all local school districts (Hallahan & Kauffman, 2003). Because of tight resources and varying philosophies of professionals in the field, some local school districts do not have the entire spectrum of services available locally and may have to transport students to other nearby districts for some services. Some school districts have minimal special education classes because they operate under the principle of full inclusion (i.e., mainstreaming all students). Other school districts are small and do not have enough students with disabilities to make it economically feasible to have a wide continuum of service delivery options. These districts may have to work with surrounding districts or purchase services from regional education service agencies (e.g., CESAs, RESAs). Larger school districts, however, do have a wider variety of services for students with disabilities.

Some professionals argue that a special education classroom might be the LRE for a particular student, especially if the student is not benefiting from the curriculum, the methodologies, or the social interaction in a general classroom. Others contend that LRE most often means placement in a general classroom. Parents may not want their child to be placed in special education if their child has what they consider to be a mild disability. Controversy surrounds the issues relating to a continuum of service options.

When students with AS get added into the mix, the issues become even more complex and controversial. Because AS has only recently come to the attention of professionals and parents in the United States, special programming and professionals with adequate training in the field are difficult to find. It can be problematic for parents of students with AS to try to get appropriate diagnoses, placements, and programs for their children. It can also be difficult for educational professionals who have not had the proper training to provide the services expected of them. IDEA (1997; 2004) specifically includes autism and Autism Spectrum Disorders (ASD) as a category for qualifying for special education services (National Research Council, 2001), but does not specifically mention AS. The use of the term ASD suggests that there is a range of related qualities that overlap in AS and autism, but at this time they are clinically distinct and separately diagnosed. The learning needs and challenges of students who have AS are often very different. Klin and Volkmar (2000) refer to students with AS in the educational setting as "orphans."

**Asperger Syndrome**

Because AS has only recently been recognized as a disabling condition, students with AS have been misdiagnosed in every conceivable way. Sometimes, because they have been labeled autistic or in the ASD category, they are put in classes with students who have severe cognitive disabilities. However, students with AS have normal or above intelligence and do not get their cognitive and academic needs met in these classes. In other cases, students with AS have been diagnosed as Learning Disabled (LD) with "eccentric features" because both groups present the same social and pragmatic language difficulties. However, students with LD are less likely to exhibit the intense, single-minded focus that students with AS do (Powers & Poland, 2002).

Students with AS have often been labeled emotionally/behaviorally disturbed (E/BD), maladjusted, or conduct disordered and have been placed in classrooms with students who have these labels. Students with AS sometimes exhibit inappropriate behaviors that may present like a student who has a behavior or conduct disorder, but these behaviors may very well be the result of sensory integration disorders. For example, a student with AS may become anxious or afraid if they hear a loud noise, encounter an aversive smell, or touch something that feels unpleasant to them. Their anxiety or fear may be exhibited in a kind of inappropriate behavior that looks like noncompliance, and the behavior can be disruptive. But, in fact, the behavior is a result of the inability of students with AS to successfully integrate the sensory experience they are having. Another reason they may seem noncompliant is if they are experiencing change in their routines and they are not prepared or if they are in uncomfortable social situations.

Frequently, the inappropriate behavior of students with AS can be eliminated if the external circumstances are changed (e.g., the loud noise or aversive smell is eliminated, the change in routine is explained, or the deficient social skills are taught). They do not need, nor do they benefit from, intervention that tries to change the behavior. For example, a student in a class for students with emotional and behavioral disabilities (E/BD) might be given a consequence for screaming because it has been determined the screaming is exhibited to gain attention (a modification of the behavior of the student). A student with AS may scream because a certain sound in the environment is physically painful to him or her. The intervention for the student with AS who screams would not be a consequence for the screaming, but rather, the elimination of the noise (a modification of the environment).

If students with AS are placed in a class with students who have emotional disabilities or conduct disorders, the students with AS easily become the scapegoats because of deficits in social skills and their naiveté in social situations (Williams, 1995). The students who have emotional disabilities are sometimes "street smart" or bullies and can therefore cause unnecessary hardship to students who have AS.

As with all students, diagnosis should not dictate the program plan for the student with AS. The program and the intervention should be based on each student's needs. Educators must understand the unique skills and deficits of each child and base programming and delivery of services accordingly. Recall that the strengths (knowledge of special topics of interests, a normal or above-average IQ) can mask the weaknesses in the social communication arena. Parents and educational advocates must pursue the appropriate educational options to meet the needs of students with AS (Klin & Volkmar, 2000).

The kind of intervention a student receives is based on diagnosis and identified educational needs, but diagnosis for an individual with AS can be subjective. A mother speaks of her experience:

> [A] diagnosis [of AS] depends on a clinician's subjective observations. What's in a name? Plenty! I've heard of parents who have taken their child to a psychologist and received a diagnosis of Asperger Syndrome; their neuropsychologist diagnosed NLD; the occupational therapist gave the same child a diagnosis of Sensory Integration Disorder; the Speech Pathologist says it's a Semantic-Pragmatic Disorder; and the pediatrician originally thought it was Attention Deficit Disorder. (Fling, 2000, p. 202)

Because students with AS may have symptoms that present like other disabling conditions, an intervention based solely on any one of them (e.g., attention-deficit/hyperactivity disorder) would not meet all the complex needs of the individual with AS.

The individualized education programs (IEPs) and the interventions for students with AS must be based on a broad continuum of service delivery options. Currently, there are few schools or classrooms specifically designed for students with AS, and there are some professionals who have been trained to work specifically with students who have AS. There are few identified schools that have programs for bright children with severe social disabilities. This makes the process of finding an appropriate program for students with AS very difficult (Klin & Volkmar, 2000). Students with AS do not necessarily need classrooms designed for them alone, as long as educational professionals receive the proper instruction to meet the needs of a student with AS.

The regular classroom may turn out to be the least restrictive environment. However, regular educators alone cannot meet all the needs of students with AS; they must have support. Gartner and Lipsky (2002) list a range of supports that are effective in an inclusive classroom, including collaborative teaming and consultation, team teachers, curricular and environmental accommodations, study skills training, cooperative learning, and inclusion facilitators. Schools that include students with disabilities in their general classrooms have to incorporate educators, parents, and administrators in the teams (Haas, 1993).

Professionals and parents must work together to find the best possible services for students with AS. Their interventions and programs will not be neatly packaged and probably will not fit into any one special education category that has been identified in IDEA (1997; 2004). They will need special education services if they are to get their educational needs met. For example, they may need to have social skills programming with a small group of students done by an SLP; a regular math class with the assistance of an aide; an alternative physical education program; or lunch in their homeroom. It is important for advocates of students with AS to search out all possible services in the area to find out which services are appropriate for each individual student. Their decisions should be based on knowledge of AS and model programs that work for students with AS (National Research Council, 2001). Parents and school personnel will also need to be very familiar with the provisions of IDEA (1997; 2004) and have knowledge of the particular student to ensure he or she is, indeed, getting a *free appropriate* public education.

# Transition Planning

> Transition is a natural process of disorientation and reorientation, caused by an event or nonevent, that alters the individual's perception of self and the world, demands a change of assumptions or behavior, and may lead either to growth or to deterioration; the choice rests with the individual. (Krupp, 1987, as cited in Michaels, 1994, p. 1)

Krupp's definition of transition serves to note the confusion that can come about by being in a transition. Students with AS find transitions particularly difficult because they prefer sameness, and they fear or are confused by change that transitions bring (Myles & Adreon, 2001). It should be noted that students experience numerous transitions in any given day. As Michaels (1994) emphasizes, it is critical to analyze and find ways to assist students in making changes, which might be as straightforward as designing transition activities (e.g., posting what changes are about to occur) and how to best meet these transitional changes using a problem-solving model.

## Educational Setting

Within the educational setting, there are three major transition points that occur. Educators should carefully consider and prepare the student with AS for these transition points. Larson and McKinley, (1995) identify these three transition points:

1. Transitioning from elementary to middle grades (or junior high school)
2. Transitioning from middle grades to high school
3. Transitioning from high school to employment or post-secondary education

Each of these transition points is illustrated in Figure 3.2 and discussed in the sections that follow.

Figure 3.2     **Major Transition Points for Preadolescents and Adolescents**

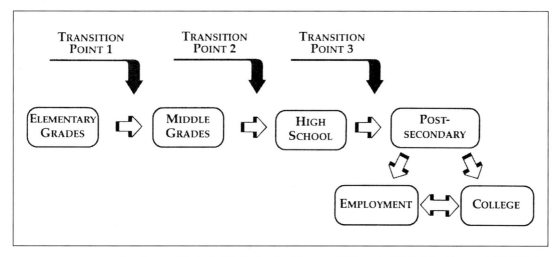

## Transition Point One: Elementary to Middle Grades

The first transition point is from elementary to middle grades (i.e., usually middle grades include 5–8 or 6–8, and junior high schools encompass grades 7–8 or 7–9). The transition from elementary school to middle school or junior high can be fairly disconcerting to students with typical development, but often is traumatic for students with AS. The changes are quite dramatic (e.g., larger class sizes, varied class schedules—without former peers or friends, numerous teachers with whom the student may spend only an hour or two a week, varied curricular subjects with different demands and textbooks, and varied classrooms located in different parts of the school). Therefore, students with AS should be assisted in dealing with interdisciplinary subject areas, flexible class scheduling, varied teachers and administrators, and new peers who are different from elementary school and who may vary from class to class. Also, each class may have its own form of "hidden curriculum" (i.e., rules and routines unique to that teacher or subject). Some of the types of activities that may assist students in making the transition between elementary to middle school or junior high include the following:

- Elementary school students with AS should visit the middle school for an information session or a school assembly.

- Elementary teachers and administrators should meet with middle school or junior high teachers and administrators to discuss how best to transition all students, especially discussing the various challenges facing the student with AS. If at all possible, the student with AS and his or her parents should meet with educators to become knowledgeable about their specific concerns and issues.

- Peer buddies from a higher grade could meet with appropriate educators, and eventually the student with AS, to discuss how they might help the student with AS make an adjustment to the new school.

- Students with AS might be given the opportunity to attend selected classes that they believe will be extra challenging, and then discuss with the teacher ways in which, as students, they might accommodate the class.

- Students with AS should be provided with visual tools (e.g., printed copies of schedules or lists of materials needed for each class in a notebook or on an index card) that are readily available to the student.

- Students with AS should have the opportunity to practice walking through the school building to find classes, restrooms, and homerooms until they feel comfortable doing so alone.

- Students with AS should be given the specific rules and routines expected in various classes and during extracurricular activities.

- Educators should clearly articulate how they will assist the student with AS in making accommodations for assignments, note taking, homework, and so on before the student has been in the class for very long (Myles & Adreon, 2001). This assistance should be reflected on the student's IEP if he or she is receiving special services.

- Educators should clearly articulate to the student what types of modifications will be made for unstructured or less structured times, such as transportation/bus, physical education, lunch, before and after school, and changing classes (Myles & Adreon, 2001).

## Transition Point Two: Middle Grades to High School

The second transition point is that from middle grades to high school, which has all the concerns expressed in the section above for the transition from elementary school to middle grades or junior high. Perhaps of even greater concern is that many times the classes and the school buildings are larger in high school than in middle grades. Often size alone is overwhelming to the student with AS. All of the activities cited above for transition from elementary to middle school apply to transitioning from middle grades to high school. Any activity that allows the student with AS to learn ahead of time about the school, scheduling, and routines will assist him or her with the transition.

## Transition Point Three: High School to Employment or Post-Secondary Education

The transition from high school to post-secondary activities is the last transition the student with AS needs to be guided through in the educational setting. In 1990, the Individuals with

Disabilities Education Act (IDEA) placed an emphasis on transition planning. This was further expanded in 1997 and 2004 when amendments were made to IDEA. IDEA 1997 legislation clearly defines the role of transition services under the law:

> "[T]ransition services" means a coordinated set of activities for a student with a disability that—
>
> A. is designed within an outcome-oriented process, which promotes movement from school to post-school activities, including post-secondary education, vocational training, integrated employment (including supported employment), continuing and adult education, adult services, independent living, or community participation;
>
> B. is based upon the individual student's needs, taking into account the student's preferences and interests; and
>
> C. includes instruction, related services, community experiences, the development of employment and other post-school adult living objectives, and, when appropriate, acquisition of daily living skills and functional vocational evaluation. (§602 [30])

It should be noted that IDEA mandates that students with disabilities begin preparing for a transition beyond high school by age 14. The transition services are to be written into every IEP, or a separate Individual Transition Plan (ITP) should be generated. More specifically, Sidebar 3.1 on page 66 delineates the responsibilities of secondary school personnel in individualized transition planning.

# Public Policy and Legal Issues

Students with disabilities have not always been educated in the public schools. Prior to 1975, students with disabilities were placed in rooms often called something like a "special opportunity class" or they were institutionalized. The first real breakthrough for students with disabilities came in 1975 with the passage of federal public law (P.L.) 94-142, the Education of All Handicapped Children Act. This law mandated a "free appropriate public education" (FAPE) for all students and resulted in much of the progress that states and localities made in meeting the needs of children with special needs (Hallahan & Kauffman, 2003).

In 1990, PL 94-142 was amended to become the Individuals with Disabilities Education Act (IDEA; PL 101-476). In that same year, the American with Disabilities Act (ADA; PL 101-336) was passed requiring that the civil rights of all individuals with disabilities be protected in the specific areas of employment, transportation, public accommodations, state and local government,

## Responsibilities of Secondary School Personnel in Individualized Transition Planning

- Form a transition team consisting of a coordinator, the student, the family, administrators, teachers, and related service personnel

- Include the student and parents in the entire planning process

- Demonstrate sensitivity to the culture and values of the student and family

- Develop an appropriate packet of materials to document the student's secondary school program and to facilitate service delivery in the postsecondary setting

- Provide administrative support, resources, and time to foster collaboration among team members

- Inform the student about laws, rules, and regulation that ensure his or her rights

- Provide appropriate course selection, counseling, and academic support services

- Ensure competence in literacy and mathematics

- Ensure that the student learns effective studying, time-management, test-preparation, and test-taking strategies

- Help the student use a range of academic accommodations and technological aids

- Help the student evaluate the need for external supports and adjust the level of assistance when appropriate

- Help the student develop appropriate skills and interpersonal communication abilities

- Help the student develop self-advocacy skills, including an understanding of his or her disability and how to use this information in communication with others

- Foster independence through increased responsibility and opportunity for self-management

- Encourage the student to develop extracurricular interests and participate in community activities

- Inform the student and family about admission procedures for diverse postsecondary settings

- Inform the student and family about services that postsecondary settings provide, such as disability services, academic counseling, and so on

- Ensure the timely development of documentation and material to meet application deadlines

- Help the student and family select and apply to postsecondary institutions that will offer both the challenge and the support necessary

- Develop ongoing communication with postsecondary personnel

*Source:* National Joint Committee on Learning Disabilities (1996)

and telecommunications. The intent of this legislation was to protect individuals with disabilities against discrimination or unfair treatment because of their disabilities. If discrimination can be documented, such individuals have the right to a due process hearing (Hallahan & Kauffman, 2003; National Research Council, 2001).

In 1997 and in 2004, IDEA was amended. In 2004, the name of the act changed from the Individuals with Disabilities Education Act to the Individuals with Disabilities Education Improvement Act of 2004. Like PL 94-142, both amendments ensure that all children receive a free appropriate public education.

In 2002, the Elementary and Secondary Education reauthorization (PL 107–110) was passed and called the No Child Left Behind Act of 2001 (NCLB). This new piece of legislation, along with the reauthorization of IDEA in 2004, make way toward resolving the differences between general and special educators. The expectation of the legislation is that teachers, both special and regular, become educators of all children (Moore-Brown & Montgomery, 2005).

The NCLB legislation implies that special educators, including speech-language pathologists, must work together with regular educators and curriculum specialists to become involved in and responsible for the learning and assessment of students with whom they work. "Students with disabilities represent a distinct subgroup under NCLB, and that means that high stakes testing is part of the work of the school-based SLP" (Moore-Brown & Montgomery, 2005, p. 13). High stakes testing is part of the work of all special educators, and students with AS are part of this group.

## Requirements under IDEA

In IDEA 2004, Asperger Syndrome is not listed as a category on its own, but is subsumed under the area of Autism Spectrum Disorder (ASD). There are several major provisions under IDEA legislation that each state and locality must ensure for each student under evaluation or already in special education (Moore-Brown & Montgomery, 2005; Hallahan & Kauffman, 2003; Kirk, Gallagher, & Anastasiow, 2000; National Research Council, 2001):

- **Identification**—All students with disabilities must be screened and identified within a reasonable time frame.

- **Free appropriate public education (FAPE)**—All students with disabilities are entitled to a free appropriate public education. That means that all students with ASD, including AS, must be provided with an appropriate education at no cost to themselves or their families.

- **Due process**—If parents or guardians are not satisfied or do not agree with the educational services their children or youth with Autism Spectrum Disorder, including AS, are receiving, they have a right to a request an evaluation from an unbiased, qualified examiner and also have the right to an impartial hearing. However, since the 2004 amendments to

IDEA, parents will no longer automatically receive the procedural safeguard notice with the IEP team notice or upon reevaluation. Parents have two years in which to exercise their due process rights after they know or should have known that an IDEA violation has occurred.

- **Nondiscriminatory evaluation**—Before students are placed in special education programs, they are required to have an individual evaluation in all areas of suspected disabilities. The evaluation must not be biased based on their culture, language, or disabilities. Students with Autism Spectrum Disorders, including AS, must be evaluated by a professional that has knowledge about the disability and the assessment/evaluation instruments being used.

- **Individualized education program (IEP)**—All students who have been identified to receive special educational services must have an IEP in place that has been determined by a team of professionals, including general and special education teachers, SLPs, other professionals with expertise, parents or guardians, and the student with AS, if appropriate. It is particularly important that a speech-language pathologist be a member of the team planning programs for students with AS because social communication and language is one of the bases of the disability. The IEP must include present level of functioning, measurable long-term goals, the special education services to be delivered, persons responsible for delivery of the services, means for carrying out the plan, how/where services are provided, any related services that have been determined to be necessary, and how the outcomes will be evaluated. In IDEA 2004, short-term goals are no longer required as part of the IEP for most students. Students with AS should have an advocate on the team that has extensive knowledge about the disability. Because AS is a relatively new diagnostic term in the United States, there are few trained professionals. That may make it difficult to ensure a coordinated approach and a consistency of programs across school districts (Cumine et al., 2001). All students with AS need a transition plan in their IEP. Some students may need a behavior plan as well, if inappropriate behaviors are getting in the way of learning.

- **Parent/Guardian participation**—Parents or guardians must be a part of the evaluation and IEP planning and must have access to all records pertaining to the student. If a parent or guardian is unavailable, a surrogate must be found.

- **Least restrictive environment (LRE)**—Students with disabilities must be educated, as much as possible, with students who are not disabled. The placement should be based on the student's educational and social needs. As with all students, students with AS should be in the general classroom as much as possible and/or should be interacting regularly with children who do not have AS. If students with AS are not interacting with nondisabled students, the reasons should be included in the IEP. In some cases, when students with AS are having problems coping in a regular, mainstreamed class, it might be less restrictive for them to be in alternate educational settings for a part of the time.

- **Confidentiality**—The results of the evaluation and placement must be kept confidential, but they must be accessible to parents or guardians.

- **Personnel development/Inservice**—General and special educators working with students who have AS should have knowledge about the disability and/or should participate in regular inservice training and educational programs.

# Litigation

One of the most controversial provisions of IDEA is the word "appropriate" in the "free appropriate public education (FAPE)" section. The school district and the parents or guardians may not agree on what "appropriate" means (National Research Council, 2001). If parents or guardians feel the plan does not meet the needs of the student, they can question the professionals, request a review of the student's IEP, and request mediation. If these steps do not bring resolution for the parents or guardians, they have the right to bring suit against the school district. If the school district decides a student should be in special education and the parents or guardians disagree, the parents or guardians have a right to file suit (Hallahan & Kauffman, 2003).

School districts may feel that the high costs of some treatment for students with AS will overburden their budgets. Parents, of course, want the best education for their children. The question becomes how to provide the most appropriate education for students with AS within the budget constraints of the school districts. "So where is the line to be drawn between optimal and meaningful services?" (National Research Council, 2001, p. 180).

The law and trends in litigation clearly show that school systems have the responsibility and the predominant role in deciding what the "appropriate" educational program is for students with a disability. However, if parents feel the school district is being "less than diligent" in providing an "appropriate education" or is violating the due process procedures, or if a consultant with expertise in the area of AS suggests the school is not doing enough or the plan is inappropriate, hearing decisions might be made in favor of the parents and against the school district (National Research Council, 2001).

Students with AS may have deficits that schools are not prepared to address, especially with the rapidly rising incidence. AS has only recently been identified as a disability, and school districts may not have professionals with expertise in AS on their staff. Treatment for students with AS may be expensive, labor intensive, and controversial. Each student with AS will have different strengths and weaknesses. In times of tight budgets, school districts may feel they do not have the resources for a special education program for a few students. Or they may not have the personnel with the expertise to develop appropriate plans for students with AS.

However, keep in mind that IEPs are not based on the services, programs, and personnel that the school districts have available. IEPs must be based on the needs of the students with AS. The school district must make every attempt to provide the services and trained personnel so that students with AS get an "appropriate" education.

If parents or guardians feel the program for their child with AS is not appropriate, they have the right to ask for an independent evaluation—free of charge—and a due process hearing. However, as stipulated in IDEA 2004, "local education agencies may seek attorney's fees against the attorney of a parent who files actions that are frivolous, unreasonable, or without foundation" (Moore-Brown & Montgomery, 2005, p. 31). The way IDEA is implemented might raise questions for parents or guardians or older students. Thus, it is critical that persons knowledgeable in the range of needs and interventions associated with ASD are consulted by these communities (National Research Council, 2001).

# Case Study: Travis

This last section provides an opportunity to apply an understanding of the federal law, public policy, and litigation that were discussed earlier in the chapter as it relates to a student with AS. The case study focuses on Travis, a sixth-grade middle school student who has been diagnosed as having AS, and has been placed in a program for students with emotional/behavioral disabilities (E/BD). Following the case study is a guide to help the reader analyze Travis's situation.

Sample IEP goals and sample interventions are also presented at the end of this section, as well as suggested interventions tied to the information presented earlier in the chapter.

## Diagnosis and Determination of LRE for Travis

Travis is a 12-year-old, sixth-grade middle school student who was diagnosed with Asperger Syndrome shortly after starting middle school. He was in a regular classroom during his elementary schooling, but when he came to middle school, he was referred for an evaluation for special education early in the fall due to volatile behavior toward his peers that his teachers could not manage in a regular classroom.

During elementary school, Travis was referred for special education twice because he had trouble getting along with others and because his behavior was disruptive in the classroom. He would usually finish his assignments with some prodding, and he did relatively well academically. He was especially gifted in math, surpassing most of his peers. However, he was always a loner, and he seemed to frequently do things that irritated his peers. He would talk to himself while doing his assignments, or he would tap his pencil on his desk throughout the day. When his peers would ask him to stop or get angry at him, he would ignore them and repeat the irritating behavior. By the time he was in third and fourth grades, he became the brunt of teasing from the other students because of his "eccentricities." He would most often

*Continued on next page*

ignore the teasing. He did not initiate conversations with others, and when his peers talked to him, he would cast his eyes down and respond quietly or not at all.

He had daily rituals in which he engaged. For example, every morning Travis would sharpen five pencils and put them in a special place in his desk. If he was prevented from doing this, he would become anxious and frustrated. He was fascinated by any kind of motor and would talk about motors every chance he got, especially with adults, and even with his peers if they would listen. However, he would not listen to his peers in return; he would talk right over them. Sometimes he would talk to himself.

As time went on, it became more apparent that Travis wanted friends. He tried to make them, but without success. His mother told his teacher that he was becoming angry and depressed about not having any friends and about the increased teasing he was getting from his classmates. By the time he was in fifth grade, he was acting out even more in the classroom. His teacher felt sorry for him and tried to protect him.

Both times that Travis was referred for special education in elementary school, he was evaluated by the school psychologist, special educators, and the speech-language pathologist, but he did not meet criterion for identification. He did marginally well in academics, so he did not qualify for learning disabilities or cognitive disabilities programming. His behavior was not severe enough to qualify for E/BD placement, nor was he acting out at home or in the community (E/BD placement requires problem behavior in at least two of the three settings of school, home, and community), so he stayed in regular education during his elementary school years.

When Travis started middle school, his life at school and at home fell apart. His mother reported that he was acting more and more depressed at home and did not want to go to school. He begged her every morning to let him stay home. He was overwhelmed with the size of the school, the number of teachers he had to relate to every day, the lack of predictability, and the increasing amount of ill will he experienced from his peers. His reactions became more intense and volatile, and most of his teachers could not manage his behavior and teach the other students at the same time. Travis was referred for special education. Again, he did not qualify for learning disability (LD) or cognitive disability (CD) services, but this time, after observations, a speech and language evaluation, and psychological testing, it was determined that he had AS. There was no program for AS at Roosevelt Middle School, but the evaluation team felt that he met the requirements for E/BD, and recommended his placement in an E/BD program. Because he was now acting out at home, as well as in school, his parents, not knowing what else to do, agreed with the placement. The evaluation team and parents also agreed that he would be mainstreamed in the general classrooms as soon as his behavior began to improve.

Travis is now placed in the E/BD program, but he does not want to be there. Several times every day he asks his teacher when he can go back to his classroom. The other students (six boys and one girl) have made Travis their scapegoat. They tease him and taunt him relent-

*Continued on next page*

**Travis—*Continued***

lessly. He gets angry and upset and cries. That escalates the teasing. Sometimes he will try to fight back, but he cannot match their combined attacks. The teacher has been ineffective in getting the other students to leave Travis alone.

Because Travis is a student who has been diagnosed as having a special education need, he must have individualized programming. The E/BD placement is not working. He does not qualify for learning disabilities or cognitive disabilities, because his IQ and academic performance are too high. His behavior interferes with his and other students' learning in the general classroom, and his placement in the E/BD classroom is resulting in depression and school avoidance.

## Analysis

Answering the following questions will help education professionals develop an understanding of the student who has had problems in school due to AS, but has not received appropriate interventions and placement. Educators, if they care to, can write their own IEP goals and develop their own intervention plans before reading the sample plan at the end of the chapter.

1. What, if anything, could have been done earlier in Travis's school years to have prevented him from being ultimately placed in a special education program for students with E/BD?

2. What are the behaviors that resulted in a referral for placement in a classroom for E/BD? Was this placement appropriate? Why or why not?

3. Who is benefiting from the E/BD placement?

4. What steps can Travis's parents take if they do not agree with this placement?

5. What can the school district do to be more responsive to Travis's needs and ensure that Travis gets an "appropriate" education?

6. What long- and short-term goals for Travis would meet the provisions of IDEA?

7. What kind of an intervention program will meet the top three goals that you have identified? Use the information in this chapter to develop the program.

## Example IEP Goals

1. Travis will learn the appropriate behavior that will allow him to return to his regular class.

2. Travis will improve his self-concept and his standing with his peers.

3. Travis will participate in a social skills group that will be developed for him and other students in the school.

# Example Interventions to Achieve the IEP Goals

**Goal #1:** Travis will learn the appropriate behavior that will allow him to return to his regular class.

1.  The assumption is that because Travis wants to be back in his regular classroom, he will be motivated to learn the appropriate behaviors so that he can return to his regular class. The program will be set up so he can go back to his regular classroom one class at a time. Math class will be first because he excels in math.

2.  The plan will use his interest in motors as positive reinforcement to increase his appropriate behavior and meet the criteria to return to a regular class.

3.  Every time Travis physically removes himself and says to himself, "I'm going to ignore their teasing," when the other students tease and bully him, he will earn 10 points and an opportunity to either talk about motors with his educators or read books and draw pictures of motors for 5 minutes. The time will be charted and, at a convenient time during the day, he will be able to use his accumulated minutes. If he does not physically remove himself from the situation, he will lose 5 points. When he earns 200 points, he will be placed in math class. Pairing points and motors will, hopefully, make the points more attractive and give him a greater incentive to "earn" his way back. (See pages 171–173 for more information about using positive reinforcement.)

4.  Travis and the educators who work with him will define what "physically removing himself" means. It will be different in every classroom. Educators will clearly summarize the agreement and give Travis a copy.

5.  When he has earned his way back to math class, Travis will be expected to physically remove himself from teasing and bullying situations in the regular classroom, as well.

6.  The plan will be repeated for every class until Travis is in his regular classrooms full time.

7.  Travis will probably need a personal aide or a counselor that will be available to give him support while he is learning to ignore his peers.

8.  Students who tease and bully Travis will be given noon-hour detention.

**Goal #2:** Travis will improve his self-concept and his standing with his peers.

1.  Allow Travis to demonstrate his academic abilities in ways that the students will see his skills. For example, ask him to answer questions that involve rote memory instead of questions that require abstract thinking.

2.  Assign Travis a "buddy." Find a student(s) in the class who shows sensitivity to Travis. Talk to them individually about AS and Travis, and ask them if they would be willing to be Travis's friend. If so, they could be seated next to each other in class. The "buddy" could "look after" Travis or befriend him between classes, in the lunchroom, etc.

3.  Praise classmates when they treat Travis with respect.

4.  When using cooperative learning groups, put Travis in a group where his strengths in math, vocabulary, memory, and so on will be emphasized.

5. Foster involvement with others. Arrange for Travis to have interaction with other students. Pair him up with a peer to do an assignment that Travis can excel at, or during free time arrange a game or activity between Travis and another student.

**Goal #3**: Travis will participate in a social skills group that will be developed for him and other students in the school.

1. A professional in the school will create a social skills group that will meet three days a week. Travis and 5 or 6 other students with varying levels of social skill will be included.

2. The activities will vary and will include, but not be limited to, modeling, role-playing, group discussions, and direct instruction.

3. Skills that will be taught will include, but not be limited to, making friends, initiating, maintaining and terminating conversations, turn taking in conversations, and making eye contact when talking and listening. (See page Chapter 4 for additional information on teaching social skills.)

# Discussion Points

1. Should students with emotional/behavioral disabilities be able to "earn" their way out of special classrooms, or should they simply be moved back to a regular class when the educator feels it is appropriate? What are the reasons for your position? Could this become an ethical issue? Why or why not?

2. What would you include in a transition program for students with AS as they move from middle school to high school and beyond?

3. Why are class meetings so important? How would a class meeting benefit students with AS? What factors could cause a class meeting to fail? How could you ensure success?

4. What is the difference between a strategy and an intervention? What do they have in common? What would be an important strategy that you could teach to students with AS?

5. On a continuum of services, which three services would be the most helpful for students with AS? Which three would be the least beneficial?

6. What is the educator's role in addressing depression in students with AS?

7. Does the federal legislation go far enough to help students with AS? Should the federal, state, and local governments mandate additional services without additional resources? Why or why not?

# Social Competence
# Intervention Strategies

## Goals

- To describe how to teach five areas of social competence skills: friendship/relationship building, selected social skills, communication skills (both oral and nonverbal), and perspective-taking

- To present 10 general intervention strategies for enhancing social competence

- To illustrate intervention strategies for social competence using case studies

For the purpose of this book, *social competence* is defined as the ability to accommodate or adapt to ongoing social situations. Although every society has a general set of social norms or rules, they are constantly changing. Social interactions demand moment-to-moment integration of multiple contextual, language, social, and emotional cues. Social interactions demand that the person be able to adjust and read the social cues within the situation on a continual basis and to adjust one's own behaviors within milliseconds of the behaviors occurring. This multitasking and reading of diverse social cues and simultaneously understanding the perspective of the people within the social situation is very difficult for the person with AS. Many social norms are not taught directly but are assimilated by students with typical development by integrating, monitoring, and adjusting to the behaviors of others as they interact within social situations. These same social behaviors that students with typical behaviors learn automatically or incidentally usually need to be taught deliberately to the individual with AS.

# Intervention Strategies for Five Areas of Social Competence

Intervention strategies to enhance social competence will entail developing skills in five areas: friendship/relationship building, selected additional social skills, and communication skills—both oral and nonverbal. In addition, intervention strategies are presented on how to develop the "theory of mind" concept by learning how to take the perspective of others.

## Friendship/Relationship Building

Friendship is a social skill that is separated out from the next section on selected social skills to emphasize how critical it is that students with AS learn this skill. Students with AS have challenges with social skills in general, and most specifically with the area of initiating and maintaining friendships. As children develop, they learn to embrace a peer group. Friendships are important for children because contact, understanding, sharing, trusting, and cooperating with others are basic human needs. Friends serve a special function that parents cannot: they play a crucial role in shaping one's social skills and sense of identity within one's peer group.

There is a reciprocal relationship between friendship and social skills (Goldstein & Morgan, 2002). All too frequently, a lack of social skills leaves one without friends and socially isolated, which in turn makes it more difficult to learn appropriate social skills from peers and friends, and this vicious spiral perpetuates. It should be noted that friendship and peer acceptance are different in that acceptance means that you are generally well-liked by your peers, but it is not a reciprocal relationship. Friendship is defined as a close and reciprocal relationship between two people who find each other unique and irreplaceable (Asher, Parker, & Walker, 1996; Bukowski & Hoza, 1989). Many researchers (e.g., Bukowski & Hoza, 1989; Hodges, Boivin, Vitaro, & Bukowski, 1999; Hodges, Malone, & Perry, 1997; Ladd, Kochenderfer, & Coleman, 1997; Newcomb & Bagwell, 1996; Pizzamiglio, Bukowski, & Hoza, 1997; Sanderson & Siegel, 1995) have noted that having even one close friend can help a child offset peer rejection from others. They have also noted that friendship has a profound, positive effect on a child's development, and perhaps—more importantly—may reduce the possibility of peer victimization and loneliness. Research (Schwartz, Dodge, Pettit, & Bates, 2000; Schwartz, McFadyen-Ketchum, Dodge, Pettit, & Bates, 1999) has indicated that if children at risk for social skill deficits or behavioral disorders form a friendship in kindergarten or first grade, then continuous positive effects will show years later. One of the premises underlying the inclusive classroom model is to prevent social isolation in students with AS and to provide them with positive social role models. This will give them the opportunity to form relationships, and hopefully, friendships with peers.

According to Attwood (2001, 2003), research has revealed a series of four typical developmental stages in friendship, which should be examined before designing a program to develop friendship skills. He describes the stages of friendship as follows.

**Stage I: 3 to 6 years (preschool)**—A time characterized by a functional egocentric concept of friendship. More specifically, children in this stage typically:

- Change gradually from playing alongside to playing with someone
- Learn some games and activities that have elements of sharing and turn-taking
- Make positive initiatives of what to do in a play situation
- Have an agenda as to what to do and how to do it as part of play

At this stage, the child with AS should be encouraged to share and invite others to join activities and make positive initiatives to play in a group or with someone. Attwood (2003) recommends that a few children of the same age with typical development be invited to play with the child with AS. This helps the child with AS learn the cues and rules of appropriate social play. In addition, cues can be identified for the child with AS by freezing the action and then by pointing out the cues in the social play. Role-playing responses to the friendship situation are also helpful.

**Stage II: 6 to 9 years (early elementary)**—A time when the child becomes aware of the value of having friends, either because of common interests or because someone is popular. More specifically, children at this stage typically:

- Understand the elements of reciprocity needed to maintain a friendship (e.g., friends come to my party, and I go to their parties)
- Realize friends fulfill needs and are helpful
- Make compliments about prospective friends
- Acquire alternative ways of dealing with conflict

The young elementary student with AS at this stage should learn to play cooperatively; therefore, more cooperative games than competitive games should be encouraged. Students can be taught cooperation using social stories or by role-playing games and then explaining actions that are friendly or not friendly. According to Attwood (2003), the relevant and typical unfriendly actions of students with AS include: interruptions, failure to recognize personal body space, inappropriate touching, and inappropriate coping with mistakes. This is a good stage to introduce students to how to read emotional cues so that they can become sensitive, caring friends.

**Stage III: 9 to 13 years (preadolescence)**—A time when friends are chosen because of their special attributes in terms of their abilities and personalities. More specifically, children at this stage typically:

- Demonstrate a gender split in their friendship (i.e., girls go with girls and boys with boys); overall peer acceptance becomes more important than parents' advice
- Base their friendship on shared interests, exploration, and emotional support
- Learn the importance of self-disclosure
- Increase awareness and concern of how they are viewed by others (i.e., peer acceptance is important)

The early adolescent with AS at this stage may not have the same gender split as do adolescents with typical development in that boys with AS may not like the games or sports that other boys their age observe or play. Therefore, they may prefer the friendship of girls, which typical male students may view as inappropriate, and may lead to teasing the student with AS (e.g., that he is a sissy) and may isolate him even more. It is important to encourage the male student with AS to play and interact with male peers. At this stage, it is important to select peers who might mentor the student with AS and to use strategies to teach teamwork, not just friendship skills. Also, this is a time when this age group should be taught observation, imitation, and acting skills to learn social skills (Willey, 1999). According to Attwood (2003), students with AS at this stage might be taught to engage in conversational scripts, to read body language and facial expressions, and to recognize the meaning in one's tone of voice. It has been found that having students with AS role-play people whom they know to be socially successful helps them to determine what are appropriate versus inappropriate behaviors (Willey).

**Stage IV: 13 to 19 years (adolescence)**—A time when the skills of friendship should solidify for the person. More specifically, children at this stage typically:

- Base friendship on how much you trust the person
- Show increased levels of self-disclosure
- Emphasize mutual or admired aspects of personality
- Move from friendship pairs to groups with shared values

Adolescents and young adults with AS at this stage should be encouraged to meet people with a wide variety of interests and should be assisted in selecting persons whom they respect, admire, and are willing to share ideas and time with. They may need to be taught, via role-playing, how they would appropriately disclose information about themselves.

Sidebar 4.1 summarizes the intervention strategies that might be used in helping students with AS become more successful at developing friendship and relationship skills. The five strategies listed are not all-encompassing, but rather present an array of strategies to be considered when developing this important skill.

1. Creating friendship files, a process encouraged by Attwood (2001), involves the child writing an index file on each peer. The index card may include:

   - Appropriate topics of conversation
   - Knowledge of the peers' attributes and how to compliment others
   - List of activities that the peer or peers might enjoy

   These index files can then be used to initiate and maintain conversations. Also, they provide insight into a peer's interests to determine if it is someone the student with AS may want to know better.

78

**Sidebar 4.1 Intervention Strategies for Developing Friendships/Relationships**

1. Create friendship files.
2. Identify friendship and relationship circles.
3. Discuss and explore characteristics of good friendships.
4. Learn the skill steps of making friends.
5. Learn the skill steps of keeping friends.

*Sources*: Anderson-Wood & Smith (1997); Attwood (2001); Myles & Adreon (2001)

2. Identifying friendship and relationship circles is another activity that may assist a student with AS. A social map of concentric circles is constructed with the child in the center. The next ring is the family, the next ring is of supporters (e.g., teachers, clergy, family doctor), and the last ring might be acquaintances and/or friends from school and the community (see Figure 4.1 on page 80). What names are placed in each concentric circle depend on the student, as will the number of circles used. Adolescents with AS should be encouraged to develop a social network. This can be accomplished by knowing several typical peers who can make up their circle of friends. These friends need to be carefully chosen to include such attributes as high-status; compliant with school rules; socially astute; and genuinely liked and interested in the student with AS (Myles & Adreon, 2001). Peers who enjoy being around people who have diverse perspectives to life may be excellent candidates to be part of the student's circle of friends.

3. Discuss and explore characteristics of good friendship as follows:

   • What makes for a good friendship (e.g., mutual interests and hobbies or participation in recreational and leisure time activities)

   • How friendships are formed and maintained (e.g., being trustworthy and supportive)

   • Why friendships end (e.g., no longer have mutual interests or are not able to trust each other)

4. The skill steps for making friends are easily assimilated by students with typical attributes, but need to be taught to those with AS. The steps for making friends are as follows (Andersen-Wood & Smith, 1997):

   • **Introduce yourself.**
     ▲ Have a friendly face and voice.
     ▲ Ask the person, "What is your name?"
     ▲ Introduce yourself by name.
     ▲ Make eye contact.

Figure 4.1        **Friendship and Relationship Circles**

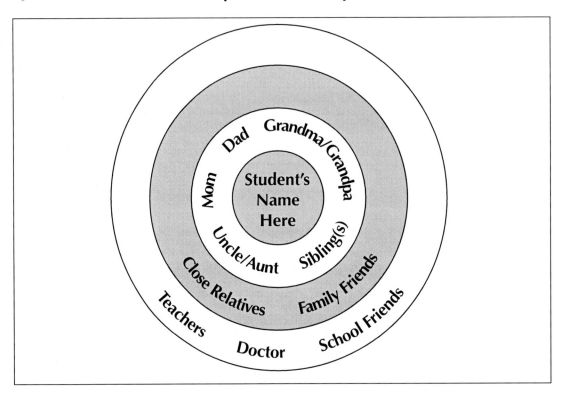

- **Start a conversation.**
  - ▲ Have a friendly face and voice.
  - ▲ Make eye contact.
  - ▲ Say hello.
  - ▲ Ask about other people's interests.
  - ▲ Tell them briefly about one of your interests.

- **Join in a conversation.**
  - ▲ Listen to know the topic of the conversation.
  - ▲ Use a friendly face and voice.
  - ▲ Make eye contact.
  - ▲ Think about what to say.
  - ▲ Wait for a pause in the conversation.
  - ▲ Say something on topic.
  - ▲ Ask a question about the topic.

- **Say just the right amount—do not bore people.**
  - ▲ Use a friendly face and voice.
  - ▲ Look for signs of boredom (e.g., yawning, ignoring you, looking away).
  - ▲ Listen to others.
  - ▲ Let others have a turn at talking.
  - ▲ Do not talk too much.

- **Listen to others.**
  - ▲ Give eye contact.
  - ▲ Face the speaker.
  - ▲ Remember what the speaker is saying.
  - ▲ Make brief appropriate comments (e.g., "Really?" "Yes," "Mm," "Uh-huh").

- **Be sensitive to the feelings of others.**
  - ▲ Tell friends if something nice has happened to you, but do it only once.
  - ▲ Thank people who congratulate and support you.
  - ▲ Remember to congratulate others for their successes.

- **Offer help.**
  - ▲ Offer to help others in need.
  - ▲ Use a pleasant face and voice.
  - ▲ Think about reasons to help others.

- **Ask for help.**
  - ▲ Use a pleasant face and voice.
  - ▲ Find someone who is not too busy.
  - ▲ Use polite words (e.g., "Please").
  - ▲ Remember to say "Thank you."

5. Making friends is only one aspect of friendship. Equally important is the ability to keep friends and cultivate the friendship. Skill steps in keeping friends are as follows (Andersen-Wood & Smith, 1997):

- **Say nice things to people.**
  - ▲ Use a friendly face and voice.
  - ▲ Think about why you might say something nice about someone.
  - ▲ Think of something nice to say about someone.
  - ▲ Think about how to say something.
  - ▲ Look at the person and make eye contact.

- **Show an interest in others.**
  - ▲ Use a friendly face and voice.
  - ▲ Make eye contact.

▲ Ask, "How are you doing?"

▲ Ask, "What have you been doing?"

▲ Listen to what others say.

▲ Make appropriate comments (e.g., "Yes," "Uh-huh").

▲ Contribute appropriately to the topic.

- **Ask—do not tell.**

  ▲ Use a friendly face and voice.

  ▲ Keep calm.

  ▲ Use polite words (e.g., "Please").

  ▲ Give a reason for the request.

  ▲ Thank the person for complying with the request.

- **Keep a secret.**

  ▲ Do not tell anyone.

  ▲ Think about if and when you should not keep a secret (e.g., illegal activity or something hurtful to someone).

  ▲ Think about why it is important to keep a secret.

  ▲ Think about how to keep a secret.

In addition to developing friends, developing more causal relationships in general is important. Adolescents and young adults with AS often struggle to develop and maintain relationships. Some suggestions to foster relationships are as follows (Pierangelo, 2003):

- Realize that you can build relationships based solely on trust, laughter, and respect.

- Involve yourself in a variety of work, community projects, and recreational/leisure time activities, which give you the opportunity to meet people.

- Be a good listener and a caring and trustworthy companion.

- Keep up on current events so that you can talk about a variety of topics.

- Be patient because developing worthwhile relationships takes time.

- Be open, frank, and informative about your disability and how it affects your social interactions.

Friendship/relationship building is critical to the social success of students with AS. It allows them to enhance and maintain self-esteem, learn appropriate social skills from observing others, and minimize being isolated or alone.

# Social Skills

Socialization is a process that takes time to learn. Social skills are learned over our entire lifetime and rely on our ability to do the following (Pierangelo, 2003):

- Observe the behaviors of others in social situations.
- Model the appropriate behavior of others in social situations.
- Practice different social skills in and across a variety of situations and then analyze them to determine which ones result in positive feedback or negative consequences.
- Be willing to discuss possible social situation options.
- Be aware, not oblivious, of one's social clumsiness.

Social skills are important because they help us interact with others, which in turn helps us understand others and make them more predictable. Typically, friendship building is included as part of social skills but was singled out in this book to emphasize its importance as a separate entity for teaching purposes. According to Gajewski, Hirn, and Mayo (1998a, 1998b) selected social skills may include, but are not limited to, the following: using manners, giving a compliment, accepting a compliment, making a request, accepting no, expressing an opinion, dealing with teasing, negotiating and compromising, and accepting consequences. Whatever the selected social skill being learned is, it is best learned if broken down into discrete steps. According to Gray (1995), a challenge to teaching social skills is that the educator or parent and the student with AS are working from two equally valid but different perspectives. Sidebar 4.2 presents an array of intervention strategies to teach social skills. The instructional strategies presented are not to be viewed as all-encompassing, but rather representative of the type of strategies that professionals might use to teach to social skills to students with AS.

## Direct Instruction

According to Myles and Adreon (2001), a six-step model for teaching social skills to students with AS is appropriate. The six steps are:

**Sidebar 4.2**  **Intervention Strategies to Teach Social Skills**

1. Direct Instruction
2. Acting Lessons (Role-Playing)
3. Social Stories
4. Social Autopsies
5. Social Groups
6. Videotaping/Audiotaping
7. Individualized Visual Social "Rule" Cards

1. **To jumpstart the learning process,** the rationale for learning the social skills should be presented (i.e., why the information is useful, how the information will be used, and where it fits with ones' current knowledge and understanding).

2. **Presentation of the social skill** should be multimodal and active (i.e., students with AS should be taught according to their learning style and in an active way, such as by role-playing, and not simply by working from a worksheet).

3. **Modeling of the correct behavior** within a social situation should be done over and over until the student understands the behavior and how to implement it.

4. **Verification should be undertaken** repeatedly by the educator to ensure that the student understands the new behavior.

5. **Evaluation should be conducted.** Since many students with AS appear to have a flat affect or emotionless expression, it is important to determine by direct assessment if the student has learned the behavior.

6. **Generalization should be determined** by asking students where else in their school, home, and community they might use the newly learned social skills, and then discuss how and why they would use them.

Gajewski, Hirn, and Mayo (1998a, 1998b) present seven critical elements needed to teach social skills instruction. The seven elements are as follows:

1. **Introduction**—The student is given time to think about the skill being taught, where it might be used, and if it has been used in the past.

2. **Guided instruction**—The skill is defined and the skill steps are introduced.

3. **Modeling**—The educator demonstrates the skill so that the students know what it looks like, feels like, and sounds like.

4. **Behavioral rehearsal (role-playing)**—The social skill is used so that the students experience the skill firsthand.

5. **Feedback**—The educator describes appropriate behaviors and gives corrective feedback in a positive, non-threatening manner.

6. **Cognitive planning**—The formula STOP, PLOT, GO and SO is used. First, the student is to "stop," think about the behavior, and stay calm. Second, the student is to "plot" or brainstorm about options and consequences. Third, the student is to "go" ahead and implement the plan. Fourth, the student is to ask "so?" which is to self-evaluate the plan by asking, "How did it work?"

7. **Transfer (generalization)**—The educator instructs students as to where else in the real world of school, home, and community they might use the newly learned social skill.

Myles and Adreon (2001) discuss an approach, Situation-Options-Consequences-Choices-Strategies-Stimulation (SOCCSS), which consists of the following six steps:

1. **Situation**—After a social problem occurs, the situation is analyzed according to who, what, when, where, and why?

2. **Options**—The student brainstorms several options for solving the social problem without the educator placing any value judgments.

3. **Consequences**—For each of the options, the student is to generate a possible consequence if that action were followed.

4. **Choices**—The student is to prioritize the options and consequences based on the outcome desired.

5. **Strategies**—The student is to develop a plan to carry out the options chosen.

6. **Simulation**—The student can practice the situation by doing such activities as talking about the plan, writing the plan down, or role-playing the options.

Winner (2000, 2002) recommends not just using a *social skill* approach, but a *social thinking* approach. This means that the student is not simply taught a social skill, but rather is taught how to think about the social skill and, in turn, is told by the professional the purpose of a given skill and when, where, and how the skill might be used within and across various social situations. She uses an I LAUGH framework of social cognition to teach social thinking and related skills. The elements of the I LAUGH intervention model are as follows:

I = Initiation of language, taught for the purpose of seeking help or clarification.

L = Listening with eyes and brain, expected from the student as a form of active listening or processing of information (particularly, interpreting and applying auditory information correctly).

A = Abstract and inferential language/communication, which can be a problem, so the professional needs to assist the student with AS to increase understanding of literal versus figurative language forms and how to read nonverbal communication.

U = Understanding perspective (i.e., the ability to understand one's own and others' emotions, thoughts, and intentions), usually acquired between 4 and 6 years of age.

G = Gestalt processing/Getting the big picture, which is the ability to see the overall task or concept before being able to break it down into small steps or units.

H = Humor and Human relatedness, as it is important for students with AS to understand humor and when it is appropriate to use it.

Gajewski, Hirn, and Mayo (1993, 1994, 1996) have designed a series of three books to teach social skills to students in grades 2 to 5: *Social Star (Books 1, 2, 3). Social Star (Book 1*; 1993) teaches general interaction skills, such as listening or body language. *Social Star (Book 2*; 1994) presents 13 skills for peer interaction such as being a friend or disagreeing politely. *Social Star (Book 3*; 1996) covers 9 higher level social skills, such as settling conflicts or making an apology.

Another valuable source is *Navigating the Social World,* which is a comprehensive program presenting 20 functional programs to work on such areas as recognizing and coping with one's own emotions, communication and social skills, abstract thinking, and behavioral issues (McAfee, 2002). Each program has background information, a set of goals, instructions, and specific activities to be used to assist the student in learning the new behaviors.

## Acting Lessons (Role-Playing)

Role-playing allows students to perform in a simulated situation before engaging in the real-life situations. Thus, role-playing activities provides a safe environment and structured format in which the student with AS learns and applies social skills. Simultaneously, role-playing allows the educator to vary the complexity of the task and social skills being acquired, while observing the learner's ability to accommodate the social situation. Often it is best to go from structured role-playing situations with a script, to a semi-structured situation where a social skill such as giving a compliment is practiced without a script, to doing the social skill in a natural real-life situation.

Role-playing or acting out various social situations can be a most effective strategy for teaching students with AS how to respond in various social situations. In her book *Pretending to Be Normal,* Willey (1999) clearly illustrates the value of being able to act your way through social situations so that you can participate in and survive them. She strongly recommends that the person with AS be taught this survival strategy.

## Social Stories

Gray (1995, 1998) has found social stories to be a successful strategy in teaching social skills to students with AS from preschool age to adulthood. The research of authors such as Attwood (2001, 2003), Paul (2003), Rogers and Myles (2001), and Winter (2003) has substantiated the value of using social stories to teach students with AS social skills. A social story describes a social situation in terms of relevant social cues and common responses, thus giving the student specific information about what happens in various social situations and why. Social stories are valuable because they personalize social situations for students, teach steps to follow in a social situation, prepare students for new social situations, and help students accommodate changes in routines. A series of steps should be followed when developing social stories.

1. Identify the problem in the social situation.

2. Visualize the goal or outcome (e.g., draw someone not interrupting during a conversation or calmly standing in line to go to the gym).

3. Write a short story about the social situation using:

   a. descriptive sentences that provide who is involved, what the person is doing, and where the person is (in other words, the facts of a social situation). It usually takes about five such sentences to every directive one. For example, "My name is Mike. I am in the first grade in school. After math class, we line up to go to the gym. In gym, we play ball."

   b. perspective sentences describing internal states or explaining the reactions and feelings of those involved in the situation. For example, "I feel crowded and don't like being touched while standing in line," or "I don't like playing ball in gym class." Another student's perspective might be, "Some kids like to fool around when they stand in line."

   c. directive sentences identifying a possible response to the social situation. For example, "I will wait in line, and if someone touches me, I will ask them to please stop," or "Even though I don't like playing ball in gym, I will try."

   d. affirmative or control sentences giving the student a way to remember what to do or say in the situation and to express a value, refer to a rule, or provide reassurance. For example, "When I wait calmly in line, my teacher rewards me by letting me go first."

Using the social story format, some wonderful insights can be gleaned about the student's ability to handle social situations and take the perspective of others (Kuttler, Myles, & Carlson, 1998; Swaggart, Gagnon, Bock, Earles, Quinn, Myles, & Carlson, 1998). Also, software has been designed that teaches social skills using a social story format. Four in particular are *Nickel Takes On Teasing* (Thinking Publications, 2003), *Nickel Takes On Anger* (Thinking Publications, 2004a), *Nickel Takes On Stealing* (Thinking Publications, 2004b), and *Nickel Takes On Disrespect* (Thinking Publications, 2005). Hagiwara & Myles (1999) investigated using a computer to teach social situations through social stories and found it successful.

## Social Autopsies

The social autopsy is an innovative strategy (Myles & Adreon, 2001) designed to get students to objectively analyze their social mistakes. Thus, social autopsies are used when a social situation did not go well. It should be conducted using a constructive and supportive problem-solving strategy. Along with the student with AS, ask the following questions to help understand the social situation and any mistakes made:

- What happened?
- What was the social error?

- Who was hurt by the social error?
- What should be done to correct the error?
- What could be done next time?

By answering these questions about each social mistake, the student becomes more aware of the problems caused by such errors and how to modify behavior in the future.

## Social Groups

Social groups can be established by carefully selecting peers with typical development as buddies. Some of the ways to recruit peer buddies are as follows:

- Write a letter to parents and/or general education teachers explaining the value of social groups for students with AS and having a peer buddy.
- Talk to students' classes, seeking volunteers for the social group (with the student with AS not present).
- Allow the student with AS to ask peers or friends to join the social group.
- Select the peers carefully from the pool of volunteers or nominees.
- Make the social groups fun, so that everyone wants to come and participate.

Social groups should have a set curriculum, such as working on greetings, conversational skills (e.g., initiating, maintaining, and terminating a conversation), or giving and getting compliments. Using such methods as social stories, comic strips, role-playing, and following scripts should facilitate the learning of these social skills.

## Videotaping/Audiotaping

Often students with AS cannot actually reflect on a given social situation, retell what happened, and then in turn tell how they might modify the response to be more appropriate in a situation. One of the methods used to assist students with AS to analyze objectively whether they have used a social skill appropriately or inappropriately is to audio- or videotape the situation. The tapes provide an actual synopsis of the situation, and can be replayed as many times as necessary, so the student can identify behaviors and then determine where to modify those behaviors so as to respond appropriately within and across situations.

## Individualized Visual Social "Rule" Cards

Using visual social "rule" cards helps some students with AS remember to use the social rules appropriately within various situations. The cards can be taped to the student's desk as a visual reminder of appropriate social behaviors to use in the classroom. Portable, laminated rule cards can be used for environments other than the classroom and at the home or in the community. Once the student understands the meaning of the rules, rules can be written on laminated index cards which the student can carry along as visual reminders of the social rules for particular social situations.

# Communication Skills

Communication is the meeting of meaning between two or more persons (Larson & McKinley, 2003). Language is a rule-governed code that consists of form (syntax), content (semantics), and use (pragmatics). Overall, communication is the act of intentionally affecting others' behavior through verbal and nonverbal means. Communication breakdowns happen when any of the following occur:

- Mismatch between verbal and nonverbal communication

- Rigidity of routines either verbally or nonverbally

- Agenda differences between verbal and nonverbal communication, or within verbal or nonverbal communication (i.e., lack of joint reference between speaker and listener)

- Inability to initiate, maintain, and terminate a topic in a timely fashion

- Deficient repair strategies in either nonverbal or verbal communication

- Inability to take turns or to interrupt appropriately

- Problems in nonverbal communication (e.g., gaze aversion, posture violations, flat facial expressions or affect), proxemics (i.e., distance from speaker), and so on.

- Information overload when information is coming in too quickly to process, when a person is unable to filter out irrelevant stimuli, or when information is too detailed or voluminous to understand its relevance.

Any of these communication breakdowns can lead to problems for the student with AS. Thus, the educator must consider a wide array of communication strategies.

Most intervention strategies will involve the use of language or communication skills, particularly of conversations and narrations. However, many students with AS do have some difficulty with understanding abstract and ambiguous language, so it would be appropriate to provide some intervention strategies for this area.

## Oral Communication

### Ambiguous Language

Ambiguous language is language capable of being used or understood in two or more contexts resulting in different meaning. Comprehension and use of ambiguous language includes, but is not limited to, multiple meanings of words; sentences with two meanings; phrases (such as idioms) that have multiple meanings; changes in stress or juncture resulting in different meanings to the same sentence or communication utterance; lack of familiarity with social or cultural elements in the situation; lack of world knowledge regarding speakers, social context, and so forth; and/or visual and auditory elements. Gorman-Gard (1992), Hamersky (1995), and Spector (1997), in their respective books, provide a wealth of information for teaching figurative/ ambiguous language. In *Saying One Thing, Meaning Another* and *As Far As Words Go,* Spector (1997, 2002) notes the importance of teaching the following skills: (1) defining words and analyzing syntactic information; (2) explaining and contrasting multiple meaning of words, sentences, and ideas; and (3) increasing world knowledge by using concrete worksheets and ultimately moving to more real-world situations. Gorman-Gard uses a variety of activities to bring to the student's awareness level of the use and misuse of figurative language in her book *Figurative Language*. And Hamersky uses cartoons to teach figurative language and humor concepts to students in her resource *Cartoon Cut-Ups*. Collectively, these materials provide visual strategies for teaching students how to use and comprehend figurative language and humor appropriately.

**Conversations**

As indicated in Sidebar 4.3, a number of activities are pertinent for teaching conversational skills to students with AS. Regardless of the conversational activity, it is important that students understand why they are doing what they are doing and how to transfer the new behaviors into new situations. For example, to know when and where the conversational rules can be applied formally or informally.

Schreiber and McKinley (1995) provide a variety of strategies to teach conversational speech. These are illustrated in Figure 4.2 and are described in detail in the pages that follow. (Note that this figure is printable from the CD-ROM as Appendix M.)

Sidebar 4.3      **Intervention Strategies to Teach Conversational Skills**

1. Teaching the rules of conversation
2. Participating as both a speaker and listener with a specified topic of conversation
3. Providing natural opportunities to converse with peers and adults
4. Initiating and maintaining a conversation
5. Improving your listening skills during a conversation
6. Experiencing topic interruptions and discussing the impact on conversational speech
7. Discussing what to do if you interrupt the speaker
8. Asking questions using the 5 *Wh*-questions and 1 *H*-question

*Source*: Schreiber & McKinley (1995)

**Figure 4.2**    **Rules of Conversation Poster**

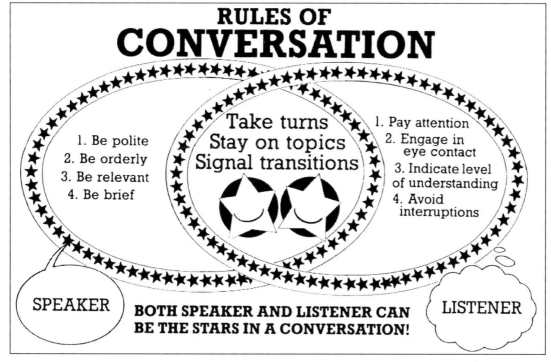

From *Daily Communication: Strategies for Adolescents with Language Disorders* (p. 135), by L. Schreiber and N. McKinley, 1995,
Eau Claire, WI: Thinking Publications. © 1995 by Thinking Publications. Reprinted with permission.

1. **Teaching the rules of conversation**—By providing students with a graphic representation of the rules (such as that provided in Figure 4.2), the student with Asperger Syndrome has a visual reminder of the rules of conversation. Review the four rules of being a good speaker: (1) be polite, (2) be orderly, (3) be relevant, and (4) be brief. Then review for the student with AS the four rules for being a good listener: (1) pay attention, (2) engage in eye contact, (3) indicate level of understanding, and (4) avoid interruptions. And last, review for the student with AS the three techniques both speakers and listeners should use: (1) take turns, (2) stay on topics, and (3) signal transitions. In reviewing all the rules, the educator provides the student with AS the opportunity to view the gestalt of conversational rules before proceeding to learn any single one of them.

2. **Participating as both a speaker and listener with a specified topic of conversation**— This can be undertaken by making index cards with conversational starters on them, such as the following:

   • "What is the most interesting TV program you have watched this week?"
   • "What is your favorite sport or TV program?"

- "What is a good place to eat in this city?"
- "What kind of job do you want some day?"
- "What are your favorite classes this year?"

The student chooses a card and speaks about the topic or the student gives a card to someone else to talk about the topic and then listens.

3. **Providing natural opportunities to converse with peers and adults**—Initially, you may have to provide contrived naturalistic opportunities like structured social groups. However, eventually, it is important to bring peers, adults, and parents together to converse with the student with AS so that he or she gets practice in participating in natural conversational situations.

4. **Initiating and maintaining a conversation**—This might be undertaken by providing the student with a situation and then asking a question for discussion. For example,

   - "Your sister is angry that your brother spilled ketchup on her sweater. What will you say to your sister?"

   - "Your friend is wearing a coat you really like. You want to find out where he bought it. What will you say?"

   - "You don't understand the directions given to play a game in gym class. You want to ask the teacher to clarify the directions. What will you say?"

5. **Improving your listening skills during a conversation**—Encourage the student to bring to a conscious level what the rules and behaviors are for being a good active listener. This might occur by discussing the following questions:

   - "What does it mean to be a good listener?"
   - "What are some of the things that get in the way of being a good listener?"
   - "Who do you know that is a good listener?"
   - "How do you know when someone is listening?"
   - "How do you feel when someone does not listen to you?"

6. **Experiencing topic interruptions and discussing the impact on conversational speech**—It is important that the student have the experience of being interrupted when talking. Follow up with these questions:

   - "How did it feel to be interrupted in the middle of a sentence or topic?"
   - "When would it have been appropriate for the listener to interrupt you?"
   - "What should the listener say if he or she interrupts you (e.g., 'I am sorry')?"

7. **Discussing what to do if you interrupt the speaker**—If you interrupt, you might say, "Excuse me. I didn't mean to interrupt you."

8. **Asking questions using the 5 *Wh*-questions (who, what, where, when, why) and 1 *H*-question (how)**—It is important that the student with AS learn what type of information is gleaned from each question (i.e., *who*, tells the person involved; *what*, the content of situation; *where*, the location of the activity or event; *when*, the timing of the event; *why*, the cause of the event; and *how*, the action surrounding the event or activity). Since students with AS can be quite blunt and abrasive, it is important that they be taught how to ask a question in a polite manner, whether in the classroom, at home, or in the community.

### Narrations

Often students with AS need to be taught narrative skills because they do not understand the more abstract dimensions to narrations or stories. A number of ways to teach narrative skills are provided in this section (see overview in Sidebar 4.4).

Strategies to help students learn narrative skills are as follows:

1. **Teach story elements as a guide for narration analysis**—Refer to Table 4.1 on page 94 to teach the various story grammar elements of the beginning (setting of the story); middle (theme of the story; events of the story; goals, motives, attempts, and reactions of the characters); and ending (conclusion) of various stories. The questions listed in Table 4.1 can serve as a scaffolding device for the student.

2. **Teach how to use story grammar elements to generate written narratives**—Written narrative development might also be undertaken by the student using graphic organizers found in the software programs *Inspiration* (Inspiration Software, 2005) or *Kidspiration* (Inspiration Software, 2005), the book *Map It Out* (Wiig & Wilson, 2001), or in Appendix N. Various word-processing software programs also can be useful in generating written

**Sidebar 4.4**  **Intervention Strategies to Teach Narrative Skills**

1. Teach story elements as a guide for narration analysis.
2. Teach how to use story grammar elements to generate written narratives.
3. Select books, audiotapes, videotapes and DVDs that have good story lines.
4. Use storytelling/formulation tasks to relate past events.
5. Use story retelling/reformulation tasks to tell stories.
6. Select bridging activities.
7. Require higher level story analysis.

*Sources:* Schreiber & McKinley (1995)

Table 4.1                    **Story Elements Guide for Narrators**

| Story Grammar Elements | Questions |
|---|---|
| **Beginning**<br><br>Setting of the Story | Who are the main characters?<br>Where does the story take place?<br>When does the story take place? |
| **Middle**<br><br>Theme of the Story<br>Events of the Story<br>Goal(s) of the Characters<br>Motive(s) of the Characters<br>Attempts of the Characters<br>Reactions of the Characters | What is the main idea (theme) of the story?<br>What happens to the characters?<br>What are the characters trying to do?<br>Why are the characters trying to reach the goal(s)?<br>What happens when the characters try to reach the goal?<br>What are their feelings? What are their plans? |
| **Ending**<br><br>Conclusion | How does everything turn out?<br>What lesson (moral) did you learn from the story? |

*Sources*: Garnett (1986); Hutson-Nechkash (2001)

documentation. The graphic organizer in Appendix N is shown in Figure 4.3 and is printable from the CD-ROM.

3. **Select books, audiotapes, videotapes, and DVDs that have good story lines**—Taking the time to choose appropriate media will help the student to have good narrative transcriptions as models.

4. **Use storytelling/formulation tasks to relate past events**—Ask the student to tell about a personal experience or to tell a story about a fictional character or about someone in history.

5. **Use story retelling/reformulation tasks to tell stories**—Ask the student to retell a story from a TV program or movie seen and/or a book read. Have the student use the story grammar element questions to see if all aspects of a story have been presented. Emphasize to the student that stories need to be done sequentially and cohesively to be understood and that it is important to include important pieces of relational information, as well as the referent in the story.

6. **Select bridging activities**—Have the student take various aspects of the story and bridge them to the student's own life. "In the story, one of the main characters felt (*state an emotion*). When is a time that you felt that emotion? What did it feel like?"

Figure 4.3    **Graphic Organizer**

**Extended Activities**

**Educational Level**

Elementary

**Objectives**

(1) Identify story characters, settings, problems, and solutions; (2) organize topics within stories to form a narrative plan; and (3) retell stories

e colored paper squares (e.g., green for characters and red for solutions)
mulate a narrative plan. The plan can move from left to right or from
Then ask students to retell a part of a familiar children's story as from
d square for that story segment. You can walk one student through all
ifferent student on each square (i.e., several students share the task of

**Completed Map**

The map shows how students in Grade 2 analyzed and organized the content of *Goldilocks and the Three Bears.*

Show the Completed Map to students and say, for example:

*This map shows what some students thought was important in the story Goldilocks and the Three Bears. Let's look at and talk about the important parts of the story, beginning with the characters.*

You may want to follow up by asking, for example:

*What else do you remember about Goldilocks? What else do you remember about the three bears? What else do you remember about the bears' house? What would you have done if you were Goldilocks?*

re of a familiar context (e.g., a circus scene). Ask them to make up
oblems, and solutions to go with the picture. Enter the students'
k them to create their own stories in response to the picture and

and guide them in analyzing it for characters, settings, problems,

familiar children's story (e.g., *The Three Little Pigs*). Then ask
n story with the same characters and similar events but set in
f might have used a bulldozer to level the houses).
f for characters, settings, and problems. Have each student use
a story. Compare the stories the students create and discuss

**Work Map**

Select a story. Show the Work Map to students and say, for example:

*This map is empty. Let's read and talk about this story. Then we'll identify the characters, settings, problems, and solutions. When we have done that, I will ask you to retell the story by using this information.*

7. **Require higher level story analysis**—Once the student can successfully use the story grammar elements, have the student summarize (e.g., "In one sentence, tell me what the story is all about"), analyze (e.g., "What are the strengths, weaknesses, or suggestions to improve the story?"), or generalize (e.g., "When might the essence of this story be applied to other aspects of your life?") the story under discussion.

# Nonverbal Communication Skills

Many students with AS have neither the ability to produce or to read nonverbal communication cues. And yet, Samovar and Porter (1991) noted that up to 90% of the social intent of a message is nonverbal. Fridlund (1994) noted that emotions are universally recognized across cultures from facial expressions. More specifically, he noted, "Happiness, surprise, fear, anger, contempt, disgust, and sadness—these seven emotions, plus or minus two, are recognized from facial expressions, by all human beings, regardless of their cultural background" (Fridlund, 1994, p. 192). Some of the nonverbal behaviors that students with typical development use automatically, but may need to be taught to students with AS, are:

- Nonverbal functions of communication, such as to repeat, complement, and contradict what one has said; substitute for a verbal action; regulate a communication event; or accentuate a message

- Movement of the body appropriately in terms of gestures, posture, touching behaviors, and so on

- Proxemics, or standing at an appropriate distance and space from the other communicator

- Using and understanding facial expressions

- Using and understanding eye contact

- Using gestures to match verbal and nonverbal communication

- Understanding others' gestures

- Physical appearance of the communicator in terms of artifacts such as clothing, perfume, and so on

- Paralanguage, including voice quality and vocalizations

- Communication environment that impinges on the interaction, such as the furniture, lighting, temperature, perceptions of time, and timing (Schreiber & McKinley, 1995)

Students with AS often have a very difficult time understanding and appropriately applying nonverbal communication to oral communication situations. Therefore, it is critical to provide specific intervention in the teaching of both the understanding and production of nonverbal communication skills. Sidebar 4.5 provides an overview of nonverbal strategies that might be used to increase students' awareness of some key nonverbal communication skills.

Schreiber and McKinley (1995) offer a number of suggestions to have students become aware of nonverbal communication use and understanding. A few of their ideas are presented below:

1. **Reading and using appropriate body language**—Students can become more aware of their body language by standing up and not saying anything, and then asking others to tell what they think the person's body language is conveying. Another strategy is to look at pictures, noting the way people are standing. Then determine by their position if they are friends, enemies, neutral/indifferent, or if you cannot judge. Then ask, "What cues lead you to your conclusions?"

2. **Using gestures to assist communication**—Have students stand with their wrists and hands inside a paper bag and then talk by answering some of the following questions: "How do you play baseball?"; "How to you get from school to home?"; "Explain how to get dressed in the morning, drive a car, or play a computer game." Discuss whether it was easier or harder to answer these questions without using gestures.

3. **Understanding how gestures assist communication**—Have students watch a movie or a videotaped TV program and then discuss how the people in it used gestures, body

**Sidebar 4.5** **Intervention Strategies to Teach Nonverbal Communication Skills**

1. Reading and using appropriate body language
2. Using gestures to assist communication
3. Understanding how gestures assist communication
4. Analyzing the effects of nonsupportive nonverbal communication
5. Discussing the effects of supportive nonverbal communication
6. Using eye contact or mutual gazing appropriately
7. Interpreting facial expressions by using contextual cues
8. Using various commands and greetings
9. Discriminating between matching and mismatching verbal and nonverbal communication messages
10. Determining comfortable physical distance during conversational speech

*Source:* Schreiber & McKinley (1995)

posture, dress, facial expressions, and other nonverbal mannerisms to convey their messages. Did their nonverbal behavior add or detract from the verbal message? Using another videotape, have students watch it without sound and try to interpret what is going on from the visual cues. Then watch it with the sound on, and determine how accurately the students interpreted the nonverbal communication.

4. **Analyzing the effects of nonsupportive nonverbal communication**—Discuss how one's personal space might be violated, invaded, or contaminated; for example, sitting too close to someone, staring at someone for a long time, or waving one's hands or arms uncontrollably.

5. **Discussing the effects of supportive nonverbal communication**—For example, how does a smile, a gentle pat on the back, or a wink add to the verbal communication?

6. **Using eye contact or mutual gazing appropriately**—Discuss situations in which appropriate eye contact took place. Study pictures of people looking at each other and decide if the eye contact or mutual gazing is appropriate.

7. **Interpreting facial expressions by using contextual cues**—Use photographs (either commercially purchased or of family and friends) to discuss various facial expressions. Using common facial expressions (e.g., happy, surprised, afraid, angry, sad, determined, and interested), ask the student to first read your face and then to attempt to do each facial expression. Note how the communication context and what types of gestures accompany the various facial expressions make it easier to read facial expressions. Explain in detail what one does with the face for the various emotions. Also use expressive facial

features like those in Figure 4.4 to discuss various facial expressions. (Figure 4.4 is represented as Appendix O on the CD-ROM.)

8. **Using various commands and greetings**—Show what type of nonverbal gesture would indicate the following: "Be silent/Hush"; "Come here"; "Stop"; "Follow me"; "Stay here"; "Hello"; "Goodbye."

Figure 4.4                                **Facial Expressions**

**Printable from the CD-ROM**

### SURPRISE

- Eyebrows are raised, curved and high.

- Skin below brow is stretched.

- Forehead has horizontal wrinkles all the way across.

- Eyelids are wide open; the sclera (white of the eye) shows above and below the iris.

- Jaw drops; lips and teeth are parted, but with no tension or stretching of the mouth.

### FEAR

- Brows are raised and drawn together.

- Forehead has wrinkles in center area only.

- Upper eyelids are raised; lower eyelids are tensed and drawn up.

- Mouth opens; lips are tense or stretched and drawn back.

### DISGUST

- Upper lip is raised; lower lip is raised and pushed up to the upper lip, or lowered and protruded slightly.

- Nose is wrinkled.

- Cheeks are raised.

- Brow is lowered; upper eyelids are lowered.

### ANGER

- Brows are lowered and drawn together; vertical lines appear between the brows.

- Eyes have a hard stare and may appear to bulge.

- Lips either pressed together firmly or open, as if shouting.

### HAPPINESS

- Corners of lips drawn back and up (i.e., forming a smile).

- Cheeks are raised.

- Wrinkles extend down the nose to the outer edges beyond the lip corners.

- "Crow's foot" wrinkles go outward from the corners of the eyes.

### SADNESS

- Inner corners of eyebrows are drawn up.

- Inner corners of the upper eyelids are raised.

- Corners of the lips are down; the lips may be trembling.

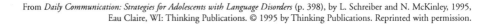

From *Daily Communication: Strategies for Adolescents with Language Disorders* (p. 398), by L. Schreiber and N. McKinley, 1995, Eau Claire, WI: Thinking Publications. © 1995 by Thinking Publications. Reprinted with permission.

9. **Discriminating between matching and mismatching verbal and nonverbal communication messages**—Show for example, frustration on your face and say, "I hate to do math" = a match; then say, "I don't like it when my brother borrows my computer" and smile = a mismatch.

10. **Determining comfortable physical distance during conversational speech**—If you know someone well, personal distance is about 2 to 4 feet; social distance is typically 4 to 12 feet. Look at pictures and determine if you can tell if the personal or social distance is appropriate. If one stands too close, how does it make you feel? If someone stands too far away, what problems are caused?

# Theory of Mind or Perspective-Taking

Theory of mind or perspective-taking is very difficult for students with AS. According to Cumine, Leach, and Stevenson (2001), theory of mind is "the ability to think about other people's thinking—and further, to think about what they think about our thinking—and even further, to think about what they think we think about their thinking and so on" (p. 19). Students with AS have difficulty appreciating that other people have mental states of intentions, needs, desires, and beliefs, which may be different from their own (Frith, 1996). Cumine, Leach, & Stevenson note that students with AS have the following difficulties:

- Predicting others' behavior, resulting in fear and avoidance of others
- Reading and understanding the intentions or motives of others
- Explaining their own behavior objectively
- Understanding their own and others' emotions
- Understanding how one's own behavior affects how others think or feel
- Realizing what others know, resulting in pedantic or overly detailed speech
- Reading and reacting to the listener's level of interest regarding their special topic of interest
- Being frank and forthright without understanding deception
- Understanding social interaction, leading to poor turn-taking, topic maintenance, and eye contact
- Differentiating fact from fiction and understanding what "pretend" means

According to Twachtman (1995), there are three broad areas of perspective-taking that should be taken into account when working with students with AS who have theory of mind difficulties: (1) perceptual, which involves the student's ability to understand that others may perceive things differently; (2) cognitive, which involves the student's ability to understand that others may have different ideas and intentions; and (3) linguistic, which involves the student's ability to adjust the form, content, and purpose of the utterance to suit the needs of the situation and/or listener.

## Asperger Syndrome

Many students with AS have a difficult time reading the minds (i.e., intentions, emotions, feelings, and points of view) of other people, resulting in the person with AS feeling stressed about how to cope with various people in social situations. Therefore, a series of strategies for teaching theory of mind or mind-reading cues are described below and listed in Sidebar 4.6.

Some tools for teaching theory of mind are to use the following:

1. **Photos of persons displaying various emotions**—Have the student look at various photos, and then ask the student to determine what emotions are being depicted by the person in the photo (by his or her facial expression or posture).

2. **Line drawings of faces displaying various emotions**—Ask the student, "If you saw this emotion, what would the person be feeling?"

3. **Videos illustrating one's own and others' emotions, intentions, and their consequences**—Have the student take the perspective of the other person in the video by their posture, facial expression, or context. Ask students to first note the emotions being conveyed and then to note what the person might be feeling given that emotion.

4. **Comic strip conversations** (Gray, 1994, 1998)—These materials allow the student to visually see the interaction between two or more persons using a comic strip format. Gray (1994) defines a comic strip conversation as "a conversation between two or more people which incorporates the use of simple drawings" (p. 1). This type of activity allows the student to practice what people say and do when talking to each other (conversational reciprocity). It also gives the learner an opportunity to visually see what people may be thinking, thus being able to visualize perspective-taking in another person (theory of mind). Gray's book (1994) is an excellent resource on how to create comic strip situations both in terms of how to structure them and what symbols to use.

5. **Referential communication activities**—This intervention strategy is sometimes referred to as "barrier games." This type of activity uses at least two people seated across from one

Sidebar 4.6          **Intervention Tools for Teaching Theory of Mind**

---

1. Photos of persons displaying various emotions
2. Line drawings of faces displaying various emotions
3. Videos illustrating one's own and others' emotions, intentions, and their consequences
4. Comic strip conversations
5. Referential communication activities

---

*Sources*: Gray (1994, 1998); Larson & McKinley (2003); Schwartz & McKinley (1987); Twachtman (1995)

another with identical material in front of them and a screen (barrier) between them. One person is the sender (speaker) who directs the receiver (listener) to perform various functions with the materials (e.g., the speaker explains to the listener how to use the materials to construct or reconstruct an identical two or three-dimensional model that only the speaker can see). The barrier is then removed and the sender and receiver compare materials to see if communication was successful. The speaker and the listener can switch roles, which allows the student with AS the opportunity to take the perspective of both sender and receiver. One of the advantages of this activity is that the arrangement of the materials allows for a visual display of what was sent and how the receiver interpreted what was being said. According to Twachtman (1995), referential communication activities provide a rich, meaningful context for interactive communication to take place, to use language to direct others' behavior, and to employ repair strategies, while simultaneously increasing one's knowledge of both literal and abstract language concepts and vocabulary. Referential communication activities can be made more or less difficult depending on the following variables (Larson & McKinley, 2003; Schwartz & McKinley, 1987): allowing questions of clarification or not allowing them; having the speaker only state directions versus state and then have the listener restate the directions; allowing gestures or no gestures; giving a partial message versus a complete message; allowing information questions versus only questions of clarification; and setting a time limit versus no time limit for the activity. For further information on referential communication or barrier games, see *Make It Yourself Barrier Activities* by Schwartz and McKinley (1987).

These types of activities allow the student with AS to practice taking the perspective of another, thus enhancing one's ability to read people and social situations more readily.

# 10 General Intervention Strategies for Social Competence

In addition to the specific intervention strategies you just read about, which should be taught to develop social competence skills, a number of general intervention strategies should also be implemented to foster the development of social competence skills across and within a variety of social situations. They are described in detail on the pages that follow and are highlighted in Sidebar 4.7.

1. **Social or communication skill groups** run by a professional (e.g., classroom teacher, special educator, SLP) to teach conversational skills; body movement and distance; perspective-taking; reading others' emotions; regulating emotions; and social problem solving of how to deal with teasing, bullying, and being left out can be most helpful (Ozonoff, Dawson, & McPartland, 2002).

Sidebar 4.7

## 10 General Intervention Strategies
## for Teaching Social Competence

1. Use social or communication skill groups.
2. Do self-awareness activities.
3. Make the abstract concrete.
4. Use social scripts for what to do and say in social situations.
5. Use social reading to teach social skills.
6. Do narrating life and thinking out loud activities.
7. Do peer coaching or peer mediation.
8. Use comic strip conversations.
9. Use role-playing activities.
10. Use scaffolding to assist performance.

*Sources*: Gray (1994, 1995); Larson & McKinley (2003); Myles & Adreon (2001); Ozonoff, Dawson, & McPartland (2002); Vygotsky (1962); Wiig, Larson, & Olson (2004)

2. **Conducting self-awareness activities** on what it means to have Asperger Syndrome helps students to recognize their strengths and challenges, to appreciate their unique differences, and to promote self-acceptance and self-advocacy (Ozonoff, Dawson, & McPartland, 2002). For example, students with AS might learn more about themselves by keeping a journal, designing a scrapbook or displaying photos about themselves, or doing a life history box (in which you put objects that represent you in some way). The purpose of these activities is to learn about themselves by answering questions such as, "Who am I?", "How do I relate to others?", and "How do others relate to me?"

3. **Making the abstract concrete** is a procedure that is very helpful to people with AS since most have normal to above-average intelligence, but become confused by abstract or implied language (Ozonoff, Dawson, & McPartland, 2002). This can be achieved by using concrete rules to elicit more abstract behaviors. For example, say, "When you initiate a conversation or ask a question, make eye contact for 5 seconds." Don't say, "You should use eye contact when you talk." This is too abstract; the rule needs to be made very concrete before exceptions to the rule can be taught.

4. **Social scripts** are written prompts or guidelines for what to do and say in common social situations (Ozonoff, Dawson, & McPartland, 2002). Most of us have learned these social scripts incidentally by observing others. We use the social scripts easily and

unconsciously (e.g., we have a script for meeting someone new, ordering food in a restaurant, answering a telephone, asking or answering questions in a classroom, and so on). Students with AS may need to be taught specifically the content, sequence, and communicative style in a social situation, or the social script. Mayo and Waldo's (1994) book, *Scripting: Social Communication for Adolescents,* teaches students a wide array of social skills using two types of scripts per social skill. Script A demonstrates the skill and the appropriate way to use the skill, and Script B's characters use the skill inappropriately so that the students can compare and contrast the differences and rewrite the scripts. Miller's (2004) book, *Scripting Junior: Social Skill Role-Plays,* is a comparable book designed for elementary students.

5. **Social reading** (Gray, 1995) consists of three instructional areas: (1) social stories, (2) social review, and (3) social assistance. All three are important in teaching social skills. Social stories are usually written by educators or parents to describe social situations and to identify social skills to be learned. Social review uses videotaped sequences to assess a child's perceptions of social situations, to present accurate social information, and to assist in developing social skills. Social assistance activities are any materials or methods that assist the child in social situations. While each of these three areas is different in its use of materials and procedures, the three are alike in that a problematic social situation is targeted; information is gathered about problem social situations and how the student performs in them; information about the perspective of social situations is shared between educators and child; and new social situations are identified by the child (see "Social Stories," beginning on page 86, for the steps in designing and implementing social stories).

6. **Narrating life** (Ozonoff, Dawson, & McPartland, 2002) is an activity that provides for the student to put their life history into a story format. Thinking out loud is an activity that encourages students to state their thoughts aloud so they can focus their thoughts and analyze them objectively (Myles & Adreon, 2001). In mediational learning, the educator serves as a mediator for the students' activities, thus focusing and framing the students' experiences as they are being experienced (Larson & McKinley, 2003). For example, something as simple as asking a student to close the door can be mediated. By simply saying, "Close the door," the educator is not mediating. But if the educator says, "Please close the door because there's a strong draft in the hallway, and I'm afraid the wind might ruin the artwork on the walls," then the educator has mediated. The educator has established a reason for closing the door that goes beyond the immediate situation. A relationship between closing the door and preventing a problem has been conveyed.

7. **Peer coaching or peer mediation intervention** is having peers with typical development interact with and coach students with AS about social situations. According to Ozonoff, Dawson, and McPartland (2002), typical peers should be explicitly taught how to initiate interactions, prompt social responses, and give feedback and reinforcement to students with AS.

8. **Comic strip conversations** (conversations which incorporate the use of simple drawings) allow the student to identify what people say and do, and also what people may be thinking, using visual supports or visualization. This activity teaches not only conversational reciprocity, but also theory of mind (i.e., perspective-taking). What symbols to use and how to structure the situation can be found in Carol Gray's (1994) book *Comic Strip Conversations: Colorful, Illustrated Interactions with Students with Autism and Related Disorders.*

9. **Role-playing** is an activity in which students are given character roles to act out, to learn how one might perform or participate in a situation before actually being put into that situation. Role-playing simulates the real-life situation, but allows the educator to vary the complexity of the task based on learner needs and abilities. Learners might begin with a script to establish the basic skills needed to undertake the task or social situation. As students with AS become skilled in using the script, they might attempt using the skill in less structured and more natural social situations. Excellent resources for scripts are *Scripting: Social Communication for Adolescents* (Mayo & Waldo, 1994) and *Scripting Junior: Social Skill Role-Plays* (Miller, 2001).

10. **Scaffolding** has its roots in Vygotsky's (1962) theory and includes the adult's use of supports to assist the student in ultimately moving from dependence to independence in a particular skill areas. Support is removed after the student is able to perform the task. Scaffolding procedures include verbal, nonverbal, visual, auditory, and tactile stimuli and may include (but are not limited to) the following (Wiig, Larson, & Olson, 2004):

    a. **Cloze procedures** require students to fill in missing words in a sentence or paragraph using the context to determine the missing word (e.g, fill in missing words using the correct verb tense marker: She plays tennis everyday. Yesterday, she _____ tennis).

    b. **Coaching** helps learners recognize when a skill should be applied, gives feedback on how the skills are being used, and provides encouragement and support for using the skills (e.g., when giving an oral presentation, how to organize and deliver the message in a clear, concise, and consistent manner).

    c. **Concept maps** use a visual structure to elicit and organize responses from students. Concept maps (also referred to as graphic organizers) show connections between pieces of information within a specified topic. *Map It Out* (Wiig & Wilson, 2001) uses graphic organizers to teach concepts (see Appendix N for an example).

d. **Cuing** provides a prompt or obvious signal to help elicit a specific verbal or nonverbal response from the student (e.g., it begins with the sounds "ba" or it is the opposite of hard).

e. **Guided questioning** uses open-ended questions to help learners focus on selected facts, details, relations, and other aspects of a task, topic, text, or situation. In guided questioning, a leading or orienting question is asked to guide students to an acceptable response (e.g., "Where do polar bears live? In a hot or cold climate? What continents have cold weather?").

f. **Modeling** provides an example for the student to copy (e.g., "Listen, then repeat what I say: 'Please pass the milk'"). Modeling is often used during practice to develop fluency in responding or to strengthen complex responses during early learning.

Students with AS have a wide array of social competency issues. Each student is different. Therefore, a variety of intervention strategies need to be considered.

# Case Studies: Jared and Max

This last section provides an opportunity to review two case studies that represent students who have various forms of Asperger Syndrome, reflecting problems with social competence. Jared best exemplifies the types of difficulties students with AS have with social communication or the use of language. Max best represents students with AS who have problems with specific social skills, specifically, relationship building. In both case studies, there is an analysis guide (via a set of questions to be considered), followed by a number of example IEP goals and suggested intervention strategies drawn from the information presented in this chapter.

## Jared: Social Communication/Pragmatics Difficulties

Jared is the school expert on pollution and how it affects food sources. He knows the pollution sources in every state and what the states or industries are doing to curb pollution. He also knows how food is grown and how livestock and poultry are raised. He is a vegetarian and will only eat organic food. It is amazing to everyone that he has this immense storehouse of knowledge.

*Continued on next page*

# Asperger Syndrome

Jared is in the ninth grade and is doing well in all his classes. As long as his routine stays the same, he can manage general education. His teachers meet with a district consultant to help them work with Jared. They understand that he needs a schedule and that if there is a change, they should let him know well ahead of time. He does his work, follows directions in class, and keeps to himself. His mother makes his lunch for him every day, so he doesn't have to worry about eating "toxic" food in the school cafeteria. Jared figures that if he decided to live alone after high school he could have a good life.

Jared does not make eye contact with anyone when he speaks and is extremely uncomfortable if he is asked to do so. Jared is very formal and pedantic is his language. He doesn't use or understand idioms or analogies, though his vocabulary is extensive. For example, a typical ninth grader might say, "Let's beat it, dude," when they are ready to leave. Jared would not know what that meant. When Jared is ready to leave he might say, "I realize it is time to leave the classroom. I will put on my jacket, get my school books, descend the stairs, and walk directly to my home." Jared also wouldn't understand expressions like "I'm keeping my eye on you" or "What's up?" He interprets everything literally.

If one of his classmates or teachers tries to engage him in conversation, he will not follow conversational rules. He will either remain quiet or take over. He will change topics inappropriately and talk about food, pollution, PCBs, or other topics on which he has expertise. Jared will go on and on without giving others a chance to speak. If someone says something that Jared knows is wrong, he will rudely interrupt, let the speaker know that he has made a mistake, and set him straight.

He is naive about relationships with the opposite gender. His mother says he is interested in girls and would like to be their friend or even ask them out on a date, but he doesn't do it appropriately. He doesn't realize that his communication is inappropriate and gets extremely sad when peers or others reject him.

Even though Jared is very bright and has extensive knowledge in certain areas, it will be difficult to get a job or live on his own when he graduates from high school. He will probably be successful in college if he doesn't need to relate to others. His future may be difficult for him because of his inability to communicate with others in a meaningful way. He will have a difficult time with job interviews, keeping a job (if he gets one), finding a partner, making friends, or living on his own.

# Analysis

The analysis questions that follow were generated to assist in focusing on Jared's needs, and thus, be better able to write appropriate IEP goals and intervention strategies.

1. What behaviors are preventing Jared from being a successful communicator?
2. What additional behaviors (e.g., friendship, social skills, executive functions) are problematic for Jared?
3. Prioritize five behaviors that need to be addressed, beginning with the ones you would work on first.
4. Develop IEP goals for Jared.
5. Create an intervention program for Jared to achieve the first three goals identified. Use intervention strategies identified in this chapter.

# Example IEP Goals

You may wish to write your own goals. The following goals are presented merely as examples for consideration.

1. Jared will understand and demonstrate the rules of conversation.
2. Jared will learn how to initiate, maintain, and terminate topics of conversation, taking the listener into account.
3. Jared will understand figurative language, including idioms and humor.

# Example Interventions to Achieve the IEP Goals

**Goal #1:** Jared will understand and demonstrate the rules of conversation.

1. The educator will present a graphic representation of the rules of conversation to a small group of students.
2. The educator will introduce the four rules for being a good speaker: (1) be polite, (2) be orderly, (3) be relevant, and (4) be brief. The educator will then talk about each rule and ask students if they understand or if they have any questions.
3. The educator will take one rule at a time and do the following: model examples, provide script situations, do role-plays with the students, and have students do role-plays with each other.
4. The educator will introduce the four rules of being a good listener: (1) pay attention, (2) engage in eye contact, (3) indicate level of understanding, and (4) avoid interruptions. Then the educator will proceed with these rules in the same way he or she taught the rules for being a good speaker.

5. Finally, students will play the roles of speakers and listeners while role-playing taking turns, staying on topic, and signaling transitions when engaged in a structured conversation.

6. The educator will help students critique each other's demonstrations.

**Goal #2:** Jared will learn how to initiate, maintain, and terminate topics of conversation, taking the listener into account.

1. Using a "deck" of cards containing conversation starters (e.g., "What is your favorite sport?") on them that are relevant to the group, the educator will model the use of the conversational starter with one of the group members.

2. The educator will ask Jared to choose an index card and will work with Jared (and then with each student) on initiating a conversation.

3. The educator will ask Jared to pick another card and to initiate a conversation with one of the group members. The students will take turns initiating conversations in pairs until the educator feels certain that the students understand the process.

4. The educator will ask the students to come back together as a group and will give each of them, one at a time, a one-sentence scenario followed by a question (e.g., "Your sister is angry that your brother spilled ketchup on her sweater. What will you say to your sister?").

**Goal #3:** Jared will understand figurative language, including idioms and humor.

1. In a small group, the educator will introduce an idiom (e.g., "It's raining cats and dogs") and then discuss with the group the literal versus abstract meanings for the idiom.

2. In the same group, the educator will tell a two-line joke and ask Jared and the other students why it is funny. The educator will discuss this joke with the students and, in turn, ask them to tell a joke they know. If they do not know a joke, the educator will provide a list of jokes for them and ask them to pick one so that the class can discuss why it is funny.

3. The educator will give students examples of comic strips and cartoons and talk about why they are funny. Finally, the educator will ask the group to work together with the educator to develop their own comic strip or cartoon.

## Max: Social Skills/Relationship-Building Difficulties

Max is a 7 year-old second grader who is characterized as being "different" because he has extreme difficulty interacting with his classmates. The other children sneer and snicker behind his back, especially when it comes to doing group or partner work, or when he shares information with them about his special interests.

*Continued on next page*

**Max—Continued**

When talking with his teacher or classmates, he has difficulty making eye contact. His teacher says that when he is reminded to look at her (and does), he looks like he is daydreaming. He has difficulty staying on task, even when he is doing work that is within his range of ability.

Max has trouble expressing his feelings to his teacher or to the other children, and he doesn't show any facial expression. It seems that he doesn't "read" others' facial expressions or gestures either. Even when his classmates look frustrated at him, he doesn't seem to notice. When he answers questions in class or gives a report, he uses "big" words and talks in a monotone voice.

If class activities include art, math, or facts that he knows or can research, he can become very preoccupied—so much so that it is difficult to get him to stop doing the activities. In addition, he has a deep passion for drawing buildings, presidents, and airplanes. During Operation Iraqi Freedom, he came to school with pictures he had drawn of the U.S. warplanes flown over Iraq, detailed pictures of mosques, and pictures of President Bush. His drawings were very well executed, and he knew an unbelievable number of facts about the war. Listening to Max, students were trying to be polite, but it was evident that from the looks on their faces that they thought he was "unusual." Max doesn't have a clue what his classmates are expressing through gestures and facial movement, because he isn't in tune with their feelings.

On the playground, Max stays by himself. He will sometimes play with a ball or just stand alone with his head down. During free time in the classroom, he usually stays at his desk or sits at a library table drawing pictures. When the teacher organizes a small-group activity, Max will either withdraw or try to make the rules. The other students often ignore him or tell him that he doesn't know what he's talking about.

Transitions from one activity to another are hard for Max. When there are schedule changes or the arrangement of the room is different, Max really struggles. He becomes anxious and verbalizes the change over and over.

It's hard for Max's classmates to have a conversation with him. Max either doesn't listen or he monopolizes the conversation. Once he takes over, he doesn't give his classmates a chance to talk. He will often interrupt inappropriately, and it seems he doesn't know that his behavior is inappropriate.

Max's mother and teacher are very concerned about his social skill deficits and want to plan a program that will help him build and maintain relationships with his classmates and others.

# Analysis

These analysis questions were generated to assist you in focusing on Max's needs, and thus, be better able to write appropriate IEP goals and intervention strategies. The questions are as follows:

1. What social skills are preventing Max from being successful in social situations?

2. What additional behaviors (e.g., forming friendships, social skills, executive functions, verbal and nonverbal skills) are problematic for Max?

3. Prioritize five behaviors that need to be addressed beginning with the ones you would work on first, second, etc.

4. Develop IEP goals for Max.

5. Create an intervention program for Max to achieve the first three goals identified. Use intervention strategies identified in this chapter.

## Example IEP Goals

1. Max will learn to read facial expressions.
2. Max will use eye contact when conversing.
3. Max will take turns in conversations.

## Example Interventions to Achieve the IEP Goals

**Goal #1**: Max will learn to read facial expressions.

1. In a one-on-one situation or in a small group, the educator will show students commercially purchased or personal pictures and ask students what expressions are being demonstrated by each person in the pictures.

2. The educator will demonstrate various facial expressions (e.g., happy, surprised, afraid, angry, sad) and ask students to identify the feeling based on the expression. The educator will then ask students to imitate the expression, noting the communication context and what kinds of gestures accompany the facial expressions.

3. The educator will explain to students what one does with the face for the various emotions.

**Goal #2:** Max will use eye contact when conversing.

1. The educator will explain to Max why it is important to use eye contact when talking or listening to someone. The educator will demonstrate how eye contact looks. The educator will give Max a mirror and ask him to look into his own eyes, then into the educator's eyes.

(If looking into the educator's eyes is too difficult for Max at first, he may look at the educator's shoulder.)

2. When the educator is sure that Max understands what appropriate eye contact is, Max will have four 5-minute sessions every day with the educator to work on Max's eye contact. The educator will have a conversation with Max on a subject of interest. Every time Max makes eye contact with the teacher during the 5-minute conversation, he will get a sticker and the educator will say, "Thank you for making eye contact with me." If Max gets 15 stickers by the end of the day, he will earn a prize.

3. As Max gets accustomed to using eye contact, the educator will fade use of the stickers, but continue to thank Max.

4. Eventually, the educator will expect Max to use eye contact in a small group and finally in the classroom, either on his own or with a verbal or nonverbal cue. Max will get positive reinforcement at the rate the educator feels is appropriate.

**Goal #3:** Max will take turns in conversations.

1. The educator will explain to Max that when he is talking with someone, he needs to take turns. The educator will set up a program for Max such that they will have a one-on-one conversation every day.

2. The educator will introduce Max to a small bean bag that he will hold when it is his turn to talk and that the educator will hold when he or she is talking.

3. When Max is talking too long (he might when he's talking about a topic such as the war in Iraq), and he does not pick up on a verbal cue (e.g., an interruption), or a nonverbal cue (e.g., turn away), the beanbag will be taken away from Max.

4. When Max is catching on to turn-taking in the one-on-one conversations, the educator will bring the beanbag into the small group and use it with Max. He or she will fade use of the beanbag when Max demonstrates that he understands turn-taking in conversations.

# Discussion Points

1. Why is the development of social competence skills so important for the success of the student with AS in school, home, and community settings?

2. How might you most effectively and efficiently assist the student to develop friendship/relationship skills?

3. Of all the social competence skills presented, which ones are the most crucial and why?

4. Social stories are valuable tools for teaching students with AS good social skills. Develop a social story to teach a student about politely asking questions in class.

5. How would you most effectively go about teaching a student to be a better conversationalist when initiating, maintaining, and terminating a conversation?

# Academic and Classroom Strategies

---

## Chapter 5

## Goals

- To provide intervention strategies for classroom structure and routines

- To describe strategies to improve student learning executive function, to maximize the learning experience, and to improve reading and writing issues

- To provide general tips for classroom teachers

---

The vast majority of students with Asperger Syndrome (AS) have great intellectual capacity to learn in school (Myles & Southwick, 1999). Students with AS have average to above-average intelligence (Jackel, 1996; Manjiviona & Prior, 1999) and good verbal skills, but lack abilities in social skills, are inflexible thinkers, and focus on narrow interests. However, in the appropriate educational setting, and with clear and concise rules and directions, students with AS can perform well. When they are taught strategies and methods that fit their learning styles, and when the need for routine is taken into consideration, the classroom can be a pleasant and productive learning environment.

As previously mentioned, it is not unusual for students with AS to become focused on one or two topics (Hewetson, 2002) and to accumulate vast amounts of knowledge on the topic(s). The knowledge can become an obsession to the point that they have little interest in learning or talking about anything else. However, this interest can be channeled to improve learning in other areas.

Recall that students with AS may also have other problems that interfere with learning. Executive function deficits are not unusual (Pennington & Ozonoff, 1996). Many students automatically develop executive function strategies without being taught. Students with AS, however, often do not acquire many of these skills automatically and must be taught the strategies and how to use them (Myles & Southwick, 1999).

Although students with AS usually do not have trouble with reading the written word, because of their problems with pragmatic language, they may have trouble reading fluently and across a variety of genres or for a variety of purposes. Pragmatic language and executive function deficits may also prevent students with AS from producing written work that requires fluency, organization, planning, composing, and editing.

The purpose of this chapter is to introduce the best practices to use in educational settings when teaching students with AS. This chapter is organized into four sections that provide (1) classroom structure and routines, (2) strategies to improve student learning, (3) general tips, and (4) a case study of a student with academic problems. Also included is a guide for analysis of the student in the case study, along with sample goals and suggested interventions.

# Strategies for Classroom Structure and Routines

Students with AS function better in a structured environment than in an environment that is unpredictable (Jackel, 1996; Myles & Southwick, 1999; TEACCH, 2005). Students with AS can allow themselves to be more flexible when they are in a predictable environment. Some students with AS have an internal structure that is very rigid, while others seem to lack any kind of organizational skills. This section will provide intervention strategies to structure classrooms to best meet the needs of these students. These strategies are described on the pages that follow and are highlighted in Sidebar 5.1.

The following strategies can help to provide structure and order in the classroom:

1. **Provide visual and physical order**—Students with AS do not try to be disorganized and messy, but often are because of their lack of organizational skills. Help students by providing a well-organized classroom environment. In elementary and middle school, specific areas can be delineated for different purposes (e.g., a reading corner, an art center, a free-time space, and other work spaces). Signs with words and/or pictures in each of the areas (e.g., "Reading Corner" or a picture of a student reading) will clarify for students what each area is used for. Be sure each area has clear boundaries. With older students, places that are to be used for free-time activities should be well marked. These places should be easily accessible. Places to put finished work should be visible.

## Strategies to Provide Structure and Order in the Classroom

1. Provide visual and physical order.
2. Assign seating so that the student is away from distractions and won't be bothered by others.
3. Create a safe place for the student to go.
4. Make materials accessible in work areas.
5. Provide space so that there is room for individual and group work.
6. Make work areas consistent for students who need them.
7. Clearly mark work areas so that they are easy to find and easily accessible.
8. Indicate a place where students can put finished work.
9. Put play or recreational areas away from exits.
10. Arrange the room so that you can see students at all times and in all places.
11. Create a visual organizer for the student.
12. Provide lists and predictable schedules for the student.
13. Provide a map of the school for the student.
14. Make arrangements for the student to arrive or leave early.
15. Make arrangements for an alternative physical education (PE) program.
16. Make arrangements for communication between home and school.
17. Use graphic organizers.

Classroom rules and expectations should be posted in obvious places and copies of them should be given to the students. When working with older students, use labels when necessary. For example, on the container that holds finished work, there might be a label that reads, "Please put your completed work here."

2. **Assign seating so that the student is away from distractions and won't be bothered by others**—It will be easier for students with AS to complete work and concentrate on learning if seated in a place with minimal distractions (e.g., away from windows, activity centers, or other students who may be distracting). If other students are teasing or agitating students with AS, try to arrange seating such that others have as little opportunity as possible to tease, bully, or bother the students (Jackel, 1996). Sometimes a place near the educator's desk or a spot in the back of the room will work. A space that is out of the way of others will benefit students with AS.

3. **Create a safe place for the student to go**—Students with AS do not come to school planning to become angry or frustrated, but they do have a myriad of obstacles to over-

come. When students with AS experience sensory overload, when confronted with changes in routines, or when other students tease or bully, they may become frustrated, anxious, and/or scared. These feelings may be presented as anger or rage. If that happens, the students will need a place that is private and safe to calm down. It is helpful to arrange for a comfortable space early on before there is a crisis. Students need to know that if they feel the possibility of becoming out of control, or are out of control, a safe place is available. This place might be a partitioned section of the room, the counselor's office, or a designated room staffed with a professional. It is important to find the right space for each student. Because students with AS have different likes and dislikes, the same place probably will not meet the needs of everyone. The key to knowing the space is right is the effect that it has on the student's behavior. Settling down in a reasonable amount of time and using the space appropriately will be evidence that the space is the right one for a particular student.

4. **Make materials accessible in work areas**—Materials that students need to complete class assignments or readings should be in a spot that is visible, easily accessible, and well marked. Labeling the space with words and/or pictures helps students identify the materials needed. Color-coding might be an additional benefit for students. Using colors to code school materials and the student's materials will help students with AS (e.g., yellow for reading, red for math, green for science). Students should be able to readily get the materials without having to ask for help. When using color-coding, take the age of the students into account. At the high school level, for example, students' notebooks or 3-ring binders might be color-coded to match the class materials.

5. **Provide space so that there is room for individual and group work**—Separate work areas should be delineated for individual and group work, if space allows. Students with AS are likely to be distracted from being on task if there are groups of students working together in the proximity of the individual work spaces. It may be necessary to specify clear boundaries to delineate the spaces (e.g., dividers or tape on the floor).

6. **Make work areas consistent for students who need them**—Students with AS almost always like consistency. They feel comfortable with sameness and may become stressed if the room is rearranged even minimally. If work areas are moved or changed, it will be important to prepare students for the change. Talking with students about an upcoming rearrangement in the classroom and showing them where the new work area will be can prevent a stressful situation. Having students discover changes with no preparation might result in anxiety, fear, and distress.

7. **Clearly mark work areas so that they are easy to find and easily accessible**—Marking a work area will clarify for students with AS where they will be working. A sign that reads "Work Area" or a picture that depicts a student at work will provide assurances for the students that they are in the right place. Be sure the signs are age-appropriate.

8. **Indicate a place where students can put finished work**—Knowing where to put finished work will provide security for students with AS. They will need to know the routine for handing in their work when they are finished. It is important that the procedure stay the same over time.

9. **Put play or recreational areas away from exits**—Students with AS may want to flee from a stressful situation. Even free time or play time can be stressful. Recreational or physical education areas should be designed so students with AS cannot easily flee. If there is an easily accessible exit and students are so inclined, getting away could be easy. Keeping the play and recreational areas away from easily accessible exits in the classroom will help.

10. **Arrange the room so that you can see students at all times and in all places**—It will be easier to monitor students with AS if they are always on your radar screen. The more visible the students, the easier it will be to prevent crises or to provide help before students experience too much stress and frustration.

11. **Create a visual organizer for the student**—Some students with AS may not be able to process written language without visual prompts. If students are having difficulty with a written schedule, provide a schedule that has words and pictures (or just pictures) that represent what they will be doing during different times of the day (e.g., a visual representation of students playing outside might depict recess). Pictures of students working, or pictures or representations of the books in which they are working, will also help.

12. **Provide lists and predictable schedules for the student**—Provide students with AS a list of assignments, steps on how to do them, and/or copies of daily or weekly schedules. This will allow them to know what to expect and feel a sense of security.

13. **Provide a map of the school for the student**—Especially at the beginning of the school year, provide students who have AS with a map. Knowing how to get from one place to another may give them a sense of security. The map must be clear and understandable and could include pictures (especially for younger students) or icons. Older students may have a clearly marked map and a list of appropriate questions that might be asked if they become lost.

14. **Make arrangements for the student to arrive or leave early**—Getting from the playground or the bus to the school room may be difficult for students with AS. Other students may tease, bully, or harass them. Arrange an early arrival or departure so the student with AS will not have to face difficult situations before entering or upon leaving the classroom. This accommodation might be taken away gradually when students with AS have learned strategies to handle teasing and bullying.

15. **Make arrangements for an alternative physical education (PE) program**—Students with AS frequently have poor gross motor skills. They are often awkward or have a clumsy gait. Students with AS need physical education, but they do not need the torment of others who will make fun of them when failing to hit the ball or score a point. Students will try hard to do it right and will be very frustrated and despairing if they do not succeed. Regular or special educators can work with physical education teachers to arrange for alternative PE programs (e.g., students with AS could help the PE teacher with younger children; several students with AS could be brought together for PE; a peer with high status and sensitivity could partner with a student who has difficulty in PE; students with AS could be asked what they would like to do in a PE program; or the students could be placed in an adaptive PE program). The bottom line is to eliminate the humiliation and teasing students with AS might encounter in a regular physical education class while learning necessary skills and behaviors.

16. **Make arrangements for communication between home and school**—It is important that the parents of students with AS and the school staff communicate regularly, effectively, and efficiently. Good communication between home and school will result in improved consistency in dealing with the students. Sharing information will prepare school personnel and parents for changes that may affect students' behavior and also provide opportunities to share successes. There are many ways that communication can be successful (e.g., daily phone calls, a communication notebook that students carry back and forth between home and school, weekly phone calls, or weekly meetings). Do what is comfortable for students, school professionals, and parents, and is consistent, frequent, and age appropriate.

17. **Use graphic organizers**—Graphic organizers are visual maps (also referred to as concept maps) that organize content material and focus on developing an awareness of concepts to make it easier for students to understand reading or oral material. Graphic organizers present abstract information in a concrete way. They work for students with AS who are concrete thinkers and have difficulty comprehending abstract material (Wiig & Wilson, 2001). These concrete maps can be used before reading or discussing content or after the reading as been completed. The graphic organizer can be created for students. After the students have read or heard the material and have discussed it using the graphic organizer, they can use it for subsequent practice (Myles & Adreon, 2001; Wiig & Wilson, 2001). See Appendix N on the CD-ROM for an example of a graphic organizer.

# Classroom Scheduling

Students with AS are most comfortable with a clear, consistent, and purposeful daily routine. They are likely to be good rule followers and will want to know the classroom rules and the parameters of the schedule. If the daily or weekly routine changes, students should be prepared ahead of time. Being well-prepared will help them accept change better, but an unexpected change can precipitate anxiety, frustration, and anger. One change is easier to accept than two. If educators are sick and there are substitute teachers in the classes, students with AS might be okay if they know ahead of time. Having a substitute teacher *and* cancelled art classes might be too much for them to manage.

It is important that students with AS know the daily schedules. Having a schedule posted in the room works well for some, while others may want a copy of their own to keep in their folder or in their desk. The needs and the developmental levels of students will determine whether the schedule should be accompanied by pictures, drawings, or icons. High school students will probably not need or appreciate pictures. Figure 5.1 on page 120 provides examples of schedules for students.

## Elementary School Schedule

Elementary students usually stay in their own classroom for most of the day. They may leave for special classes like art or physical education, for a special education class, or for a speech-language session. In the elementary schedule in Figure 5.1 on page 120, the student with AS is taken out of the classroom for small group social skills training and speech-language intervention. Transitions from one classroom to another need to be addressed at the beginning of the year and whenever there is a change. Planning for the transitions with students will likely have a positive effect. Even when students with AS stay in their homeroom, they will still need accommodation and preparation for transition from one subject to another because of their difficulty to adapt to change.

Students with AS will also need to have weekly schedules so that they can be aware of the differences in days with special classes (like physical education and art). A weekly schedule would include the daily schedules and highlights for any modifications on certain days of the week. Because some students with AS think in wholes rather than details, a monthly schedule might be useful for their understanding the big picture.

## Middle School Schedule

Middle grades are more complicated for students to navigate than elementary school—especially for students with AS. Not only do students in middle grades change rooms many times a day, but they also have different teachers, different classmates, different routines, and different rules in each

## Example Schedules for Elementary, Middle, and High School Students

Figure 5.1

| Elementary School Schedule | Middle School Schedule | High School Schedule |
|---|---|---|
| **8:00** School begins, put belongings away, go to desk, and sit down | **7:35–8:05 Period 1** Homeroom Rm. 324 | **7:05–7:55** Calculus I |
| **8:15** Morning meeting | **8:09–8:54 Period 2** Social Studies Rm. 113 | **8:05–8:55** Wood Shop/Aide present |
| **8:30** Group reading | **9:00–9:55 Period 3** General Science Rm. 229 | **9:05–9:55** World History |
| **9:00** Individual reading | **9:59–10:54 Period 4** Speech-language | **10:05–10:55** Phy Ed/Music |
| **9:30** Break/Recess | **10:58–11:53 Period 5** Study Hall Rm. 333 | **10:55–11:35** Lunch |
| **9:45** Social skills | **11:53–12:37 Lunch** Cafeteria | **11:35–12:25** English Literature |
| **10:30** Speech-language | **12:37–1:32 Period 6** Social Skills | **12:35–1:25** Social & Communication Skills |
| **11:00** Free time | **1:36–2:31 Period 7** Phy Ed/Music | **1:35–2:25** Life Skills |
| **11:30** Prepare for lunch | **2:35–2:45 Homeroom** Rm. 324 | **2:25** Dismissal |
| **11:45** Lunch/Recess | **2:45 Dismissal** | |
| **12:45** Math | | |
| **1:15** Individual math | | |
| **2:00** Story time | | |
| **2:45** Dismissal | | |

class. They have short periods of time to change classes and often they have to stop at their lockers to get specific material for individual classes. This can be a nightmare for students with AS. It is very important that there is a support person to help them at the beginning of the middle-grade experience with followup as needed. Students with AS should be assigned to a counselor, special education teacher, or paraprofessional, who will work with them to transition from one class to the next, organize a locker and/or backpack, and provide support during lunch and free time. Depending on the level of the student's disability, the qualifications and willingness of the special education personnel, and the atmosphere in the classroom, the student may be assigned to an appropriate special education program for part or all of the day.

## High School Schedule

By the time students with AS reach high school, they are usually knowledgeable of changing classes and understanding that each class will have different requirements, different peers, and different teachers. However, depending on the needs of the students, transitioning from one class to another might be challenging. Bullying and teasing from peers may require students with AS to receive ongoing support from school professionals. Support may come from special educators, speech-language pathologists, school counselors, or regular educators. It is important to give students the help and support they need in order to receive the best education possible. It is likely that even though students have reached the high school level, they will still need social and communication skills training and extra help in some classes. This may be provided in a special setting (e.g., in a speech-language class, in a regular class with an aide or a speech-language pathologist present, or in a special education classroom). The programs developed for students with AS will depend on their needs and, as always, the student and his or her parents should be an integral part of the planning process.

# Intervention Strategies to Improve Student Learning

Being in the school environment is difficult for students with AS. The school is a very complex place: educators have different classroom rules, schedules change without warning, and the behavior of peers can be unpredictable. If educators understand AS and can use their understanding to make the classroom a comfortable place, students with AS can have an easier time in school.

Frequently, students with AS have difficulties with tasks requiring executive function skills (e.g., dialing a telephone number while trying to hold the number in memory, or holding phonetic rules in mind while trying to comprehend a story). Students with AS have problems planning, self-monitoring, organizing, inhibiting responses (waiting to be called on), exhibiting behavioral flexibility, completing tasks, staying focused, and being patient. Students with AS also have difficulty dealing with the ups and downs of life, readjusting behavior, and thinking when things are not working (Powers & Poland, 2002).

There are other factors that interfere with learning in students with AS, including having narrow interests, experiencing problems working with others, understanding meaning of materials, generalizing across tasks, and having pragmatic language deficits. Because they are not intuitively aware of their own learning processes (a metacognitive task) and learning strengths and weaknesses, it may be difficult for them to automatically employ strategies for learning.

As mentioned earlier, teaching cognitive strategies is one approach that will help students. Learning cognitive strategies can change the students' learning processes (Hallahan & Kauffman, 2003). Students can apply cognitive strategies to help change unobservable or internal thought processes (e.g., a student may learn to count to 10 before raising his or her hand). In addition to providing cognitive strategies for overcoming executive function deficits, this section will also describe strategies to maximize the learning experience in the classroom and to address reading and writing issues.

# Cognitive Strategies to Address Executive Functions

Most students automatically develop executive function skills that help them maximize their learning. However, students with AS typically have deficits that effect classroom performance. Sidebar 5.2 lists classic behaviors of students with executive function deficits.

Additionally, most students also learn the behavior of others through modeling or imitation. Students with AS, however, are often not aware of their cognitive behavior. Because students with AS are typically more interested in objects than people, learning from modeling or imitation of others often does not happen. Consequently, students with AS do not automatically learn the strategies needed to be successful in the classroom. Educators need to be prepared to use methods to help students achieve success in the classroom and to teach specific strategies so that students can learn to problem solve without help from others (Cumine, Leach, & Stevenson, 2001).

In this section, strategies are suggested to address the executive function tasks (see overview in Sidebar 5.2). Each strategy is labeled **GEN** (general strategy), **COG** (cognitive strategy), or **C/E** (curricular or environmental strategy) to help educators understand whether the change is internal or external to the students.

1. **Completing assignments.** Completing assignments is important for students to be successful in school. The following strategies can help students accomplish this:

   - **Check assignment levels (C/E)**—Make sure the assignments are at the students' developmental level. If assignments are too hard, long, or overwhelming, students may become frustrated and give up. If the work is appropriate and if the directions are understood, but students are still unsuccessful, you will need to use more than one strategy.

   - **Divide the assignments into small segments (C/E)**—Give the segments (parts) of an assignment to students one at a time. Ask the students to check with you after finishing each part, so the work can be monitored and they can receive feedback.

   - **Give the students a reward for completing the entire assignment (GEN)**—It can be tricky to find the appropriate reward, so be patient. Try to use the students' special interests in ways that are rewarding (e.g., more time in the library to do research on a special topic after they finish an assignment). (See pages 171–173 for details on how to increase positive behavior using behavior modification techniques.)

Sidebar 5.2    **Difficult Tasks for Students with Executive Function Deficits**

1. Completing assignments
2. Thinking flexibly
3. Organizing personal classroom space
4. Making plans to accomplish goals and to solve problems
5. Remembering a sequence of events
6. Waiting patiently to be called on in class when the teacher asks a question
7. Staying focused on a topic, issue, or problem until it is resolved
8. Seeing the big picture
9. Starting and stopping an assignment or project
10. Self-monitoring their learning behaviors
11. Learning abstract concepts
12. Doing self-evaluation
13. Using self-instruction

*Sources:* Attwood (2001); Cumine, et. al. (2001); Grandin (2001); Hallahan & Kauffman (2003); Myles & Adreon (2001); National Research Council (2001); Williams (1995); Winter (2003)

2. **Thinking flexibly.** Students with AS are often rigid and inflexible thinkers. They do not like changes in a routine, making mistakes, or to experience ambiguity or unpredictability. Some of the following strategies can be tried to help students become more flexible.

- **Encourage them to make mistakes (GEN)**—When mistakes are made by students, explain that mistakes are good opportunities for learning, then give a concrete example of using a mistake to learn. Support and reassurance that it is okay to make mistakes will help students become more comfortable with the mistake and will help them understand that mistakes can be expected and accepted. Everyone makes mistakes. Students can correct their mistakes, learn from them, and then forget about them. Let students know that educators make mistakes, too, and that it is okay. (See page 88 for information on how to do a social autopsy to learn from mistakes.)

- **Encourage students to change their schedules around every so often (GEN)**—Give them support when they change their schedules. Do not force students to make a change, but give lots of support when they do.

- **Give students support when the unexpected happens (GEN)**—When something unexpected does happen, make every attempt to be with the student and to offer support and understanding. The goal is that, eventually, the support can be reduced and then eliminated.

3. **Organizing personal classroom space.** Because students with AS lack organizational skills, they usually have messy desks and lockers and have a hard time gathering materials for class. They often come to class with the wrong book or notebook and incomplete assignments. To help them, try one of the following strategies.

   - **Color-code materials (C/E)**—Use different colors for each subject (for example, folders, book covers, and notebooks for math could be yellow; for reading, green; and so on.) Students may be better able to come to class with the correct materials if they are color-coded.

   - **Create templates (GEN)**—You can create templates to help students organize their spaces. Masking tape, labels, colors, and maps can be used to show them where particular materials belong. Creating a template for reports or other assignments may also be helpful. For example, you could develop templates for book reports. These could be single sheets of paper indicating what needs to be included in the reports and the places to enter the information, including the name of the book, the author, the date written, the setting, the main characters, the plot, and so forth.

4. **Making plans to accomplish goals and to solve problems.** Students with AS have difficulty planning ahead. They need to be taught to make a plan and follow it. These steps will help students in the planning and problem-solving process.

   - **Work with students who have AS to set a goal (GEN)**—Start with a fairly short-term goal like finishing a reading assignment by the end of the day or by the end of the week. You will need to help students develop realistic goals that can be attained fairly quickly.

   - **Ask students what steps they would need to take to achieve the goal (GEN)**—Help students develop realistic steps, such as the following.

     *Step 1:* Every day at 9:30, I will get my science book out of my desk. I will find a quiet place to read, where I won't be disturbed.

     *Step 2:* I will set the timer for 5 minutes.

     *Step 3:* When the timer goes off, I will note whether or not I was actually reading and then mark it on the chart my teacher has given me.

     *Step 4:* I will ask myself what I read about. If I can answer the question, I will set the timer and keep reading for another 5 minutes and follow the steps again. I will continue to do this until 10:00.

*Step 5:* I will know that I have met this goal if I finish and understand my reading assignment and can answer questions about it. If I can't answer the questions, I will read the assignment again or ask the teacher for help.

- **Give students a copy of the steps they can put in an accessible place (GEN)**—Remove steps from the paper copy one at a time until the students have achieved their goals. This will encourage them to remember the step(s) that have been taken away. Remove steps and cues from the sheet as they are ready. The students' behavior should guide the pace. The long-term goal is that they will automatically do the steps and, ultimately, generalize them to other situations.

- **As students become comfortable with the tasks, use the scaffolding process to help them learn the tasks and become independent (COG)**—Scaffolding is defined by Hallahan and Kauffman (2003) as a cognitive approach in which the teacher provides temporary support as the students are learning the task and then removes the support little by little as students are able to perform the task.

5. **Remembering a sequence of events.** There are several strategies students can be taught to help remember a sequence of events.

   - **Mnemonics (COG)**—A mnemonic is a technique used for assisting memory, in this case, letters of the alphabet will cue key words for the students to help them remember a strategy. If preparation for math class is an important expectation, this sequence of events for students to learn might be appropriate:

     1. Get your completed assignment out of your math folder.
     2. Get a pencil from your pencil case.
     3. Sharpen your pencil.
     4. Get your math book out of your desk.
     5. Walk to the math area.
     6. Sit down.
     7. Be quiet.

     Pick a key word out of each step that will give them a clue to the directive in the step. For example:

     1. assignment
     2. pencil
     3. sharpen
     4. book
     5. walk
     6. sit
     7. quiet

Then take the first letter from each word and use those letters for making words that will form an easy-to-remember sentence such as: *At Parties Some Boys Will Sit Quietly.* Ask the students to help make the sentence. They might write the sentence on a piece of colored paper or an index card and keep it in their math folder. When it is time for math class, give the students the first step, getting the assignment out of the math folder. When they do this, their sentence on bold paper will cue them to follow the sequence for math class.

Use any variation on this theme that works for students. Writing the key words on a paper may work as well as mnemonics, but may not be as easy to remember. The success that students experience in using the strategy will indicate whether the mnemonic strategy works for the student.

- **Use visual cues (GEN)**—Another way to teach students how to remember a sequence of events is to draw or find a picture that will demonstrate what the student needs to do at each step. The visual cues can be posted in the room, or a copy can be given to the students.

  Practice is important in learning to remember a sequence of events. Go through the sequence several times to make sure the students understand. After they have practiced enough to feel comfortable with the cues, begin fading the cues (e.g., remove one or two cues at a time, and when they are successful at each step, remove another cue). The trick is to remove the cues at just the right time. If the timing is too fast or too slow, the students will let you know directly or indirectly by their behavior. Go back a step if it is apparent that cues are being removed too quickly. The students' success will be your gauge. You may decide that it is okay for students to use cues all the time.

6. **Waiting patiently to be called on in class when the teacher asks a question (inhibiting correct responses).** Students with AS may have a hard time waiting to respond to a question when they know the answer. Students may realize that they should raise their hand and wait to be called on, but the second their hand goes up, they blurt out the answer. The following strategies will help students learn to wait until called on to give the answer.

   - **Make a rule (GEN)**—Always try the easiest way first. Make it a class rule that a student cannot answer a question until called on. Students with AS are usually good rule followers (Fling, 2000), and the rule may be all that is needed to inhibit their responses.

   - **Teach students to change thinking patterns (COG)**—If the rule approach does not work, ask students to do a simple internal strategy, like counting silently to 10, or silently repeating a rhyme after raising their hand and before blurting out a response. Calling attention to the problem and offering specific strategies should help students inhibit their responses. If a visual prompt is needed, write the strategy on a note card that the student can keep with him or her or post in the room, or give the student a personal cue.

7. **Staying focused on a topic, issue, or problem until it is resolved.** Students with AS may have a hard time seeing a topic or issue through to resolution. Finding a way to stay focused is the issue.

   - **Give an overall view (GEN)**—Start by giving students with AS an overall view of the problem and an estimated length of the conversation or discussion. Try negotiating a time with them. Ask if they could stay on topic and be a part of the discussion for 5 minutes (or however long is realistic for them to be involved in the resolution). When the allotted time is up, stop the conversation, even if you have not reached a resolution. Make plans to meet again to finish the topic, and be sure to follow up.

   - **Use positive reinforcement (GEN)**—Another method is to have the discussion without setting the stage as described above, but rather use reinforcement when the students stay focused until the end of the discussion.

   - **Try a combination of the two (GEN)**—Set the stage, and tell students that they will get a reward (e.g., free time or the chance to play a game on the computer) if they keep their part of the bargain by staying focused.

8. **Seeing the big picture.** Because students with AS may lack flexibility in their thinking, they are often limited to only what is right in front of them. Putting an issue or problem in context may help them develop a broader perspective. Expand on topics by using social stories, social autopsies, social groups, or role-plays to help students get a bigger picture. (See pages 86–88 for specific strategies for using social stories, social autopsies, social groups, and role-playing.)

9. **Starting and stopping an assignment or project.** Students with AS may have difficulty starting projects because they may not be interested, may be distracted, or may not understand the task at hand. On the other hand, they may have difficulty stopping because of a tendency to perseverate on tasks. You need to provide an incentive to start promptly and end when asked. This could be done by putting the expectation in a rule format or giving a reward for starting and stopping. Another approach might be giving them a cue or signal for starting and stopping, (e.g., you could say "start now" or "end now").

10. **Self-monitoring their learning behaviors.** Self-monitoring is a cognitive strategy that can change a student's internal thinking about the process needed to complete a task or change the way of approaching a task. You can use cues that will remind the student to stay on task. For example, a timer can be set at random intervals, and each time it goes off, the student can record whether or not he or she was on task. Another variation is to record some random beeps on an audiocassette tape recorder; put the cassette player near the student's desk; play the tape; and each time the player beeps, have the student note whether he or she was on task. Having students record their own behavior on a chart might

be rewarding. (See Figure 5.2 and Appendix P on the CD-ROM for a Self-Monitoring Chart and corresponding Teacher Recording Form.) The steps you can use to teach students to monitor their own behavior are listed below.

**Step 1:** Identify the behavior to be monitored (e.g., being on-task, comprehending reading material, interrupting, raising their hand before speaking). The behavior must be defined, and the timeframe for monitoring must be identified. (If you use the Self-Monitoring Chart in Appendix P, add the behavior and the time-frame [e.g., 30 minutes] to the form. Also identify questions you will ask to determine if the student was successful. (Add the questions to the Self-Monitoring Chart).

**Step 2:** Explain to the student to record his or her behavior. For example, during a reading period, a student might be asked to check his or her understanding of the reading material. A reminder to check comprehension could be cued by random beeps on an audiotape played during the silent reading time. When the audiotape beeps, the student will determine if he or she is comprehending the reading passage. Teach the student to say silently "Do I understand what I am

Figure 5.2     **Self-Monitoring Chart and Teacher Recording Form**

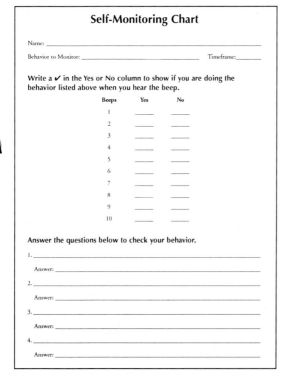

reading?" If the answer is 'Yes,' he or she will make a check in the Yes column and go on reading. If the answer is 'No,' they will make a check in the No column and will reread what they just read.

**Step 3:** Have the student answer the questions you generated in Step 1. The answers will indicate if he or she was successfully using the new behavior.

**Step 4:** Keep a file or a chart to record the information gathered by the students over time. You can determine if the student needs to be rewarded intermittently or each time the timer rings and he or she is on task. If a reinforcer is needed to motivate the students, you can reward the successful recording of behavior and reading comprehension. The information could also be sent home so that the parents can administer a reward. A Teacher Recording Form is also shown in Figure 5.2 and is provided for you as Appendix P on the CD-ROM as a way to monitor progress over time.

11. **Learning abstract concepts.** Students with AS often have difficulty understanding abstract concepts and abstract information. Using visual cues to illustrate concepts (e.g., drawings, pictures, or written words) is helpful for understanding. Be concrete in your demonstrations. If the concept can be related to students' personal experiences or interests, the concepts and information will be more easily understood.

12. **Doing self-evaluation.** It is important to learn what students with AS know about their own learning, behavior, progress, or feelings of self-worth. Two or three times a semester, you can have meetings with students to determine whether their evaluation is realistic. Here are some questions that could be asked:

    * Are you working as hard as you can on your school work?
    * Are you doing your best work?
    * What is your favorite subject?
    * Where do you think you need the most help?
    * How are you getting along with your classmates?
    * Do you have a best friend?
    * What would you like to do when you grow up?
    * Do you think you have made a realistic choice?

13. **Using self-instruction.** Students with AS might learn better if they think aloud. Encourage this behavior if it helps, and ask them to use a soft voice; a whisper. If this bothers the other students, students with AS can do their work in a study carrel or in an isolated part of the room. You can give encouragement to students to use their own learning style (Winter, 2003).

# Strategies to Maximize the Learning Experience

In addition to executive function deficits, students with AS may have other problems that prevent them from being successful academically. Students with AS may demonstrate excellent rote memory skills or vast knowledge of a particular topic, but may not work well in groups, may have problems self-monitoring, or have difficulty generalizing what is learned. They may need instruction to ensure acquisition of skills that facilitate self-awareness, self-calming, and self-management (Myles & Southwick, 1999).

The pages that follow describe 11 strategies (highlighted in Sidebar 5.3) addressing ways to use learning groups, help students generalize, and use students' special interests to motivate them to do other, less enjoyable things. Using these strategies with students who have AS may help them develop awareness of their own thinking patterns and learn rote ways of approaching problem-solving (Connor, 1999; Grandin, 2001; Jackel, 1996; Winter, 2003).

1. **Select work groups**—If you ask students to choose work groups, students with AS are likely to be the last ones chosen. If you choose who will be in each group, students with AS will not have to suffer the embarrassment of being the last to be chosen. You will know what students will best work together and will interact with each other. You can choose the students that will work best with students with AS. One student might be a good model for social skills, another may be patient, and another may have compassion or be fair-minded. With the right people in their groups, students with AS can thrive.

**Sidebar 5.3**   **Intervention Strategies to Maximize the Learning Experience**

1. Select work groups.
2. Use cooperative learning groups.
3. Ensure all tasks are manageable and within the students' attention span.
4. Provide practice in newly acquired skills in different settings to foster generalization.
5. Use various means of presentation.
6. Use the students' special interests to motivate.
7. Allow students to use their own methods.
8. Keep a notebook of things students do not understand.
9. Do regular check-ins with teachers.
10. Choose seating carefully.
11. Help students comply with classroom rules and expectations.

2. **Use cooperative learning groups**—The idea behind cooperative learning groups is that the whole group will work together and be equally responsible for the finished product or for meeting the group goals. Students with AS can be valuable members of a cooperative learning group. If the group's topic happens to be a special interest of the student with AS, the student with AS will have a vast amount of information to contribute to the group. They may also be good researchers, or good group monitors, because of their rule-following capabilities. In turn, their skills will be viewed as assets, which will enhance their status in the group, making them more likely to be accepted by the others (Williams, 1995). Students with AS may also be able to learn appropriate group behavior, including turn-taking and reciprocity, from a carefully selected group.

3. **Ensure all tasks are manageable and within the students' attention span**—Do not give students with AS work that is too easy, too hard, or too lengthy. Doing so has the potential to cause frustration, boredom, acting-out behavior, or a reason to give up. Communicating with previous educators can help determine the proper work level and length of assignments. Observing students' body language, ability to stay on task, and moods when they are working will provide helpful information about the appropriateness of the assignment. It is good to remember that acting-out behavior may be the result of assignments that are developmentally inappropriate, rather than a ploy to get attention or to be unpleasant. Students with AS do not necessarily want to cause problems in the classroom.

4. **Provide practice of newly acquired skills in different settings to foster generalization**—Generalizing skills from one setting to another can be difficult for students with AS, so it is important to provide practice in different settings with real materials. If students with AS are learning how to change money in their math workbook, give them the opportunity to make change in a real setting (e.g., working in the school store, paying for hot lunch, taking a field trip to a store to purchase an item). Let the parents know what the students are learning, so they can provide opportunities for generalization, as well. The greater the number of environments where a student with AS can practice the newly developed skill, the greater the chance that the behavior will last and will generalize to different settings. Be sure to use age-appropriate experiences when practicing. A young student may work in the classroom store, and an older student may do an exercise with real money in a commercial setting.

5. **Use various means of presentation**—No two students with AS learn in exactly the same way. While all hold the major characteristics of social communication deficits, even the way the social communication deficits are exhibited vary from child to child. Their learning styles are also different. Some students may learn better visually, while others like an auditory approach. The key to determining the best approach for teaching specific students with AS is through direct observation and through gathering information from

parents or other professionals. Watch carefully how students respond to each approach, and use the one in which they are the most successful. Interviewing students about which learning style they like better may also be valuable (see Appendix C on the CD-ROM for a questionnaire). It may take some time to determine what works best—the students' behavior will be the best guide.

6. **Use students' special interests to motivate**—Students with AS can become obsessed with a special interest and want to be completely immersed in it. Make it clear to them that their special interests and vast knowledge are respected, and that when their assignments are completed, they will have an opportunity to talk, read, write or do research about them. Making special interest work contingent on getting normal school tasks done will help the student get other tasks accomplished. Also, using the special topic in reading or science lessons, for example, may increase the student's interest in learning to read or do science. Knowing the special interest will be indulged may motivate them to finish other work. Also, allowing them to teach their special topics to others could be a good motivator, assuming the learners are interested in the topic.

7. **Allow students to use their own methods**—If students with AS have abilities in math, science, computers, or other subjects that are at or above grade level, but do not always use the same problem-solving strategies that you or other students use, allow them to use their own strategies. Students need to know that it is okay to use their own methods as long as their answers are correct. Expecting students with AS to use strategies they do not understand may cause frustration and anxiety. Pay attention to the strategies the students with AS use, and try use these strategies occasionally to teach the rest of the class. Students with AS may feel proud that their strategies are being used by others in class.

8. **Keep a notebook of things students do not understand**—Ask students with AS to keep notebooks of things that happen during the day that they do not understand. It may be a metaphor or a simile, a math problem, an event during recess, or a social situation. Take time each day to go over the items they have recorded and help them understand the concerns.

9. **Do regular check-ins with teachers**—Ask students with AS to check in with teachers every day at a specified or a random time, whichever works better. Students with AS can count on this time to get help from you and other teachers, get answers to questions, or get a chance to vent or chat. This will help them build a trusting relationship with educators and get needed support.

10. **Choose seating carefully**—It will be easier for students with AS to complete their work and concentrate on learning if seated in a place with minimal distractions. Sitting away from windows, an activity center, or other distracting places will allow students to focus on the task.

11. **Help students comply with classroom rules and expectations**—As mentioned before, students with AS are most often excellent rule-followers. The consistency of rules gives them a feeling of security. Students who have AS will be the first ones to notice when rules are not being followed by others. If they are not following a rule, there is probably a good reason. The rule may involve a stimulus that they cannot handle—for example, too much noise, too little space, or an aversive smell. It is important to check out every possibility. If nothing is found in the environment that explains the noncompliance, using behavior management strategies would be in order. First try positive reinforcement for compliance or a consequence for noncompliance (see Chapter 7 for more information about reinforcement strategies and consequences).

# Strategies to Address Reading and Writing Issues

Students with AS are usually good at reading the written word. However, they sometimes do not understand what is being read, the purpose for the reading, or how to get more out of their reading. Students may also have difficulty expressing themselves in writing. They may be good spellers because of good rote memory, but they have difficulty producing written language and adjusting writing to various audiences. This section explains five strategies (highlighted in Sidebar 5.4) you can use to help students with AS address the issues of reading and writing to learn, rather than learning to read and write.

**Sidebar 5.4**    **Intervention Strategies to Address Reading and Writing Issues**

**Teach students to:**

1. Produce cohesive written language required in various academic, social, and vocational situations by gathering and organizing information, composing, editing, and gathering feedback.

2. Be fluent speakers.

3. Comprehend from printed symbols in various academic, social, and vocational situations.

4. Read fluently across a variety of genres (e.g., narratives and expository text)

5. Read fluently for a variety of purposes (e.g., to be informed, to be persuaded, to be entertained)

*Sources:* Harris & Graham (1996); Larson & McKinley (2003); Westby & Clauser (1999); Wiig & Wilson (2001)

## Asperger Syndrome

Teach students to:

1. **Produce cohesive written language required in various academic, social, and vocational situations by gathering and organizing information, composing, editing, and gathering feedback.**

    - Do not assume students with AS know what to write about and are ready to start. Begin with prewriting strategies like discussing the topic and gathering information. Allow plenty of time for teaching these prewriting skills—weeks or even months.

    - Formulate strategies for organizing the information. After studying the information gathered, help students with AS formulate a map or outline. Computer software such as *Inspiration* (Inspiration Software, 2005) can be helpful to students with AS who have difficulty with executive function skills, like organization. You can also develop a plan-think sheet that will help students organize their material. According to Westby and Clauser (1999) a plan-think sheet might look as follows:

    The Topic
    **Who:** Who am I writing for?
    **Why:** Why am I writing?
    **What:** What do I know? (Brainstorm a list of what is known about the topic.)
    **How:** How can I group my ideas?

    - Teach students with AS strategies that will help them compose the material that has been gathered and organized. It is important to encourage students with AS to express their ideas and not worry about grammar, spelling, and formulating sentences and paragraphs in the first draft. Westby and Clauser (1999), as cited in Larson & McKinley (2003), recommend that during the writing process, "the students be taught to use self-regulating behaviors, such as (1) focusing attention and planning by thinking 'I need a topic sentence and supporting details'; (2) self-evaluating and error correction by thinking, 'I didn't say that clearly; I know I can do better'; (3) coping and self-control by thinking, 'I'm not going to start all over until I think more about this topic'; and (4) self-reinforcement by thinking, 'This is one of my best sentences'" (p. 362). Students with AS need to know up front that they will have to produce more than one draft. That knowledge will prevent a problem that could occur if students feel they are finished after the first draft and then find out they must do another draft or two.

    - Teach students with AS strategies for editing. During the editing stages, students clean up the composition, looking for grammatical, spelling, and mechanical errors. Word-processing software can help students edit mechanics if they are unable to do it themselves. Word-processing software can be a good self-checking procedure after the final checking is done.

- Students also need to learn to edit for meaning, clarity, and organization. Harris and Graham (1996), as cited in Larson & McKinley (2003), suggest the following procedure—called SCAN—for revising and editing text: "(1) Does it make **S**ense?; (2) Is it **C**onnected to my central idea?; (3) Can I **A**dd more detail?; and (4) **N**ote errors" (p. 363).

- Students with AS need to understand that writing is a way of communicating thoughts and ideas to others. Having another student read or listen to the other's work and give constructive criticism can work well. You can also have writing conferences with the students to give them feedback. Students with AS may not be able to organize, compose, and edit meaningful text without feedback from others that can be easily understood and then incorporated into future writings. Your comments on the composition alone will not result in better writing from the students with AS. They will also have to be given strategies and feedback in a logical and sequential way. Even the best writers may have difficulty expressing themselves on paper and need feedback.

2. **Be fluent speakers.**

- Students with AS usually have good verbal language skills (i.e., syntax and semantics) and are almost always very knowledgeable about a special interest. They can talk to others about a topic at great length and are fluent speakers for the most part. However, they lack pragmatic skills, so they do not know how to "read" audiences or speaking partners very well (e.g., they have difficulty knowing when they have said enough, when the audience or speaking partner is getting bored or tired, or when information is not at the level of the audience). They rarely engage in eye contact, may interrupt, and often are not brief once they have started talking. You need to teach them how to get cues from audiences or speaking partners, how to be relevant, how to be brief, and how to engage in eye contact. (See pages 90–93 for more detailed strategies on conversational rules.)

- In addition, students need to organize, plan, deliver, and edit remarks when making presentations. This process will follow many of the steps (explained earlier) for the writing process. If speaking about special interests, they will probably not need to gather information, but if speaking about things that are unfamiliar, they will have to go through the stage of gathering information. Students will have to organize the material, plan what to say, make an outline or a map, practice delivering the information, and receive feedback. Other students and educators can give them constructive and positive feedback. The feedback should contain specific and concrete steps that can be followed to improve skills.

3. **Comprehend from printed symbols in various academic, social, and vocational situations.**

- Reading comprehension for younger students with AS will focus on learning reading skills, including word, sentence, discourse, and metacognitive (i.e., understanding one's own learning process) levels and comprehending what has been read. Reading comprehension for older students with AS will focus on reading for meaning and metacognitive skills. To teach and improve comprehension at both levels, the reader must have prior knowledge of the subject or the setting, and the characters (Larson & McKinley, 2003). Having an oral discussion that focuses on these areas is a good way to introduce the reading assignment and to introduce knowledge and facts that will help students better understand.

- While students with AS are reading, they can be taught to self-monitor their comprehension. (See pages 127–129 for more information about self-monitoring; see Appendix P on the CD-ROM for printable forms.)

- To enhance comprehension, a student may be provided with graphic organizers. "The graphic should show the overarching organization of ideas (or story) presented by the writers, the main ideas and relevant details, and their relationship to one another.... Once the graphic is developed, have students practice discussing the main idea of the author(s) by referring to the visual they have created" (Larson & McKinley, 2003, p. 357). (See Appendix N on the CD-ROM for an example graphic organizer. For additional graphic organizers, see Wiig and Wilson's book titled *Map It Out,* 2001).

- Another way to enhance comprehension is to use Bloom et al.'s (1956) taxonomy (as cited in Wiig & Wilson, 2002). Using Bloom's taxonomy to provide students who have AS with opportunities to answer higher level questions can be helpful in increasing the comprehension skills of the reader (e.g., in addition to asking who, which, what, or when questions of general knowledge, ask a student to apply, analyze, synthesize, or evaluate the information from the text). You will need to proceed slowly with students who have AS, because they may have difficulty dealing with information that is not concrete.

4. **Read fluently across a variety of genres (e.g., narratives and expository text).**

   - To read expository text fluently, begin by having students with AS identify their prior knowledge. If little or no prior knowledge exists, lead an oral discussion about the reading that will provide an orientation to the content of the text (Larson & McKinley, 2003).

   - To read narrative text fluently, ask students about their knowledge of the setting, the characters, the author, and the title. If little or no prior knowledge about the text exists, lead an oral discussion about the reading that will provide an orientation to the content of the text (Larson & McKinley, 2003).

   - For both expository and narrative reading, provide a list of concrete and higher level questions for students with AS to answer as they read the text. This will help organize their thinking and make them more aware of their comprehension during reading.

- Graphic organizers can also be used. The graphic organizer might show the overarching organization of the ideas and their relationship to one another. Or they can be used to present abstract or implicit information in a concrete manner. (For example, if students with AS are having problems with word meaning, you might use a graphic organizer that asks for the grammatical class, category, action word, or the uses and functions of the word, attributes, or any other aspects of the word that is being defined. (See Appendix N on the CD-ROM for an example graphic organizer.)

- Minskoff and Allsopp (2003) suggest several reading strategies for students to enhance their comprehension (see Sidebar 5.5): the **ABCDE** strategy for getting the overall idea;

Sidebar 5.5          **Reading Strategies to Enhance Comprehension**

---

**ABCDE**
- **A**cclimate—determine what you know about the topic.
- **B**efore reading—Survey the headings, pictures, graphics.
- **C**reate questions—Ask yourself "teacher-like" questions.
- **D**uring reading—Answer the questions.
- **E**nd of reading—Summarize.

**RAP-Q**
- **R**ead a paragraph/passage.
- **A**sk yourself, "What was the main idea?"
- **P**ut the idea in words and tell someone else (i.e., paraphrase).
- **Q**uestion yourself about what you've just read.

**ASK 5 Ws & 1 H & Answer**

While taking notes or in a graphic organizer, ask detailed questions about each main idea by using these questions as headings:

- **W**ho?
- **W**hat?
- **W**here?
- **W**hen?
- **W**hy?
- **H**ow?
- **Answer** the question using the notes taken, or using the graphic organizer made while reading.

---

*Sources*: Minskoff & Allsopp (2003)

the **RAP-Q** strategy for understanding the main ideas of what was read; and **ASK 5 Ws & 1 H & Answer** strategy for comprehending details of what was read.

5. **Read fluently for a variety of purposes (e.g., to be informed, to be persuaded, to be entertained).**

- Discuss with the students who have AS the purpose of the writing by the authors.

- Discuss emotional reactions students may have had, and talk about what the authors did to cause those reactions.

- Have students think about what skills they used to understand the story.

- Ask students questions (based on Larson & McKinley, 2003) to determine if they are comprehending the material they are reading such as:

  ★ "The purpose of the material was to inform you. What else do you read that informs you?"

  ★ "The author succeeded in helping you feel angry about someone being treated unfairly. What else have you read that made you feel like that?"

  ★ "As you read this passage, there were many words with multiple meanings. What words were they? What are the meanings?"

Students with AS usually have good basic reading and writing skills, but without the understanding of pragmatics, their own comprehension, and purposes and genres of reading and writing, they will not fully grasp what they need to know to be successful in school. Using the strategies presented above will help students with AS to be better readers.

# General Tips for Educators

Even if an educator has knowledge about teaching students who have AS, he or she is responsible for many other students who all have unique abilities and needs. You will need a great deal of support when students with AS are in class. These following tips from (Church, Alisanski, & Amanullah, 2000; Grandin, 2001; National Research Council, 2001; Powers & Poland, 2002; Pyles, 2002; Quill, 1995; Willey, 1999; Williams, 1995; Winter, 2003)—in addition to the specific strategies covered earlier in this chapter to address executive function deficits, to maximize the learning experience, and to address issues involved in reading and writing—are not specific to academics, but rather cut across all content areas to help educators provide the best possible learning environment for students with AS. A description and explanation of these general tips for educators is presented in this section and are summarized in Sidebar 5.6).

**Sidebar 5.6**    **General Tips for Educators**

1. Focus students' attention before communicating.
2. Use visual prompts whenever possible.
3. Be patient with students' responses to questions.
4. Give students directives instead of offering choices.
5. Use concrete speech; avoid metaphors and similes.
6. Make requests or instructions clear and simple, and check for understanding.
7. Do not take misbehavior personally.
8. Prepare students for changes.
9. Be consistent with rules.
10. Provide predictable schedules and routines.
11. Use prompts for participation in discussions.
12. Create a code for students to use to ask for help.
13. Allow students to burn off anxiety.
14. Do not assume students will want to please.
15. Pick your battles.
16. Allow students to practice the skills they need to learn.

*Sources:* Grandin (2001); Moreno & O'Neal (2002)

1. **Focus students' attention before communicating**—Students with AS are often more interested in objects than people. It might be difficult for students to know if an educator is talking to them if they are not looking at the educator. Be sure to get students' attention before you begin talking to them. Ask students if they are attending. Educators may have previous agreements with students that are in the form of a nod or another signal to indicate they are paying attention.

2. **Use visual prompts whenever possible**—Students with AS most often are visual thinkers (Grandin, 2001). They attend to visual representations of schedules, routines, or directions better than oral representations. When making schedules or classroom rules or giving directions, use pictures or drawings wherever possible. Pair it with print when appropriate. Also, educators can use visual cues and signals as memory aids.

3. **Be patient with students' responses to questions**—Because students who have AS likely have deficits with language—especially pragmatics—they may not understand a question unless it is asked in a direct, understandable way. Rephrase questions if students do not seem to understand. Refrain from using idioms and metaphors in your questions unless you are confident students understand their meanings. Students most often will interpret a metaphor or idiom literally.

4. **Give students directives instead of offering choices**—Students with AS will frequently have difficulty making choices. If presented with choices, they may become frustrated and agitated. These feelings could lead to anger or despair. Students with AS are good rule-followers. An educator who makes a directive statement (instead of offering choices) or proclaims a rule will help students feel more comfortable.

5. **Use concrete speech; avoid metaphors and similes**—Students with AS have very literal interpretations of language. If you tell them "to keep an eye on the ball," for example, they may pick up the ball and hold it to their eye. Students must be taught about the pragmatics of language—its function and use—to enable them to use and understand more complex language.

6. **Make requests or instructions clear and simple, and check for understanding**—Even though students with AS can be very articulate, translating meaning from the spoken or written word may be difficult. Give instructions one at a time. When two- or three-step directions or complicated directions are given, the level of understanding of students with AS must be checked. If students do not understand, educators must repeat the directions—as many times as needed—write them on the board, or give the students a copy of them. When checking for understanding, it's not enough just to ask the students if they understand. Instead, ask them to repeat the instructions back to you or to explain the meaning. For younger students with AS or nonreaders, pictures can be used to illustrate the directions.

7. **Do not take misbehavior personally** (Moreno & O'Neal, 2002)—Students with AS will most likely not be manipulative. Most of the time, their inappropriate behavior results from frustration, stress, and feelings of low self-esteem. When students are angry, there usually are good reasons, but they may not be able to articulate them. Be supportive. Help them find the reasons for their misbehavior, develop prevention plans that may work in the future, and work on coping strategies.

8. **Prepare students for changes**—Changes in schedules and routines can be very difficult for students with AS. They want predictability in their lives. If the routine changes, if the room is rearranged, or if there is a substitute teacher in the room, students can become anxious and afraid and may act out fears in ways that are distracting and inappropriate in school. You can minimize or prevent anxiety by preparing students ahead of time. (As an example, if you will be absent and will be replaced by a substitute teacher, talk to students with AS about it ahead of time. Explain as much as you can about the sub and what the day will be like. Remind students over and over about the upcoming change. Parents need to be alerted, so they can talk to their children about the change, also. Even with advanced preparation, students still may experience anxiety and fear. Alert the sub, too, so he or she is aware of the problems and can address them directly.)

9. **Be consistent with rules**—Setting rules and boundaries is important. Students with AS are rule-followers and will be comfortable knowing what the rules are. However, they might not respond well to changing rules. Try to keep the classroom rules clear and consistent. If there are consequences for breaking the rules, be sure to present the consequences every time. Inconsistency can cause fear and anxiety.

10. **Provide predictable schedules and routines**—Students with AS like routines and predictability. Try, as much as possible, to keep daily and weekly routines the same. Have schedules posted so that students can easily check to see what is next.

11. **Use prompts for participation in discussions**—Students with AS may not know when it is appropriate to speak in a group. They may interrupt, blurt out an answer, or not speak at all. Have students hold a prompt of some kind (e.g., a ball, a hat, a piece of paper, or something that is easy to pass from one student to another) to start a discussion or to answer a question. Students will make their responses or comments while they are holding the prompt, then pass it on. The next person to receive the prompt will be the next speaker. Do this until everyone has had a turn. The prompt will give students with AS a concrete cue for knowing when to speak. They will realize that they cannot speak whenever they want to, but rather have to wait until they are holding the prompt. With your help, this behavior can be generalized to other areas. Explain to the students that the prompt gives them permission to speak. When in situations where there are no prompts, students can be taught to be aware of other cues for the appropriate time to talk (e.g., when someone makes eye contact, when there is a gap in the conversation, or when the student is called on).

12. **Create a code for students to use to ask for help**—Students with AS may be embarrassed to ask you or other adults for help. You and the students can develop an inconspicuous code that can be used when help is needed (e.g., raising their finger in the air). They may need to be reminded that you will look for the agreed-upon code.

13. **Allow students to burn off anxiety**—Students with AS need to have opportunities to burn off anxiety. When anxiety is building, look for ways the students can exert themselves to get rid of their stress. Going to the gym or playing outside will help. Letting students "run loose" or engage in activities like running laps, playing tag, dodge ball, or other noncompetitive games can be helpful in burning off anxiety. Also, provide opportunities for students to vent frustrations and anger. Educators who are willing to listen compassionately can play an important role in the treatment of students with AS.

14. **Do not assume students will want to please**—Students with AS are often more interested in objects then people. They may not care if they please educators because they may

not think very much about them. This should not be taken personally; most people will not be very important to them. Other incentives must be found to encourage the students to work, behave well, and so on.

15. **Pick your battles**—Students with AS have many issues to face that will be challenging to them and to you. You will not be able to deal with everything, so it is important to address the issues that are of the highest priorities first. If students with AS exhibit some behaviors that are eccentric, but are not affecting themselves or others, you may want to ignore those behaviors and stick to the most important issues.

16. **Allow students to practice the skills they need to learn**—Teach students with AS the skills they need to learn, and then give them every opportunity to practice. Once they learn the skill, they will likely remember it. It is important to harness this strength.

Students with AS have varying abilities and learning styles. A variety of strategies have been presented in this chapter. Not all of them will work for every student with AS, so it is important to try a number of strategies to find one or two that work for each student.

# Case Study: Alan

This last section provides an opportunity to apply the skills that have been addressed earlier in the chapter. The case study focuses on Alan, a fourth-grade student with AS who has executive function deficits. Following the case study, there is a guide to help analyze Alan's deficit areas. Sample goals and suggested interventions are also presented.

### Alan: Executive Function

Alan walks into his fourth-grade classroom most days with his hair rumpled, his shirt untucked, his shoes untied, and papers flying out of his backpack. Oblivious to others around him, he first touches the light switches next to the door, spins the globe on the table, then goes to his desk to begin the day. This is a morning ritual that he practices routinely. He has other rituals throughout the day that seem meaningless to others but are of the utmost importance to him. If the teacher or his classmates try to interfere with his rituals, he gets anxious and angry.

When the teacher asks students to turn in their permission slips to go on the class field trip the next day, Alan immediately starts rummaging through his school bag, throwing papers on the floor. He goes through his desk throwing papers hither and yon, and then back

**Alan—*Continued***

to his school bag. He is lucky this morning and finds what he needs at the bottom of his bag, wrinkled and torn, but it's there, and he's relieved. And now he's left with papers, pencils, rulers, and books everywhere. He organizes his belongings the best he can and sits down to start the day.

During first period reading class, Alan is expected to silently read the story and answer the comprehension questions at the end of the story. The teacher is working with another reading group. Alan starts reading, but soon is distracted by Marcia, who walks by his desk on her way to sharpen her pencil. The teacher, from her chair in the reading group, reminds Alan to get back to work. He does, but while he has his head in the book, he says in a whisper, "You're chubby, you're chubby, you're chubby, chubby, chubby." Joe, sitting in front of Alan says, "Shut up, dummy!" Alan says, with his eyes still on the book, "Teacher, teacher, Joe called me a dummy. Tell him to stop it." The teacher gets up and goes over to Alan and Joe and tells them nicely to get back to work. Joe does, but Alan, with his head down, starts laughing and fiddling with his watch. By the end of the allotted time, Alan has not finished reading the story, nor has he answered the comprehension questions. And so goes the day.

Alan seldom asks for help. Sometimes he inappropriately has an outburst about the "stupid story" or an "impossible question." When he is interested in a topic, he will do more work than usual, but doesn't do it quietly. He talks incessantly to himself or to the classmates who sit near him about his work. When the teacher tells him to stop, or gives him constructive criticism about how he could more appropriately have a discussion about the topic, he becomes frustrated and says, "I know that already."

The teacher, needless to say, is frustrated. She has tried many different approaches to get Alan to stay on task and finish his work. She knows he has the ability to do it.

# Analysis

Addressing the following analysis questions and exercises will help you develop an understanding of a student with AS who has executive function deficits. You can write your own goals and develop an intervention program before reading the examples at the end of the chapter.

1. What are the behaviors that are keeping Alan from being a successful student?

2. In what categories of characteristics do his problems fit (e.g., social and communication skills, academic, psychomotor, behavioral)?

3. Prioritize the behaviors that need to be addressed, beginning with the ones you would work on first.

4. Develop long- and short-term goals for Alan.

5. Create an intervention program to help Alan achieve the top three goals that you have identified. Use the interventions that have been described in this chapter.

## Example IEP Goals

1. Alan will come into the classroom each morning with his school materials organized.
2. Alan will monitor his on-task behavior.
3. Alan will complete his assignments.

## Example Interventions to Achieve the IEP Goals

**Goal #1:** Alan will come into the classroom each morning with his school materials organized.

- Alan will organize his materials using a color-coding strategy. He will use color-coding so that each of his classes (math, reading, language arts, etc.) has the same colored text, folder, and notebook. The teacher and parents will work together to help Alan leave school and return to school with his materials organized.

- Alan and his teacher will organize his locker so that each subject has a different compartment. There will also be a special holder for pencils, erasers, colored pencils, paper clips, etc.

- After the organization plan is complete, Alan, his teacher, and his parents, will work together to set up a program in which he will earn rewards for staying organized.

**Goal #2:** Alan will monitor his on-task behavior.

- Alan's teacher will explain to Alan that he will record his own on-task behavior.

- She will define for Alan what constitutes on-task behavior. So there is no misunderstanding, she will write the definition on paper for him to keep at his desk. The definition might be: "On-task behavior means you are sitting at your desk reading or writing. You will not be talking to your classmates, be gazing around the room, or be out of your desk."

- Alan's teacher will set a kitchen timer on her desk. She will set it for the number of minutes she thinks Alan can work without being distracted. It is important to set it for the amount of time Alan can be successful at the beginning of the intervention and keep his spirits up. The teacher can increase the number of minutes as Alan gets acclimated to the program.

- When the timer goes off, Alan will determine if he is on task. If so, he will make a check on a form on his desk. The teacher will also record whether Alan is on task. Alan and the teacher can compare notes at the end of the work period.

- The teacher and Alan will reset the timer and repeat the procedure until the work period is over.

- At the end of the period, Alan will get a reinforcer if he is successful.

**Goal #3:** Alan will complete his assignments.

- Alan's teacher will analyze the assignment to make sure it is at Alan's developmental level.

- The teacher will break Alan's assignment into smaller segments so that he can finish each one in a relatively short period of time. She will tell him how many parts he has to do, but only give him one part at a time so he is not overwhelmed.

- When he finishes each part, he will have his teacher check it and give him the next part.

- The teacher will discuss a reinforcement with Alan. It could be a positive statement, points to use for a larger reinforcer, candy, free time, or anything that is acceptable and works for Alan. The teacher will reward Alan in some way after he completes each part.

- Alan will self-monitor his homework completion.

# Discussion Points

1. Students with AS wouldn't have a disability if they didn't have to deal with other people. Do you think this is true? What does this mean?

2. How can AS affect the academic performance of students?

3. Many students with AS are very intelligent. How can we, as a society, help them to realize their potential for their own good and the common good of all citizens?

4. What are the biggest problems students with AS have to face in the school environment?

5. How can parents and educators work together more effectively to help students with AS and themselves?

6. Have you seen individuals with AS portrayed in the media, including movies, TV, books, the news, and others? Where? How were they portrayed?

7. Should students with AS be placed in general education or special education classes?

8. Do you think AS should be a category onto itself, including teacher certification in AS and special education classrooms for AS students? Explain your reasoning.

# Sensory and Motor Intervention Strategies

---

## Goals

- To present problems that students with AS have due to sensory and motor differences

- To present classroom implications of sensory and motor processing problems

- To discuss intervention strategies that will improve student learning

---

The way people hear, see, smell, and taste gives them information about their world. Everyone perceives sensations differently, even when they receive the same sensory information (Pyles, 2002). They use their senses to avoid pain or stress or to increase comfort. Most people perceive their senses at the automatic level. They do not have to think about processing the information they take in. If they encounter an aversive smell, they hold their breath or move away. If they hear a loud noise that is disturbing, they will plug their ears or go somewhere else. If people taste something that is pleasant, they will eat more. If they touch something that feels good, they will probably keep touching it for a while, without thinking very much about it.

Sensory integration is the organization of the sensations for use (Ayres, 1979). The way individuals respond to sensations and situations is the outcome of the sensory integration process. Sensory systems work together to help us understand our world.

There is evidence to suggest that a large percentage of those who have AS have abnormal sensory sensitivity and difficulty with fine and gross motor coordination (Ehlers & Gillberg, 1993; Garnett & Attwood, 1995; Ghaziuddin, Tsai, & Ghaziuddin, 1992; Gilberg, 1989; Tantam,

1991; Wing, 1981). Some studies indicate that over 40% of individuals with autism have sensory integration problems (Pyles, 2002). A study of 42 children and youth with AS supported the hypothesis that sensory processing is a distinct problem area for them (Myles, Dunn, & Orr, as cited in Myles, Cook, Miller, Rinner, & Robbins, 2000). More than 50% of the participants with AS had difficulties in the auditory (hearing), vestibular (balance), proprioceptive (body awareness), tactile (touch), gustatory (oral), visual, and multisensory areas. Approximately two-thirds of children and youth with AS in this sample evidenced emotional and social difficulties or problems related to their sensory processing. According to Attwood (2001), the most common sensitivities for students with AS are smell and touch, while some may express minimal reaction to high levels of pain and temperature.

After reading Grandin's (1995) book *Thinking in Pictures,* a mother of a child with AS understood for the first time the reasons behind many of her son's behaviors, stating,

> Now I understand why Jimmy put his fingers in his ears when a baby cried!…Now I understand why he avoided rambunctious play! The sensory stimulation was overloading his nervous system. Now I could empathize with my son over his rigidity when it came to clothing choices and food preferences. His skin is ultra sensitive to textures. (Fling, 2000, p. 128)

This chapter will address the seven individual sensory systems, how students with AS may be affected at school by problems in each of these systems, and the interventions that can eliminate or reduce troublesome sensations or help students cope with their sensory issues.

# Sensory and Motor Intervention Issues

All the sensory areas—tactile hyper- and hyposensitivity, vestibular hyper- and hyposensitivity, proprioception, visual, auditory, gustatory, and olfactory—are related and, when effectively processed and integrated, contribute to success in school, at home, and in the community. (NOTE: "Hyposensitivity" is rarely mentioned in the literature in any of the sensory areas except tactile and vestibular; thus, this distinction will be made for only these two topics in the sections that follow.)

On the other hand, if children have sensory processing problems, they will most likely experience difficulties in home, community, and school settings. Students with sensory processing difficulties may not be able to play physical games very well; may be "picky eaters"; experience severe anxiety from certain noises; become annoyed when bumped in line at the school cafeteria; or avoid places that have strong smells, like the perfume counter at a department store or the school cafeteria (Pyles, 2002). When sensory processing systems do not work efficiently, children's entire lives are affected. They can experience problems in paying attention, learning, and understanding the intentions of others (Myles, Cook, Miller, Rinner, & Robbins, 2000). "All the behavior modification in the world is not going to stop a child from screaming if the sound of the bell hurts" (Quill, 1995, p. 39).

# Tactile
## Tactile Hypersensitivity

Some students with AS are very sensitive to touch, and they strongly dislike particular tactile sensations (Asperger, 1944). Tactile hypersensitivity can have many affects on students with AS at home, at school, and in the community. Table 6.1 lists some of the tactile hypersensitivity problems students with AS often face, the impacts of such problems, and intervention ideas for avoiding or remediating them.

Some general intervention requirements for students with hypersensitivity may include teaching them compensatory strategies, usually of a verbal nature, such as teaching them how to ask peers not to stand too close, or providing occupational and physical therapies to promote learning of visual-spatial concepts such as order, causation, sequencing, and left-right orientation.

## Tactile Hyposensitivity

Some students with AS have the opposite reaction to touch than students with hypersensitivity have: They do not feel anything when other people or things touch them. These students frequently learn

Table 6.1     **Tactile Problems, Impacts, and Interventions**

| Hypersensitivity | | |
|---|---|---|
| **Problem** | **Impact** | **Intervention** |
| **They avoid contact and being touched by anyone or anything** | • Students may have "meltdowns" if they have to stand too close to others in line for fear of being touched or bumped. | • Require all students to leave an appropriate amount of space in line. Respect the students' need to physically distance themselves from others so they will not be accidentally touched. Let them be first or last in line, and avoid entrances in busy, crowded places. Let them enter at the rear so they can control where they are standing or sitting. |
| | • They may refuse to work in groups to avoid social contact, for fear that someone might touch them. | • Teach students with AS how to ask their peers, educators, and others to warn them if they need to touch them. |
| | • They may be particularly sensitive to their seating assignment, wanting plenty of space around them. | • If other students, the airflow of heating or air-conditioning, or the movement of curtains or other things bothers students with AS, allow them to move their workspace away from objects that may touch them. |

*Continued on next page*

Table 6.1—*Continued*

| Problem | Impact | Intervention |
|---|---|---|
| They do not want to touch substances like glue, paste, finger paint, clay, paper maché, grit, rubber, or other tactile stimuli. | • Students may refuse to do art or class projects that require them to touch unusual textures.<br><br>• They may not want to participate in physical education class. | • Find an alternative project for these students, or let them use different materials. If the student likes to squeeze or scrunch things, try various materials such as a package of rice or beans, a soft rubber ball, a Nerf ball, play dough or bread dough, modeling clay, a balloon filled with flour or flour and rice, or a balloon filled with sugar or cornstarch to see how they respond. Have these materials available, then move slowly and do not force students to touch things they do not like.<br><br>• Some students with AS will not participate in ball games because they do not like the feeling of the ball. Do not force them to do the things they feel strongly about not doing. |
| They do not like certain kinds of fabric (e.g., wool or linen). | • Students may refuse to wear a plastic art smock, a gym uniform, or certain clothes or tennis shoes. | • Work with the parents to ensure that students with AS wear clothing that does not aggravate them or their skin. Find fabrics they like and advise parents to try to buy clothing made of these fabrics, suggesting that it might be a good idea to buy several articles of the same piece of clothing so there is always one available.<br><br>• Advise parents to introduce new materials slowly. Sometimes introducing a new material to the child's feet first, or lightly rubbing their arms and legs with a new and similar fabric will help increase tactile tolerance. |
| | Hyposensitivity | |
| They may not notice or respond to being touched. | • They do not respond to warmth shown via a pat on the back or a light touch on the arm. | • Use verbal reinforcement or verbal cues. If you are out of their visual field (e.g., behind them) move to a place where they can see you before you start talking, or say their name to get their attention. |
| They do not seem to feel pain at the same intensity as peers do (e.g., scrapes, bruises, stomachaches, or other physical injuries). Some students do not notice pain that others would find unbearable. | • They may hurt themselves and not realize it. | • Teach them to recognize signs on their bodies that should cause pain (e.g., blood, bruises, hot skin, hoarse voice). Teach them to tell their parents, teachers, and other adults when they notice these symptoms. |

**Table 6.1—*Continued***

| Problem | Impact | Intervention |
|---|---|---|
| **Because touch may be their most reliable sense, they may frequently touch other people and things to get their bearings.** | • Others may be annoyed because their personal space or property is being invaded. | • Before entering an area where there are people or things that should not be touched, try to calm the students. If they are not calm, they will want to touch everything. Provide deep pressure by using a weighted vest or by rubbing their shoulders, backs, or palms to calm them. |
| **They may have low muscle tone and, as a result, appear clumsy.** | • They may not be successful in games that require coordination skills and, consequently, may be the last picked for a team. | • Use educator-chosen teams. Work with parents and other school staff to arrange opportunities for the student with AS to practice and learn motor coordination skills. |
| **They seek sensory sensations, so they may bite themselves severely or they may pick at their faces, noses, mouths, and scabs.** | • They may injure themselves trying to feel sensations. | • If students with AS need to stimulate sensitive nerve endings around the mouth, encourage them to chew on paraffin wax that is not softened, thick rubber tubing, gum, or heavy plastic straws. Pencils and pens do not work very well as they may splinter or break in their mouths. |
| **They may wear clothes that are too small because they like how their skin feels when the clothing presses against their skin.** | • Wearing clothes that are too tight may result in teasing or rejection from other students. Also, this may restrict movement and may further negatively impact motor coordination. | • Parents can use personal hygiene routines for sensory input instead. Firmly scrub their arms, legs, or bodies when appropriate with differently textured bath brushes and washcloths. |
| **They may fidget or be in constant motion to get stimulation.** | • They may not be able to sit still in class, and their academic performance may suffer. | • Use deep pressure to calm hyposensitive students who are fidgety. Use a weighted vest to calm the central nervous system. For best results, let the student wear the vest for 20 minutes or so and then remove it for a few minutes to prevent the nervous system from adapting to it. Another method is for students to carry weights in their pockets. |

*Sources:* Attwood (2001); Cumine et al. (2001); Grandin (1995, 2001); Klin & Volkmar (2000); Myles, Cook, Miller, Rinner, & Robbins (2000); Willey (1999)

by touching other things or people and may need more tactile input than students with typical development. Table 6.1 on pages 149–151 lists some of the tactile hyposensitivity problems that students with AS encounter, the impact those problems can have, and some intervention techniques for addressing them.

# Vestibular

## Vestibular Hypersensitivity

Students with vestibular hypersensitivity tend to have a low tolerance for activities that involve movement. Activities that are dependent on the vestibular senses are movement, posture, vision, balance, and coordination of both sides of the body (Myles, Cook, Miller, Rinner, & Robbins, 2000). Klin, Volkmar, Sparrow, Cicchette, & Rourke (1995) found a high proportion of students with AS have fine and gross motor skills deficits. Table 6.2 outlines some of these problem areas, the affects they can have, and the interventions that may be required.

## Vestibular Hyposensitivity

Students with vestibular hyposensitivity have a high tolerance for activities that involve movement. They are in constant motion in order to get the stimulation externally that they are not getting internally. Table 6.2 highlights several problems students with vestibular hyposensitivity can have, the affects of such problems, and several corresponding intervention ideas.

Table 6.2      **Vestibular Problems, Impacts, and Interventions**

| Hypersensitivity | | |
| --- | --- | --- |
| **Problem** | **Impact** | **Intervention** |
| They are most comfortable standing with both feet on the floor. They do not like changing direction or speed. | • They will not want to participate in activities that require changing direction or speed. | • Allow students to stand during activities if they are more comfortable than when moving around.<br><br>• Provide opportunities for large motor activities (e.g., touching their toes, pulling, or pushing).<br><br>• Incorporate movement into sedentary activities (e.g., allow students to run in the gym before watching a movie.) |

**Table 6.2—*Continued***

| Problem | Impact | Intervention |
|---|---|---|
| **They do not like participating in games in which there is a lot of movement in many different directions (e.g., soccer, football, tag, basketball, or hockey).** | • They are not very competent in physical activities and most likely will not be chosen to play on teams with others. | • Provide opportunities for large motor activities such as jumping jacks, hopping, or skipping. |
| **They have poor eye-hand coordination.** | • Their academic work may be negatively impacted since they may have problems copying from the board to a piece of paper on their desk, may often lose their place when they are reading, and/or may have problems with handwriting. | • Provide opportunities for them to practice copying from the board, or, if they are unable to succeed, provide them with printed materials instead of asking them to copy. If they often lose their places while reading, give them blank strips of paper to put under lines of text.<br><br>• Encourage them to use their fingers to help them keep their places. |
| **Students with AS may try to avoid activities in which they are uncomfortable. They may feign illness or try to flee if they are forced to participate.** | • They may not want to go to school if they are uncomfortable with academics and physical activities. | • Provide programs that are comfortable for them. Make sure that their academic and physical activities are at their developmental level. |
| | **Hyposensitivity** | |
| **They are constantly in motion (e.g., swinging around, rocking back and forth) even when they are sitting.** | • They don't listen to or follow directions.<br><br>• They can't concentrate or stay focused, so they often do not do or finish their work, because they are always moving.<br><br>• They distract others. | • Teach students a cue (e.g., hand signal or a squeeze on the shoulder) that you will use when students need to attend, because you will be giving a direction.<br><br>• Prepare in advance for active students in the classroom (e.g., put away and out of sight things that are breakable or distracting).<br><br>• Use a hand-fidget materials (soft ball, modeling clay) to help decrease anxiety or enhance self-regulation.<br><br>• Teach the child a "self-talk" strategy to get through difficult times. (This strategy would be appropriate for older students, and would have to be taught in steps, over time.)<br><br>• Allow students to move, swing, or rock while doing certain school activities (e.g., flash cards, spelling practice, or other activities that don't require written work). |

*Continued on next page*

**Asperger Syndrome**

Table 6.2—*Continued*

| Problem | Impact | Intervention |
|---|---|---|
| **They often exhibit awkward movements; they may be clumsy and may have difficulty starting and stopping activities that involve movement.** | • They may be in danger of hurting themselves or others. | • Break movements down into small steps and start teaching them the most basic movements, adding steps slowly. Try to make sure they feel safe as they perform the tasks in the learning process. |

*Sources*: Attwood (2000, 2001); Ehlers & Gillberg (1993); Grandin (1992); Manjiviona & Prior (1995); Myles, Cook, Miller, Rinner, & Robbins, (2000); Tantam (1991); Wing (1981); Klin et al. (2000)

# Proprioception

Proprioception is being aware of one's body in space. It is what allows people to walk through a room without bumping into desks and tables and other people, to sit down in a chair without looking back, or to keep balanced when walking or running—without even thinking about it. Some individuals, however, may not be able to judge where their bodies are in relation to others. They need to be taught and to be given opportunities to practice (Myles, Cook, Miller, Rinner, & Robbins, 2000). Table 6.3 lists some of the problems that students with a lack of body awareness may encounter, the impact of the problems, and intervention tips for each.

Table 6.3    **Proprioception Problems, Impacts, and Interventions**

| Problem | Impact | Intervention |
|---|---|---|
| **They have poor posture.** | • They may do damage to their bodies, internally and externally over time. | • Arrange for practice of proper posture.<br>• Define "proper posture" and break the skill into small steps. |
| **They are unbalanced when they walk or get up from a chair or the floor, so they need to steady themselves.** | • They bump into other people and things in the room. | • Teach students to visually monitor their movements in the environment.<br>• Put weights in their pockets or around ankles or wrists, or use a weighted vest to make the students more aware of their bodies. |

154

**Table 6.3—***Continued*

| Problem | Impact | Intervention |
|---|---|---|
| **They get confused about left and right.** | • They may have trouble following directions and interpreting messages that include left and right. | • If students are young, put cues on right and/or left hand (e.g., "L" & "R" or the words right and left). For older students, make sure the cues are not visible to others or are associated with a watch or ring, for example. |
| **They get confused about finding a place on a page.** | • They have difficulty copying from the board or another paper.<br><br>• They have difficulty writing. | • Have them practice starting with small steps (e.g., one word or one letter at a time), gradually increasing the expectation. If they don't make adequate progress, give them printed materials so they don't have to copy and let them use the computer so they don't have to write. |
| **They have difficulties in physical education.** | • They do not want to engage in games with others.<br><br><br><br><br><br>• They engage in rough play because they have an unclear understanding of their own strength. | • Rather than participating in contact sports, allow students to participate in gross motor activities like jumping, running, or tug of war. Or do structured recess activities like an obstacle course, jumping rope, jumping over lines on the ground, or other activities that can be practiced in isolation without calling the attention of other students.<br><br>• Do activities like role-plays, cartoons, and social stories that emphasize the importance of knowing their own strength and being considerate of others. |
| **They do not play on monkey bars or bridges.** | • They may feel inadequate. | • Teach them alternate physical skills that they can master. |
| **They have difficulty climbing stairs.** | • They are unable to get to places that require stairs. | • Arrange for them to use escalators or elevators. Practice climbing stairs. |
| **They have difficulty getting their jackets or coats on.** | • They will be dependent on others. | • Teach them to put on their jackets and coats. Allow time for practice. |

*Continued on next page*

Table 6.3—*Continued*

| Problem | Impact | Intervention |
|---|---|---|
| **They seem tired or lack energy.** | • They will not be able to keep up academically or physically in school. | • Work with parents for students to have physical exam to determine if there is a medical reason.<br>• Check on the student's nutrition.<br>• Reduce expectations, if necessary.<br>• Provide reinforcement for effort. |
| **They are slow in movement and in completing tasks.** | • They do not finish tasks or assignments on time. | • Break tasks into small pieces and reinforce students for finishing work.<br>• Use areas of special interest to teach content (e.g., math, history, reading). |
| **They cannot imitate the movement pattern of others.** | • They do not learn social and physical skills in an automatic way. | • Use direct instruction to teach skills not learned automatically. |

*Sources:* Attwood (2001); Grandin (2001); Meltzoff & Gopnick (1993); Myles, Cook, Miller, Rinner, & Robbins. (2000); Rogers & Pennington (1991)

# Visual

The area of visual perception seems to be a relative strength for students with AS (Myles, Cook, Miller, Rinner, & Robbins, 2000). However, some students with AS experience visual problems related to sensory processing (e.g., brightness or dimness of light, perceiving visuals in unusual ways; Attwood, 2001). Klin et al. (1995) found evidence of visual-motor integration, visual-spatial perception, and visual memory deficits as a result of reviewing the records of 40 individuals with AS. Table 6.4 lists problems encountered by students with poor visual sensory processing, along with the impact of these problems, and intervention ideas for handling them.

Table 6.4    **Visual Problems, Impacts, and Interventions**

| Problem | Impact | Intervention |
|---|---|---|
| **They frequently cannot find what they are looking for, even if it is right in front of their eyes.** | • They may have problems with organization, word retrieval, and academic performance.<br>• They may not want to be in crowded areas. | • Teach students to put their hands around their faces so they can only see what is directly in front of them when they are in crowded areas.<br>• Teach students to look down at the floor directly in front of them while being guided through crowds. |

**Table 6.4—*Continued***

| Problem | Impact | Intervention |
|---|---|---|
| **They have writing problems that are visually based (e.g., their writing is sloppy or they have difficulty copying from the board, staying on the lines, or maintaining consistent spacing between letters).** | • They may have problems with academic performance because of difficulties with writing. | • Provide opportunities for writing practice.<br><br>• Let them use a computer to word process their work.<br><br>• Provide them with materials so they don't have to copy. |
| **They may have attention problems because they are distracted by the visual stimuli.** | • They are sensitive to florescent lighting or bright sunlight. The flickering of the light is distracting and may hurt their eyes. | • Have sunglasses available for students who are sensitive to sun or bright lights.<br><br>• Experiment with different kinds of lighting and /or light bulbs to see what is most comfortable, using colors that appeal to students with AS.<br><br>• Avoid placing students in areas where they will experience full glare of the sun or bright lights. |
| **They sometimes have trouble reading because they skip lines and words. They may move their heads across the page to follow the words.** | • They may have problems with academic performance because of difficulties with reading. | • Teach them to use their fingers to point to and follow what they are reading.<br><br>• If moving their head across the page helps them read, encourage them to do that. |
| **They frequently don't make eye contact with others.** | • They may have poor social skills. | • Make them aware of the importance of eye contact.<br><br>• Teach them to have eye contact, if possible. |
| **They are visually distracted.** | • They may miss visual cues that are necessary for success (e.g., assignments posted on the board or signs posted). | • Provide slight auditory or tactile cues to encourage visual attention. |

*Sources:* Attwood (2001); Myles, Cook, Miller, Rinner, & Robbins. (2000); Willey (1999)

## Auditory

There is evidence to suggest that many students with AS have some kind of auditory perceptual problems (Garnett & Attwood, 1995; Rimland, 1990). A study done by Myles, Cook, Miller, Rinner, & Robbins (2000) found that 85% of the students they tested had some kind of auditory processing problems. These problems do not result from auditory acuity, but rather from auditory processing. These students were either hyper- or hyposensitive to auditory stimulation. It is possible that a student can have problems at both ends of the continuum, depending on the type of stimuli they are trying to process. Hans Asperger (1944) wrote that "the same children who are distinctly hypersensitive to noise in particular situations, in other situations may appear to be

Table 6.5     **Auditory Problems, Impacts, and Interventions**

| Problem | Impact | Intervention |
|---|---|---|
| **They may respond negatively to loud noises (e.g., fire alarms, fire crackers, sirens). They may be terrified if confronted with a loud noise and may obsess over the anticipation of the noise.** | • They may obsess over the anticipation of an aversive noise which interferes with their learning. | • Allow students to leave class early so they don't hear the bell and aren't confronted with crowds and loud noises. |
| **They may be distracted by either loud or soft noises or they may not be able to concentrate if there is any noise at all. Some students may find even soft sounds aversive (e.g., material rubbing together, chalk on the blackboard, some kinds of music/instruments, or chairs scraping against the floor).** | • They may not be able to stay focused and complete assignments due to auditory distractions. | • Make ear plugs available to cushion sounds—don't use cottonballs or tissue, as they may create their own disturbing frequency.<br>• Move students with AS away from noise.<br>• Avoid areas where many noises merge together like sports stadiums, concert halls, busy malls, large cafeterias.<br>• Have stereo headphones available for students to mask other noises.<br>• Eliminate background distractions and noise from the environment as much as possible.<br>• Allow students to go to the lunchroom early to avoid crowds and noise.<br>• Allow students to eat lunch in the classroom if the cafeteria is too noisy. |

**Table 6.5—***Continued*

| Problem | Impact | Intervention |
|---|---|---|
| **There are some students who have AS who do not respond to noise at all. They act as if they don't hear what is being said, even though they have normal hearing acuity. They sometimes drift away in conversations.** | • They may not hear directions, so they don't follow them. | • Provide auditory cues to direct attention. |

*Sources*: Attwood (2001); Grandin (1995, 2001); Myles, Cook, Miller, Rinner, & Robbins. (2000)

hyposensitive. They may appear to be switched off even to loud noises" (p. 80). Table 6.5 lists problems for students with auditory sensory processing issues, along with the impact of these problems and intervention ideas for handling them.

# Gustatory

Some students with AS have problems with processing taste sensations. They are fussy in their choices of food, avoiding certain tastes that are typical of a child's diet and eating foods with certain other tastes (Attwood, 2001; Myles, Cook, Miller, Rinner, & Robbins, 2000). They often have a preference for sweet or sour foods and do not like vegetables or dairy products. Most children with AS outgrow their sensitivity as they get older, but some adults with AS have a very constricted diet (Attwood, 2001). Table 6.6 on page 160 lists problems encountered by students with taste-processing issues, the impact of such problems, and some intervention techniques to try.

Table 6.6        **Gustatory Problems, Impacts, and Interventions**

| Problem | Impact | Intervention |
|---|---|---|
| **Certain foods, like vegetables, fruit, or dairy products, are avoided.** | • Students have increased illness due to poor nutrition. They may have more broken bones because of low levels of calcium. | • Work with nutritionists to make sure the diet is balanced and healthy.<br><br>• Positively reinforce students with AS for eating healthy food.<br><br>• Use vitamins and calcium supplements to ensure appropriate intake of healthy nutrition and calcium.<br><br>• Encourage students to lick and taste (rather than chew and swallow) when trying a new food.<br><br>• Give students the opportunity to try new foods when they are relaxed or distracted. |
| **Teeth-brushing is a problem because of the taste of tooth-paste.** | • They have increased cavities due to poor dental hygiene. | • Positively reinforce students for brushing their teeth. |

*Sources*: Attwood (2001); Myles, Cook, Miller, Rinner, & Robbins. (2000)

# Olfactory

Some people with AS have a sensitivity to certain smells. Smells can be so overpowering to these individuals that they will do almost anything to avoid them. Because smells are present in everyone's daily life, they can create serious problems for students with AS (Attwood, 2001; Myles, Cook, Miller, Rinner, & Robbins, 2000). Table 6.7 lists problems encountered by students who have issues with their sense of smell, the manifestation of such problems, and intervention methods to help with these issues.

Table 6.7            **Olfactory Problems, Impacts, and Interventions**

| Problem | Impact | Intervention |
|---|---|---|
| **Strong cooking odors are aversive.** | • Students may refuse to eat lunch in the cafeteria or to be near the cafeteria. | • Allow students to eat in another room if the cafeteria smells are aversive. |
| **The odors of people or places are aversive.** | • They may not want to go to physical education class because the smells in the locker rooms are aversive to them. | • Arrange alternative physical education.<br>• Arrange for a locker in an area with better ventilation. |
| **Materials used in art or classroom projects may be aversive.** | • They may avoid certain projects or classes. | • Allow students to do alternative projects where they will not encounter the smells that bother them.<br>• Try to identify the smells that are aversive to students with AS and eliminate as many as possible. |
| **Cleaning supplies and chemicals used in school rooms, halls, and bathrooms are bothersome.** | • Students may not want to go to school at all because there are cleaning and chemical smells that are aversive to them. | • Introduce certain smells in small increments so students with AS can get used to them gradually. |
| **The colognes and perfumes of adults or students in the school are annoying.** | • They may want to avoid certain classes or certain adults and peers. | • Wear a cologne that doesn't effect the students, or eliminate colognes or perfumes.<br>• Don't require students to be in a place that smells offensive to them. |

*Source*: Myles, Cook, Miller, Rinner, & Robbins (2000)

# Case Study: Sally

The last section provides an opportunity to apply the skills for intervention that have been addressed in this chapter. The case study focuses on a fifth-grade student named Sally, who was diagnosed as having AS when she was in fourth grade. Sally's major problem (in addition to language and social skills) is in the area of sensory integration. Following the case study, there is a guide to help analyze Sally's problems.

## Sally: Sensory Integration Disorders

Sally was diagnosed with Asperger Syndrome when she was in the fourth grade, after having problems in school since kindergarten. She and her family moved from Pleasantville over the summer, so she would be starting a new school in Greenfield this fall. Sally's mother asked for a meeting with Greenfield's school staff before school started to help understand what Sally would need to be successful in fifth grade.

Reports from Pleasantville describe Sally as a student with above-normal intelligence, reading at grade level, and doing math about a year above grade level. She is a quiet, shy student who doesn't interact with her peers or teachers very much. She usually walks with her head down, with her eyes cast downward, and with an awkward gait. Her previous teachers reported that she was fairly shy and quiet, except for times when she would get very agitated. Then, she might burst out crying or nervously ask to leave the classroom. Her teachers did not understand what might be bothering her, and Sally would not or could not tell them.

Sally rarely got her assignments done on time throughout her first three years in school. She was easily distracted by typical classroom noise and did not attend to tasks. In spite of this, she did not fall behind in her ability to read or to do math.

Sally's gross motor skills are below average. She doesn't like to go to physical education, and sometimes refuses to go to school on days when she has physical education. She refuses to eat lunch in the cafeteria. Starting in first grade, she didn't want to take hot lunch, so her mother always packed her a lunch. The students were required to eat their lunch in the cafeteria, even if they had brought their own lunch. Sally could not be forced to go to the cafeteria from the first day of school. She would have a temper tantrum and would act out verbally and physically when she was forced to go. Consequently, arrangements were made to allow her to eat lunch in the classroom in Pleasantville.

Sally also doesn't like art class. She might do some projects, but not all of them. She would sometimes ask to leave the room or would act out so she would be sent to the principal's office before art class. Other times she would act out during art class, probably with the hope of getting sent to the principal's office.

The educators working with Sally in Pleasantville all knew she had problems, but they were unable to pinpoint what they were. She didn't do her assignments, but she tested at grade level or above. She acted out or had temper tantrums when she was forced to do things she didn't want to do, and she was a loner who had minimal interaction with her peers and other school personnel who worked with her. Teachers noted that she would cover her ears when there were certain loud noises, like the recess bell, the fire alarm, or too much noise in the classroom. She would always get in line last and tarry behind the other students.

Each year there was discussion about what the best program for Sally would be, but school personnel really couldn't determine what she needed or whether she would fit in special education. By the middle of third grade, her temper tantrums were increasing in frequency and duration, and she wasn't getting any of her assignments done. Her mother reported that she cried every morning because she didn't want to go to school. At the end of third grade in Pleasantville, her teacher referred her for a special education evaluation. The evaluation team was puzzled about the appropriate placement for Sally. An emotional/behavioral disability (E/BD) placement seemed to come the closest, but Sally's mother was very reluctant to have Sally in an E/BD class.

In Pleasantville, the discussion between the evaluation team and Sally's mother was very productive. The educators talked about Sally's difficulty with gross motor skills, her seeming discomfort with loud noises, her distractibility, her confusion about left and right, and her strong refusal to eat in the cafeteria. Her mother talked about how Sally didn't want to go to school—especially on physical education days—her refusal to go to department stores or crowded places, her strong reaction to the smell of some foods, her lack of energy, and her aversion to loud noise. They also discussed her difficulties in making friends and her disinterest in people.

The speech-language pathologist (SLP) in Pleasantville had recently attended a conference on Asperger Syndrome (AS) and, after listening to the reports of the educators and the mother, she suggested that perhaps Sally had some of the characteristics of a student with AS. Under the guidance of the SLP, Sally was evaluated by school personnel during the summer, and educators and Sally's mother completed checklists and evaluations. In the fall of her 4$^{th}$ grade year, a functional behavior assessment (FBA) was completed by the school psychologist to try to determine what the cause of her problems might be.

After all the information was gathered, it was hypothesized that Sally could be a student with AS. She met the *DSM–IV–TR* criteria in that she exhibited a qualitative impairment in social interaction, and she had no significant delay in language or cognitive development. She did not engage in restricted patterns of behavior. However, she did exhibit behaviors that led the team to think she might have sensory integration problems in the auditory, tactile, and maybe proprioceptive (body awareness) areas. The SLP knew that many students with AS had sensory integration problems, even though it is not a characteristic listed in the *DSM-IV-TR*. She was not placed in special education, because she didn't meet the criteria for any of the special education programs in the Pleasantville School District. The team recommended that she stay in regular education, and the teacher and other professionals worked together to put in place the appropriate interventions to help Sally be more comfortable in school and benefit more from the learning experience.

Now that she is starting fifth grade in Greenfield, the educators—with the help of Sally's mother and the records from her old school—are working to plan a program for Sally.

## Analysis

Discussing the analysis questions and doing the exercises will help you develop an understanding of a student with AS who has sensory integration problems. Write your own goals and develop an intervention program before reading the samples.

1. What behaviors does Sally exhibit that indicate she has a sensory integration problem and AS-like behaviors?

2. In what categories of characteristics do her problems fit (e.g., academic, behavioral, sensory and motor, social and communication)?

3. Prioritize the behaviors that need to be addressed, beginning with the ones you would work on first.

4. Do you think Sally belongs in a special education classroom? Why or why not?

5. What kinds of modifications would have to be made in a regular classroom to meet Sally's needs?

6. Develop long- and short-term goals for Sally.

7. Create an intervention plan to help Sally achieve the top three goals you have identified. Use the intervention strategies that have been described in this chapter.

## Example Goals

1. Sally will finish her daily assignments.

2. Sally will learn to recognize the sounds and noises in her environment that she has difficulty integrating, and will remove herself quietly from the sounds that are offensive.

3. Sally will improve her gross motor skills.

## Example Interventions to Achieve the Goals

**Goal #1:** Sally will finish her daily assignments.

- Sally will be provided with a study carrel in a partitioned space in the classroom that is relatively quiet where she can do her work. She will have access to it whenever she feels it is necessary, but she won't be forced to use it.

- If the study carrel is not quiet enough, a quiet place in the library will be made available to her.

- Ear plugs will be made available to her.

- Headphones with sounds of her choice will be made available to block out the noise.

- When she finishes her work, she will receive a reinforcer of her choice.

**Goal #2:** Sally will learn to recognize the sounds and noises in her environment that she has difficulty integrating, and will remove herself quietly from the sounds that are offensive.

- Educators, Sally, and Sally's mother will work together to identify noises that irritate Sally.

- Educators will work with Sally to eliminate the noises that are aversive. When the noise or sounds can't be eliminated, Sally will be able to leave the area where the sound is occurring. She will use a signal to let the educator know she is leaving.

- She will go to a comfortable area and stay there until the noise is over. She will not disturb other students or the teacher as she comes and goes.

- Sally will be notified when there will be a fire drill, so she can either find a comfortable place in the building to go, or she can stay home when the fire drill is scheduled.

- Sally will be able to eat lunch in the classroom to avoid the noisy cafeteria.

**Goal #3:** Sally will improve her gross motor skills.

- Educators will arrange an alternative physical education class for Sally. They may refer her to an adaptive physical education program if there is one available that meets her needs.

- Sally will be encouraged to do exercise that she and the educators agree is appropriate for her.

- She will participate in activities that include jumping, pulling, pushing, and others that will improve her large motor problems.

# Discussion Points

1. If students are bothered by loud noises, should you try to eliminate the noises or work to desensitize students to the noise? What is your rationale?

2. How do sensory integration processing deficits affect a student in school?

3. Should students with AS be integrated into the regular classroom, or should they be placed in special education? Discuss your rationale.

4. Is it the regular educator's job to eliminate the environmental incidents that cause sensory integration problems, or should students with special needs be in special education? Why or why not?

5. Are you sensitive to any sounds, smells, tastes, sights, or touches? Explain how they affect you.

6. Should students be allowed to have alternative classes (e.g., physical education, art), or should they have the same experiences as everyone else? Why or why not?

7. Have you ever worked with students or have you known people with sensory integration problems? Talk about your experiences.

# Behavior Management Strategies

---

## Chapter 7

## Goals

- To provide strategies for behavior management

- To describe a method of functional behavioral assessment

---

Behavior management practices are options to be used only after other curricular and environmental adaptations have been tried. The purpose of this chapter is to introduce the basic elements of increasing and maintaining positive behavior and reducing and eliminating negative behavior. This chapter is organized into three sections that provide educators with information about (1) performing an effective functional behavioral assessment, (2) increasing and strengthening positive behaviors, and (3) reducing and eliminating inappropriate behaviors. The end of the chapter includes a case study of a student with AS who has behavioral problems, an analysis of the student's behavior, example IEP goals, and suggestions for interventions.

Many students with AS have sensory integration deficits and need a supportive environment to thrive. These students should be spared from being in an environment that is sensory-aversive (Heflin & Alberto, 2001). Inappropriate behavior exhibited by students with AS is frequently a result of frustration from having different perceptions of the world than people with typical developments, and frustration from being unable to communicate about their differences. Their behaviors are not willful, but stem from sensory, social, and communication delays. Trying to force a different behavior may feel hopeless (Pyles, 2002).

Their misbehavior most often does not result from their wanting to be irritating or annoying. They come to the classroom, as most students do, wanting to be the best they can be. As educators of students with AS, it is important to change the curriculum and the environment to fit the needs of the student, not to change the student to fit into the school's curricula and environments. Students should be aware of their behavior and the changes educators are making in the environment and curriculum (National Research Council, 2001; Simpson & Myles, 1998; TEACCH, 2005). This will help them monitor their own behavior and needs (Cyr, 2002).

A behavior management system is an important tool for professionals who work with students who have Asperger Syndrome. The system can be used to increase and strengthen positive behaviors and to eliminate or reduce inappropriate behaviors. Behavior management techniques work extremely well for students with AS when it is determined that some behaviors need to be changed or modified.

Behavior management needs to be clear, consistent, and concrete. It should be rule-governed (students with AS are good rule followers). Other techniques for changing behavior may include too much discussion or be too complex (e.g., insight-oriented psychotherapy; Klin & Volkmar, 2000). If educators are consistent in using the straightforward behavioral management strategies put forth in this chapter, there is a good possibility that they will be successful in changing or modifying the behavior of students with AS.

Behavior management should be used mainly to support curricular and program goals. When students with AS are exhibiting behavior that enhances their learning, promotes positive interpersonal relationships, or demonstrates good use of leisure time, their program should be set up so that they maintain or increase these behaviors. This can be done using positive reinforcement. When students are exhibiting behavior that is inappropriate in the school setting or on the playground, this behavior can be reduced or eliminated using behavior modification techniques.

The purpose of this chapter is to give basic information and simple and effective strategies that can be used to change the behavior of students with AS without you needing to be an expert in the field. For more technical and detailed approaches to behavior modification, consult Attwood (2001), Cyr (2002), Green (2001), and the National Research Council (2001). To make behavioral changes as effective as possible for students with AS, first do a functional behavioral assessment (FBA) to determine the cause and effect of the behavior should be complete. An FBA is required in the 1997 Individuals with Disabilities Education Act (IDEA) amendments, as well as IDEA 2004. The next section describes how to complete an FBA.

# Completing a Functional Behavioral Assessment

To gain an understanding of the rationale and purpose for doing an FBA, refer to page 43–45. An FBA gathers information about a problem behavior to understand and describe the reason why it occurs (Drasgow & Bradley, 1999; Hallahan & Kauffman, 2003). The following are steps for completing a FBA. (Sidebar 7.1 provides an example FBA.)

1. **Identify and describe the behavior to be observed**—To do an FBA, the behavior that needs to be changed must be identified and carefully described. It must be a single behavior that has a beginning and an end, and one that can be observed and measured. A few examples of behaviors that fall into this category are on-task behavior, temper tantrums, hitting, biting, talking out of turn, running away, or interrupting. A few examples of behaviors that do not have parameters and cannot be observed or measured are "understanding," "being bad," and "being good."

2. **Determine how the behavior will be counted**—Once the behavior to be assessed has been identified, you will determine how it will be assessed or counted. Will it be the

**Sidebar 7.1**　　　　**Example Functional Behavior Assessment (FBA)**

---

**Step 1: Identify and describe the behavior to be observed.**

**Statement from the teacher:** "Jeremy does not complete his work. During work time, he is distracted by everything. He gazes around the room, looks out the window, looks at what the other students are doing, and digs in his desk. He does everything except what he's supposed to be doing. I would like to know how to get him to do his work during work time."

**Behavior to be observed and measured: On-task behavior**

**On-task behavior is defined as Jeremy sitting at his desk with:**

- His eyes fixed on his book as he is reading;
- A pencil in his hand and a paper on his desk with his eyes fixed on the paper; or
- A pencil in his hand writing on the paper.

**Step 2: Determine how the behavior will be counted.**

The behavior will be counted at 30-second intervals.

**Step 3: Determine how the behavior will be recorded.**

- The observer will record Jeremy's behavior at 30-second intervals. If Jeremy is on-task, the observer will write a "Y" in the column labeled "Behavior." If Jeremy is not on-task, the observer will write "N" in the column labeled "Behavior."

---

*Continued on next page*

- Immediately after the behavior is recorded, the observer will record in the column labeled "Consequence" what Jeremy was doing or what was happening in the proximity of his desk.

- Before the next 30-second interval, the observer will record in the column labeled "Antecedent" what Jeremy is doing or what is happening in the proximity of his desk. If this behavior is the same as the consequent behavior, the observer will mark the column with an "X."

**Step 4: Decide when the observations will take place.**

During math seat work (9:00–9:30 AM, Monday through Friday)

**Step 5: Do the assessment by observing the behavior, the antecedent, and the consequences.**

**Step 6: Analyze the results.**

The teacher and observer work together to try to determine what is causing or preventing Jeremy's off-task behaviors. From the very preliminary data on the chart, one might assume the teacher's attention resulted in Jeremy's behavior becoming on-task for a minute. The FBA should be done over at least 4–5 days. Subsequently, the data from the week is analyzed and a behavior management program is planned and implemented based on the results of the FBA.

Name of Student: _____Jeremy Smith_____

Behavior to Be Observed:___On-Task Behavior_____

Date and Time: _____Monday, October 2, 9:00 to 9:30_____

Interval: _____30 seconds_____

| Interval | Antecedent | Behavior | Consequence |
|:---:|:---:|:---:|:---:|
| 1 | | N | Peer standing by J's desk |
| 2 | x | N | Peer standing by J's desk |
| 3 | x | N | Room is quiet |
| 4 | Alan sharpens pencil | N | J watches Alan; teacher tells J to get to work |
| 5 | Teacher walking toward J's desk | Y | Teacher says, "I'm glad you're working" |
| 6 | x | Y | Teacher walking away |
| 7 | x | N | J watching teacher |
| 8 | x | N | J gazing into space |

numbers of times it occurs or the duration or length of time the behavior lasts? It depends on the behavior. For example, will it be important to know the number of times students get out of their seats or the total amount of time students are out of their seats? That will need to be determined by you. Will it be important to know the number of temper tantrums exhibited, the length of the tantrums, or both? These are questions that must be answered up front by professionals.

3. **Determine how the behavior will be recorded**—The behavior, the antecedent, and the consequence can be recorded on the form provided on the CD-ROM in Appendix K. You may also adapt your own form, but it should suit the behavior that is being counted and will depend on what is being measured. Talking out loud in class might be measured by duration (length of the talking out loud incident) or frequency (number of times the talking out loud incident occurs) or both. Different recording charts need to be developed depending on what they are recording.

4. **Decide when the observations will take place**—Observe and measure the behavior every day for a number of days to get a representative sample. Students may not exhibit the behavior all the time, so it is important to observe the behavior over a period of time— approximately a week to 10 days. It is not necessary to observe the student every minute of every day. Choose a time period, an academic class, physical education, or recess when the behavior occurs. If the behavior always occurs during one particular period of the day, observe the student during that period and perhaps another period when the behavior does not occur to determine if there are different antecedents, consequences, or setting events.

5. **Do the assessment by recording the behavior, the antecedent (what triggers the behavior), and the consequence (what purpose the behavior serves)**—This step involves observing the behavior and recording the data. You may not be able to teach the class and gather the data at the same time. In this case, a teacher's aide, a school psychologist, or another teacher may gather the data. It is important to have all the equipment that will be needed, perhaps a stopwatch, two writing utensils (in case one breaks or runs out of ink), and the appropriate forms.

6. **Analyze the results**—After the observations for the FBA are completed, the information can be analyzed and, only then, can you determine the kind of behavior management program to put in place and what goals should be set for the student.

7. **Develop a behavior management plan**—After looking at the analysis of the results, you will decide to increase, maintain, reduce, or eliminate the particular behavior. The methods used will depend on what is maintaining the behavior and what goals are set for the student.

# Increasing and Strengthening Positive Behaviors

Schools have rules that students are required to follow. Each educator also has his or her own set of rules and expectations. Students with AS might be expected to raise their hands before they speak, to walk (not run) in the halls, to be respectful to others, to be on-task, or to keep their desks clean. The expectations are numerous, but usually make sense in the environment. A classroom requires a certain amount of order for everyone to function to the best of their ability. Some students may have problems following all these rules, and some of the rules might not make sense for some students. Students with AS are basically good rule followers (Fling, 2000). When they do not follow the rules, it is not because they are incorrigible students, but because the rules may not make sense to them and the way they perceive the world, or because the rules may get in the way of their routines. Because of this, it might be necessary to develop a behavioral management plan to help the students get along better in school. The behavioral management plan is developed after the FBA is completed. If you include the students with AS in the development of the plan, there will be a greater chance of success (Simpson & Myles, 1998). Sidebar 7.2 outlines some points to consider when developing a behavior management plan to increase positive behaviors.

1. **Try a positive approach first** (Autism Society of America, 2003)—It is almost always better for the self-worth of students with AS to use a positive approach (giving them something they like) rather than a negative one (taking away something they like or giving them something they do not like; Simpson & Myles, 1998). For example, students with AS may blurt out the answer to a question before they raise their hands and/or wait to be called on. Using a positive approach, the students would be reinforced when they do raise their hands. If they never raise their hands and the behavior is not in their repertoire, it would be explained to them that raising their hands is important and expected in the classroom,

**Sidebar 7.2**      **Principles to Consider to Increase Positive Behaviors**

1. Try a positive approach first.
2. Establish a baseline using a functional behavioral assessment (FBA).
3. Choose a reinforcer that increases the positive behavior.
4. Reinforce the positive behavior every time it occurs.

*Sources*: Autism Society of America (2003); Dewey (1991); Simpson & Myles (1998)

and that every time they raise their hands and wait to be called on, they will receive a reinforcer. Using a negative approach, a consequence (something they do not like) would be presented to the students when they did not raise their hands. The former approach will have the most positive effect on the students. However, if the inappropriate behavior is deeply ingrained, combining both positive methods and negative consequences will achieve the result faster than using positive reinforcement alone. Positive reinforcement, when used properly, can change the behaviors of students with AS (Dewey, 1991).

The behavior that is expected of students with AS almost always exists in the students' behavioral repertoire, but it may not be strong enough to be consistently applied across situations. For example, you might want to increase the students' time on-task. Chances are the students spend some time on-task—maybe half of their time—but they are not able to get their work done in that amount of time. You will want to find a reinforcer that you can use to increase the amount of time on-task. If the behavior does not get stronger, the reinforcer is probably not effective and a different reinforcer should be found.

2. **Establish a baseline using a functional behavioral assessment (FBA)**—Before trying to change the behavior of a student with AS, information about the behavior must be gathered. From the information collected during an FBA, a baseline of the behavior can be determined. A baseline is defined as the number of times or percentage of time the behavior occurs without any changes in the environment and before you implement the behavior management plan. Subsequently, you will compare the behavior after implementation of the plan to the original baseline to see if changes have occurred. (See pages 43–45 for more information about FBA).

3. **Choose a reinforcer that increases the positive behavior**—Reinforcers are defined by their effect on the behavior. If hand-raising behavior increases when you give reinforcement in the form of points every time the student raises his or her hand, it is evident that the points work. If the behavior does not change or decreases after you present points to the student with AS, then a different reinforcer should be used (e.g., a sticker). There is no single reinforcer that works for all students with AS. The key is to discover what the student with AS likes more than what you are asking him or her not to do. One student may like free time, another candy, still another playing a game or having computer time. Students with AS often do not find praise from educators or free time to spend with peers to be reinforcing, because of their lack of interest in people. They may, however, want time to work on a special interest or have time on the computer. It will be important to ask the student, the parents, or previous teachers about ideas for what might be reinforcing. Don't limit yourself to points or free time. There are a host of things that can be used for reinforcers. Ask the student to brainstorm a list of things they would be willing to work for with you. Several different reinforcers might have to be tried before one is found that actually works.

Some educators tend to worry about fairness to other students when they have a special program or reinforcer for one or two students. If you tell the other students the truth in a gentle and respectful way, they almost always understand. The message must be that all students are different and need the kind of program that will be best for them. It might be pointed out that many students in the classroom already have a variety of learning and behavioral expectations. The important message is that all students need the best program for them so that they can have the best possible school experience, and those programs will be different in some ways.

There are a few other things to keep in mind with reinforcers:

- The student with AS may tire of the reinforcer, so something new will have to be found that will maintain the positive behavior.

- Something or someone else might be a stronger reinforcer that will interfere with the success of the behavioral management program. For example, if students with AS long for friendship, their classmates may be able to keep them off-task just by having their attention. In that case, the other students will have to be included in some way in the behavioral management program.

4. **Reinforce the positive behavior every time it occurs**—After the behavioral management program is introduced to the student with AS, there must be consistency about presenting the reinforcers. If there is no consistency, the behavior is not likely to change. The reinforcer must be presented every time the behavior occurs until it stabilizes. Subsequently, the reinforcement can be withdrawn slowly. For example, when working with the time-on-task behavior, the period could be broken into small intervals and the student's time-on-task could be reinforced if it is occurring at the end of each time interval. Once the student is meeting the goal (measured against the baseline percentage), the number of reinforcers could be reduced to being given every other time or every third time. Intermittent (unpredictable) reinforcement will maintain the positive behavior over time. However, if the target behavior begins to decrease, it will be evident that the reinforcer was withdrawn too soon, and it will be necessary to go back to an earlier level of reinforcement.

# Eliminating or Reducing Inappropriate Behaviors

Sometimes it is impossible or impractical to change behavior by changing the environment or using positive reinforcement. However, it is important to try those approaches first. There are some behaviors students exhibit at school that are inappropriate and that need to be reduced or eliminated in order for the student to be successful. Inappropriate behavior can be reduced or eliminated using consequences or extinction (withdrawing attention). Consequences should not be physically or emotionally harmful to the student with AS. Consequences should be used only if other approaches (e.g., changing the curriculum and the environment) have not worked. Nonaversive behavior management techniques used in a favorable environment can be very effective in reducing inappropriate behavior (Trehin, n.d.).

# Using Consequences to Reduce or Eliminate Inappropriate Behaviors

A consequence can be defined as the presentation of something the students with AS do not like or taking away something they do like. There is not one consequence that works for all students with AS. A consequence is defined by its effect on the behavior and is administered only after the behavior has occurred. Sidebar 7.3 lists five things to consider when using consequences to reduce or eliminate negative behavior. Each item is explained in the paragraphs that follow.

1. **The consequence should be something the student with AS does not like (e.g., staying after school, or being removed from the classroom)**—As with positive reinforcers, the consequences are determined by the effect they have on the behavior. If the behavior occurs less often after the consequence has been administered, you will know the consequence is effective. If the behavior continues at the same rate as before the consequence, you will know you must find a different consequence. Keep in mind, though, that a consequence must be given for some time before it can be determined whether it works. Do not give up on the consequence too quickly (e.g., a few days) as it might take a while for the student to understand the cause and effect of what is happening.

2. **The consequence should be administered in a neutral way, not in anger**—A simple statement or action is all you need. Say to John, "You just lost a point for talking out of

---

**Sidebar 7.3**   **Things to Consider When Using a Consequence**

The consequence should:

1. Be something the student with AS does not like
2. Be administered in a neutral way, not in anger
3. Be administered as soon as the behavior has occurred
4. Take away something the student with AS does not want to lose
5. Be appropriate for the offense

*Source:* Mather & Goldstein (2001)

175

turn," or you can simply remove the point if John knows that you are doing it and why he is losing it. It should not be presented with a lecture or with moralizing. It will be more effective if it is presented in a neutral manner with little or no discussion.

3. **The consequence should be administered as soon as the behavior has occurred**—This is particularly important with younger students. Be sure the students know why they are receiving the consequence. If it is administered some time after the behavior occurs, a positive intervening behavior may have occurred, and the students might be confused about why they are receiving the consequence.

4. **The consequence should take away something the student with AS does not want to lose**—Make sure students with AS always have something to lose. In a point system or token economy, if the students have lost all their points, they may continue to exhibit negative behavior because they have nothing left to lose.

5. **The consequence should be appropriate for the offense**—Use small consequences for small offenses and bigger consequences for bigger offenses (e.g., use a verbal warning for talking out of turn; use detention for skipping school).

## Using Extinction to Reduce or Eliminate Inappropriate Behaviors

All behavior—negative and positive—is maintained by positive reinforcement. So it follows that a behavior of students with AS would be reduced or eliminated if the positive reinforcement was withdrawn. Extinction is the process of withdrawing positive reinforcement from the inappropriate behavior. Extinction has the best results in eliminating or reducing unwanted behavior, but it is the most difficult to administer.

1. Identify the behavior to be eliminated or reduced.

2. Do a functional behavior assessment (FBA). Observations of the behavior will need to be carefully done. (See functional behavioral assessment on pages 43–45, 168–171.)

3. Analyze the data from the FBA to determine what is prompting or maintaining the inappropriate behavior.

The following is an example of a student with AS, who talks out loud, and the extinction strategy his teacher used to eliminate this behavior:

Bob talks out loud when he is working at his desk. The educator wants to eliminate the talking out loud because it disturbs other students. The FBA indicates that the students around him are annoyed by this behavior and tell him to stop it. Sometimes they call him names, tell him to "shut up," or make derogatory remarks. The observation shows that even though the behavior of the other students is unkind and disrespectful, Bob likes the attention. He will glance at the students when they respond, and sometimes he will exhibit a half grin. In most other cases, the other students just ignore him.

The hypothesis is that Bob is talking out loud when he does his work because he gets attention from the other students. If that is true, it means that if you remove the reinforcer from his behavior—getting the students around him to stop responding to his talking out loud—he will stop talking out loud when he does his work.

There are a couple of ways to test the hypothesis: (1) Bob could either be isolated (put in a different place when he is doing his work) so he does not get the reinforcement (attention from peers), or (2) his peers could be asked to stop responding to him when he talks out loud. Always try the easiest intervention first—isolate Bob when he is doing his work.

If he is angry or does not want to be isolated, and the talking out loud does not stop, try working with the other students. Reinforce them for not responding to Bob, or move them to a different location. If other students willingly move to another location, Bob will be isolated, and you will avoid a potential power struggle with Bob, and—through extinction—you will remove the positive reinforcer for Bob's behavior.

There are several things Bob's teacher should consider when using extinction:

1. The reinforcer has to be controllable. If Bob's peers will not ignore him, even with positive reinforcement, then the program will not work.

2. The reinforcer needs to be eliminated every time the negative behavior occurs. If Bob gets reinforced by his peers some of the time, Bob's negative behavior will get stronger, because he will try harder to get the attention that he wants.

3. If the program is working, the behavior will get worse before it gets better. This could be compared to getting food out of a vending machine: It is expected that every time someone puts money into a vending machine, the treat will be forthcoming. If the treat is not delivered, one might put more money in. After putting money in three or four times and not getting results, one might become aggressive and pound on or kick the machine. Bob will feel the same way when he does not get the attention he is used to getting. His behavior will escalate to try to get it.

4. This is where carrying out an extinction program really gets sticky. The program will succeed only if the reinforcer is kept from the students even after the behavior escalates. Eventually, students will give up the behavior if the reinforcement does not occur. If one gives in to the escalating behavior, it will be strengthened at a more intense level and Bob's behavior will get even worse.

5. The extinction program should not be started if you are not prepared to "go the distance." The worst behavior must be anticipated before the program is started and you must be

determined to see it through, even in the worst-case scenario. If this commitment cannot be made, an extinction program should not be started.

## Using Response Cost to Reduce or Eliminate Negative Behavior

Response cost involves taking something of value away from students. For example, Susan, a student with AS, earns points throughout the day for finishing her assignments. When she gets enough points, she gets to choose an item from a reinforcement menu. Susan loves to earn points and get rewards. If she loses points, she feels very bad. Taking points away from Susan would be an example of response cost.

Things to consider when you are using response cost:

1. Be sure that the students with AS value what will be taken away.

2. Be sure that the students with AS do not lose everything at any time. If they do, they will have nothing to lose and there will be no reason for them to stop exhibiting the undesirable behavior.

3. Taking things away from students with AS can make them feel bad. Some will not be able to emotionally handle losing something they really care about, so response cost could make matters worse.

4. When something is taken away, you must be neutral and clear about what is happening and why. An educator might say, "Susan, you are losing 10 points because you talked out of turn." Lectures are not necessary. A simple statement about why she's losing the points will do.

Using behavior modification with students with AS to increase positive behavior and to decrease or eliminate negative behavior will work if you follow the suggestions delineated in this chapter. Students with AS like to have an orderly, predictable, and dependable world. Using behavior modification can help create that world for them so that they will be more successful in school.

# Case Study: Nathan

The last section provides an opportunity to apply the skills for intervention that have been addressed earlier in this chapter. The case study focuses on Nathan, a sixth-grade student with AS who has behavioral problems. Following the case study, there is a guide to help analyze Nathan's problem behaviors.

# Nathan: Behavior Management Issues

Nathan enters his sixth-grade classroom every day like he was shot out of a cannon. He runs into the room, hangs up his coat, and proceeds to run around the diameter of the room in the same pattern every day. Then he makes a trip to the restroom. Any deviation of this pattern can set him off.

Nathan is in a regular classroom, but his teacher is in the process of referring him to special education. He has recently been diagnosed as having Asperger Syndrome. It is not clear what the best placement for Nathan is. The school psychologist, the principal, Nathan's mother, and his teacher have talked together about how the school can best meet his needs in relation to his Asperger Syndrome. His behavior is too demanding to be in a regular classroom, but he doesn't qualify for Learning Disabilities (LD). He has a slightly above-average IQ, and has also been diagnosed with attention-deficit/hyperactivity disorder (ADHD), but refuses to take medication. He wouldn't fit well in the emotional disorders (ED) classroom, because it is filled with predominately tough boys. Nathan could easily become the class scapegoat. In the meantime, Nathan's teacher has been given an aide for four days a week to help with Nathan or the other children if Nathan is taking up the teacher's time.

Nathan has always been in regular education, but has only recently become a serious behavior problem. Previous teachers have put up with his routines and rigid behaviors. While he has always moved around the room a lot, he would not bother his peers and they pretty much left him alone. He has always had great difficulty with social skills, and he is clumsy. He has no friends, to speak of. One of the girls in his class, Sara, sometimes takes him under her wing and tries to take care of him. He seems to like Sara's attention, but doesn't very often respond to her overtures or suggestions.

His behavior has taken a turn for the worse in sixth grade. He has become boisterous in the classroom and is frequently aggressive toward other children. If they get in his way, he will yell at them and tell them in no uncertain terms to leave him alone. If any of his routines get interrupted, he gets very anxious, may cry, or may have an outburst. He has taken to biting himself or others if he gets angry.

Nathan has recently developed a keen interest in raptors. He uses the internet and the library to find information, and he devours everything he finds. He has become quite an expert. He likes nothing more than to get into a conversation about them (which quickly becomes a monologue). He also loves music. Sometimes when he is anxious, he will go to the back of the room and listen to music with headphones.

Because Nathan has become more aggressive, his peers don't put up with his eccentricities like they used to. They tease and harass him and try to pick fights with him. He usually takes the bait, gets into the fray, and comes out on the losing end.

He is lonely and depressed much of the time.

# Analysis

Answering the following analysis questions and doing the exercises will help you develop an understanding of a student with AS who has behavioral problems. You can write your own goals and develop your own intervention program before reading the samples at the end of the chapter.

1. What behaviors are keeping Nathan from being accepted by his peers?

2. What are the behaviors that have resulted in a referral to special education?

3. Which of his behaviors are you most concerned about?

4. In what categories of characteristics do his problems fit (e.g., social and communication skills, academic, psychomotor, behavioral)?

5. What kind of special education placement would you recommend for Nathan?

6. Prioritize the behaviors that need to be addressed, beginning with the ones you would work on first.

7. Develop long- and short-term IEP goals for Nathan.

8. Create an intervention program to help Nathan achieve the top three goals that you have identified. Use the intervention strategies that have been identified in this chapter.

# Example IEP Goals

1. Nathan will stop biting himself and others.
2. Nathan will make one new friend this semester.
3. Nathan will learn to ignore his peers when they harass him.

# Example Interventions to Achieve the IEP Goals

Before any interventions are planned, the educator in the classroom will do a functional behavioral assessment (FBA) to determine the antecedents and consequences of the behaviors that are targeted in Nathan's IEP goals. The intervention plan will be based on the results of the FBA.

**Goal #1:** Nathan will stop biting himself and others.

- Biting can be injurious to self and others, so this behavior should be reduced quickly with the ultimate goal to eliminate it.

- A consequence will be presented each time Nathan bites someone else. A consequence might be having a timeout in the classroom, going to the principal's office, or serving an in-school detention, or some other thing Nathan doesn't like. The consequence will be presented (1) every time the behavior occurs, (2) as soon as the behavior occurs, and (3) in a neutral way.

- A reward system will be put in place to reinforce Nathan for a period of time when he doesn't bite himself or another student. Every day (or every half day, hour, or whatever period of time works), reward Nathan for not biting. He will earn points, food, a trip to the library, time to listen to music, or whatever seems to help reduce the behavior.

**Goal #2:** Nathan will make one new friend this semester.

- Nathan's teacher and the SLP will develop a social skills program for Nathan and a few other students.

- Friend-making behavior will be divided into several categories (e.g., eye contact, initiating a conversation, being a good listener).

- Nathan will get reinforced for learning to do the behavior in each category.

- When Nathan completes the social skills program and has developed an in-school friend, the teacher will reinforce the whole social skills group. A group reward (such as a movie, a pizza party, popcorn, or a field trip) would be appropriate.

**Goal #3:** Nathan will learn to ignore his peers when they harass him.

- The teacher will talk to Nathan about what ignoring means and how the best way to get the other students to stop harassing him is to ignore them.

- Every time Nathan ignores being harassed, he will immediately get a reinforcer that not only he likes, but that the other students might like too. The harassers will see that Nathan is being rewarded for ignoring their behavior. Nathan will need a lot of support for ignoring his peers because he probably likes the attention even though it is negative. Diverting him to some other activity would help.

- At the same time, the teacher should consider rewarding the students for not harassing Nathan. This is a controversial idea, but if it works, it would be worth the effort. Some educators say that other students will start acting up so they can get a reward to stop the negative behavior. The teacher needs to be firm about every student having different needs, and talk about this openly with students.

# Discussion Points

1. Are regular education teachers prepared to deal with students who have the kinds of behavior problems Nathan has? Why or why not?

2. What responsibilities do regular and special educators have for students like Nathan?

3. Some critics say that giving students reinforcements for appropriate behaviors is plain and simple bribery. Do you agree? Why or why not?

4. How can educators help students without disabilities be more understanding and supportive of students with disabilities?

5. Are classroom teachers equipped to do an FBA and behavioral modification programs? Do you believe behavioral modification programs can change behavior? Discuss your beliefs.

6. The numbers of students being diagnosed with AS are growing at a rapid rate. Are schools equipped to address the needs of these students? If yes, explain. If no, what should be done to help teachers be better prepared?

# Glossary

ABSTRACT LANGUAGE. Language that is ambiguous; may have multiple meanings or the referent may not be present.

ANXIETY DISORDER. A disorder in which the person is overly apprehensive, uneasy, fearful, etc. for no apparent reason.

ASPERGER SYNDROME (AS). A neurologically based disorder that to be diagnosed in the United States, must meet the criteria put forward by the American Psychiatric Association in the *DSM–IV–TR* (2000).

ASSESSMENT. A dynamic ongoing process that uses both formal tests and informal procedures; a process to determine the existence, type, nature, and severity of the problem. Once it is determined that a problem exists, the purpose of assessment is to select a service delivery model and to design a program (e.g., write an individualized education program) that best meets the needs of the individual.

ATTENTION-DEFICIT/HYPERACTIVITY DISORDER (AD/HD) A neurologically based disorder characterized by deficits in attention and/or hyperactivity/impulsivity. Under the criteria listed in the *DSM-IV-TR* (2000), there are three subtypes: (1) attention-deficit/hyperactivity disorder, combined type; (2) attention-deficit/hyperactivity disorder, predominantly hyperactive-inattentive type; (3) attention-deficit/hyperactive-impulsive type.

AUTISM. A neurological disorder that usually appears in the first three years of life and has characteristics such as those listed on the checklist from the Autism Society of America

AUTISM SPECTRUM DISORDERS (ASD). Suggests that there is a range of related qualities that overlap but are clinically distinct and separately diagnosed. Core characteristics differ in how they are manifested in terms of number and severity of the characteristics.

**BEHAVIOR MANAGEMENT.** Using antecedent or consequent events to either increase and maintain positive behavior and/or reduce and eliminate negative behavior.

**BEHAVIORAL OBJECTIVE.** A statement that provides instructional information about what the learner is to do, under what conditions the learner will do the behavior, and the criterion for success.

**BENCHMARK.** A measurable statement of a student's intermediate performance on reaching an annual goal, usually measured as a function of time in which the student will attain mastery and stated on an individualized education program (IEP).

**CHECKLISTS.** Tools used to determine a person's strengths and challenges as they pertain to a certain area of development or overall functioning.

**CLASS MEETING ROUTINES.** An intervention approach that establishes certain routines that are used at the beginning, middle, or end of intervention sessions to provide consistency.

**CLASSROOM STRUCTURE AND ROUTINES.** The daily structure and routine that a teacher uses to keep students on task and working productively.

**COGNITIVE ABILITIES.** Knowing, thinking, learning, and judging. Includes such areas as attention and memory, conceptual thinking, problem solving, verbal and nonverbal reasoning, and acquired knowledge.

**COGNITIVE STRATEGY.** A strategy or group of strategies used to perform an academic or social skills task such as visualization, verbalization, making associations, chunking, questioning, scanning, underlining, accessing cues, using mnemonics, sounding out words, and self-checking and monitoring.

**CONCRETE LANGUAGE.** Language that has a specific referent and conveys an object or event that is in the here or now or is tangible.

**CONTINUUM OF SERVICE DELIVERY.** A broad range of services available for students who have been diagnosed with a disability and in need of special programming.

**CONVERSATIONS.** A dialogue between two or more people that is rule-governed in which one person initiates a topic, maintains it until a topic shift is initiated and ultimately a topic is terminated. Also, the conversational partner or listener engages in such behaviors as maintaining eye contact, head nodding, etc. The two conversational partners take turns, use appropriate topic shifts, and attempt to mutually understand how to engage in the topic at hand.

**COUNSELING.** A process that allows individuals to gain insights about situations and/or themselves thus being more effective in handling problems, issues or challenges.

**CUING STRATEGY.** Either a visual or verbal prompt that reminds the student to learn something or reminds the student what he or she has already learned (e.g., an educator may say "manners" to remind the student to give a compliment to a peer).

**DIFFERENTIAL DIAGNOSIS.** A process whereby the examiner, using a variety of formal and informal tests and working with the student, determines what is the most appropriate diagnosis by noting what the diagnosis is or is not.

**DIRECTED TASKS.** Informal procedures designed to assess a specific skill. The focus is on the process that the student goes through to complete the task and not on the product that the student generates. Directed task assessment is another name for dynamic assessment in that the focus is on determining how the student is learning and on identifying some teaching or scaffolding that helps the student learn the task at hand.

**DUAL DIAGNOSIS.** A determination that the person has more than one disability (e.g., Asperger Syndrome and attention-deficit/hyperactivity disorder).

**EXECUTIVE FUNCTIONS.** The ability to plan, organize, shift attention, to do multitasking successfully, inhibit inappropriate responses, use feedback, and suppress distracting stimuli. It is "the ability to maintain an appropriate problem-solving set for attainment of a future goal" (Luria, 1966, p. 27). "It refers to many skills required to prepare for and execute complex behavior, including planning, inhibition, mental flexibility, and mental representations of tasks and goals" (Ozonoff & Griffith, 2000, p. 86).

**EXPOSITORY TEXT.** Discourse that conveys sequenced or categorized factual or technical information; occurs with a higher frequency in school after third or fourth grade; includes seven types of text: (1) descriptions, (2) enumerations, (3) sequential/procedural text, (4) comparisons and contrasts, (5) problem-solving text, (6) persuasive text, and (7) cause-and-effect descriptions.

**EXTINCTION.** The process of eliminating a behavior, usually by withdrawing positive reinforcement.

**FORMAL/STANDARDIZED TESTS.** A type of test that is (1) norm-referenced (in which large numbers of children were sampled on a given item and the scores are used to compare students), and (2) criterion-referenced (in which a predetermined criterion has been established and in which most children are successful, thus, a criterion is established).

**FRAGILE X.** A condition in which the bottom of the 23rd pair of the X chromosome is pinched off resulting in a number of physical abnormalities such as a large head, large flat ears, narrow face, prominent forehead, etc. as well as cognitive disabilities.

**FUNCTIONAL BEHAVIORAL ASSESSMENT.** An assessment of behavior to determine the factors that account for a student's misconduct in school (Hallahan & Kauffman, 2003); examines behavior maintained by antecedents (events that happen before the behavior is exhibited), consequences (events that happen after the behavior), or setting events (the context in which the behavior occurs).

**GRAPHIC ORGANIZER.** Visual maps that organize content material and focus on developing an awareness of concepts to make it easier for students to understand academic material. Graphic organizers present abstract information in a concrete way.

**GUSTATORY.** The sense of taste.

**HEARING IMPAIRMENT.** An inability to hear because of damage to the structure of the hearing mechanism or to the auditory nerve resulting in air conduction or sensori-neural hearing losses.

**HIDDEN CURRICULUM.** The rules of the classroom and the routines that are part of the school day that are not taught explicitly but that students are expected and assumed to know (Myles & Adreon, 2001; Paul & Sutherland, 2003).

**IDEA 2004.** The federal law that provides for education of students with disabilities; provisions are made for students whose behavior impedes their learning or that of others.

**INDIVIDUALIZED EDUCATION PROGRAM (IEP).** A written statement describing the special education program and placement of each child with a disability that is developed, reviewed, and revised in a meeting in accordance with 34 Code of Federal Regulations (C.F.R.) SS 300.341-300.350.

**INFORMAL PROCEDURES.** Evaluation procedures that include but are not limited to: interviews; questionnaires; checklists; observations at school, home, and community; profiles; oral and written language samples; rubrics; portfolios; directed tasks; and functional behavioral analysis.

**INTERVENTION.** A program that provides a student with methods, procedures, and materials that allow the person to grow, develop, and overcome his or her challenges.

**INTERVIEWS.** A face-to-face interaction between two or more people (usually an interviewer and the interviewee) where responses to specific questions or statement are recorded; can be either structured (questions and comments are predetermined and there is more control over the interview session by the interviewee) or unstructured (questions and statements are not predetermined and open-ended discussion is pursued).

**LEARNING DISABILITY.** A disability in which the person has average or above-average intelligence but has a discrepancy between his or her ability and achievement.

**LEARNING STRATEGY.** A set of steps needed to accomplish a particular task (such as taking a test, writing a story, giving an oral presentation, or listening to a lecture).

**LEARNING STYLE.** Information describing how, what, where, and when an individual learns best.

**META-ABILITY.** The ability to know that we know. Meta-abilities can be categorized into the abilities of metalinguistics (talk about talking); metacognitive (thinking about thinking);

metapragmatics (being aware of cultural rules for using language appropriately within and across various social context); and metanarrative (being aware of story elements and how to intentionally manipulate them).

METACOGNITIVE STRATEGY. The students' understanding of how well they understand their own learning process. This would include how to use strategies to accomplish tasks and the process by which the learner oversees, monitors, and even critiques his or her use of strategies (also referred to as self-regulation).

MODELING. An instructional method that provides an example for what the child should imitate.

MOTOR SKILLS. Skills that consist of fine motor skills, as needed for holding and using a pen or pencil, to gross motor skills, such as walking and running.

NARRATIONS. Real or imaginary time-ordered descriptions of sequences of events that are interrelated in some way and can be analyzed using a story grammar approach or via a developmental sequence.

NEUROTYPICAL. A typical neurological system that results in typical cognitive, academic, social, sensory-motor, language/communication, and development (Attwood, 2002).

NONVERBAL COMMUNICATION. The ability to communicate using gestures, body language, facial expressions, intonation, and stress to supplement or supplant oral communication.

OBSESSIVE COMPULSIVE DISORDER (OCD). A neurologically based psychiatric disorder that is characterized by obsessions and compulsions that interfere with the person's daily life socially, academically, and/or vocationally.

OLFACTORY. The sense of smell which determines if odors and fragrances have a pleasant or unpleasant smell.

OPPOSITIONAL DEFIANT DISORDER (ODD). A disorder characterized by recurrent defiance, disobedience, and hostility over a period of time, usually for at least six-months. According to McAffee (2002), at least four of the following eight behaviors must be present and reoccurring for the diagnosis to be made: (1) losing your temper; (2) arguing frequently with adults; (3) defying or refusing to comply with requests or rules of adults; (4) deliberately doing things to annoy others; (5) blaming others for one's mistakes; (6) being easily annoyed; (7) being angry or resentful; or (8) being spiteful or vindictive. These behaviors occur more frequently than is typical for the person's age; and interfere with his or her personal-social, academic, or vocational potential.

PEDANTIC. A term used to refer to using speech and language in a very stilted, rigid, inflexible manner and more like a monologue than a dialogue.

**PERVASIVE DEVELOPMENTAL DISORDERS** (PDD). Describes a broad classification of disorders: autistic disorder, Asperger's disorder, childhood disintegration disorder (CDD), Rett's Disorder, and PDD-Not otherwise Specified (PDD-NOS).

**PORTFOLIO.** A purposeful collection of student work that exhibits the student's efforts, progress, and achievements in one or more areas. The collection must include student participation in selecting contents, the criteria for selection, the criteria for judging merit, and evidence of the student self-reflection (Paulson, Paulson, & Meyer, 1991).

**PRAGMATICS.** The ability of the person to use language in various contexts and within and across various social situations to accomplish goals or intentions.

**PREVALENCE.** The percentage of a population that is affected with a disability at a given point in time.

**PROMPT.** An instructional method that provides a verbal or visual instruction that tells an individual what to do (e.g., say, "Please").

**PROPRIOCEPTION.** Awareness of one's body in space; awareness that allows people to walk through a room without bumping into desks and tables and other people, to sit down in a chair without looking back, to keep balanced when walking or running; body awareness.

**PUNISHMENT.** A consequence that decreases the likelihood of a behavior to occur.

**QUESTIONNAIRES.** Assessment tools that are generated to ask an interviewee a series of questions about a given topic or topics to ascertain the overall strengths and challenges facing the person.

**READING.** A system of decoding (i.e., a word recognition process that transforms print to words) and a comprehension process by which words, sentences, and discourse are interpreted through the written code (Catts & Kamhi, 1999).

**REFERENTIAL COMMUNICATION.** The communication act of "informing;" requires production and understanding of messages (Schwartz & McKinley, 1987).

**REINFORCEMENT.** A consequence that increases the likelihood of a behavior to occur.

**RESPONSE COST.** Involves taking something valued away from the student.

**ROLE-PLAYING.** An activity in which students are given character roles to act out, to learn how one might perform or participate in a situation before actually being put into that situation. Role-playing simulates the real-life situation but allows the educator to vary the complexity of the task based on learner needs and abilities.

**RUBRICS.** Scoring guides which measure increasing levels of difficulty on selected tasks, typically presented in a 4" × 4" grid and resulting in qualitative measures of performance.

**SCAFFOLDING.** Use of supports to assist a student in ultimately moving from dependence to independence in a particular skill area; support is removed after a student is able to perform the task. Scaffolding procedures include providing verbal, nonverbal, visual, auditory, and tactile stimuli (Wiig, Larson, & Olson, 2004).

**SEMANTIC-PRAGMATIC DISORDER.** A disorder in which the person has difficulty with understanding the meaning of the language and the use of the language in social situations.

**SENSORY INTEGRATION** (SI). The process by which incoming sensations are interpreted, connected, and organized; these characteristics are necessary for the child to feel safe and comfortable in the environment and to function effectively within the environment (Ozonoff, Dawson, & McPartland, 2002).

**SOCIAL AUTOPSY.** An intervention approach designed to get students to objectively analyze their social mistakes; used when a social situation does not go well; breaks the social situation down using a constructive and supportive problem-solving strategy to determine what when wrong and how to do it differently in the future.

**SOCIAL COMMUNICATION.** The ability to know what to say, who to say it to, where, when, why, and how to say it across and within a variety of social situations; the ability to select the appropriate syntax and semantics and then use it appropriately within social situations. To use communication appropriately within social situations one needs to know about the speaker, the listener, the social and physical setting, as well as the social and cultural norms that apply within a given situation.

**SOCIAL COMPETENCE.** The ability to accommodate or adapt to ongoing social situations. Social interactions demand moment-to-moment integration of multiple contextual cues, language, social and emotional cues, and demand that the person adjust and read social cues within the situation on a continual basis and adjust one's own behaviors within milliseconds of the behaviors occurring.

**SOCIAL SKILLS.** Skills that allow students to develop positive relationships, cope with the demands of various settings, and communicate one's desires, needs, and preferences effectively. Gajewski, Hirn, and Mayo (1998a, 1998b) noted a number of social skills, that need to be taught directly to people lacking social competence, that typical students appear to learn incidentally. Some of these skills are using manners, offering and asking for help, controlling anger, giving and receiving compliments, accepting no, and making an apology, to name only a few.

**SOCIAL STORIES.** An intervention strategy that describes a social situation in terms of relevant social cues and common responses, thus giving the student specific information about what happens in various social situations and why. A series of steps should be followed when developing social stories: (1) identify the problem in the social situation; (2) visualize the goal or outcome; and (3) write a short story about the social situation using descriptive sentences, perspective sentences, directive sentences, and affirmative or control sentences.

**STRATEGY-BASED INTERVENTION.** Refers to the fact that a strategy is a tool, plan, or method for accomplishing a given task (Beckman, 2002). According to Beckman, a variety of strategies comprise a strategy-based approach to instruction; including: cognitive, cuing, learning, and metacognitive strategies.

TACTILE HYPERSENSITIVITY. Having a strong sensitivity to touch (e.g., an aversion to having hair washed, wearing particular fabrics such as wool or linen, standing too close to others for fear of being touched, touching substances like glue or play dough).

TACTILE HYPOSENSITIVITY. Having a lack of sensation or response to touch (e.g., a pat on the back or a light touch on the arm).

THEORY OF MIND. "The ability to think about other people's thinking and further, to think about what they think about our thinking and, even further to think about what they think we think about their thinking and so on" Cumine, Leach, and Stevenson (2001, p. 19).

TOURETTE SYNDROME. A neurological disorder (usually three times more prevalent in boys than girls) in which repetitive motor movements, such as facial tics, are accompanied by vocal outbursts, such as grunts or socially inappropriate words or sentences that cannot be controlled by the individual.

TRANSITION. The movement of a student from one level to another, especially the movement from preschool to elementary school or from high school to postschool.

VESTIBULAR HYPERSENSITIVITY. Having a low tolerance and balance for activities that involve movement.

VESTIBULAR HYPOSENSITIVITY. Having a high tolerance for activities that involve movement. People with vestibular hyposensitivity are in constant motion in order to get the stimulation externally that they are not getting internally.

VISUAL IMPAIRMENT. An inability to see because of damage to the eye or the visual nerve.

WRITING. A system of using graphemes to communicate to a reader the message conveyed.

WRITTEN COMMUNICATION. The communication system that requires decoding graphemes to convey messages to a reader or using graphemes by a writer to convey a message.

# References

Alley, G., & Deshler, D. (1979). *Teaching the learning disabled adolescent: Strategies and methods.* Denver, CO: Love Publishing.

American Psychiatric Association. (2000). *Diagnostic and statistical manual of mental disorders* (4th ed., text revision). Washington, DC: Author.

Americans with Disabilities Act (ADA), 42 U.S.C. § 12101 *et seq.* (1990).

Anderson-Wood, L., & Smith, B. R. (1997). *Working with pragmatics.* Bicester, Oxfordshire, UK: Winslow Press.

Asher, S. R., Parker, J. G., & Walker, D. (1996). Distinguishing friendship from acceptance: Implications for intervention and assessment. In W. M. Bukowski, A. F. Newcomb, and W. W. Hartup (Eds.), *The company they keep: Friendships in childhood and adolescence* (pp. 366–405). New York: Cambridge University Press.

Asperger, H. (1944). Die "autistischen psychopathen" im kindesalter, archiv fur psychiatrie und nervenkrankheiten (U. Frith, Trans.). *[Autism and Asperger syndrome]* (pp. 117, 76–136). Cambridge, MA: Cambridge University Press.

Attwood, A. J. (2000). Strategies for improving the social integration of children with asperger syndrome. *Autism: The International Journal of Research and Practice, 4*(1), 85–100.

Attwood, A. J. (2001). *Asperger's syndrome: A guide for parents and professionals.* London, UK: Jessica Kingsley Publishers.

Attwood, A. J. (2002, July). *Navigating the social world.* Paper presented at the annual conference of the Autism Society of America, Indianapolis, IN.

Attwood, A. J. (2003). Social skills programs to teach friendship skills for children with Asperger syndrome. *Perspectives on Language Learning and Education, 10*(4), 16–19.

Autism Society of America. (2003, July 15). Tips to ensuring a successful positive behavior plan. ASA-Net [E-newsletter].

Ayres, A. J. (1979). *Sensory integration and the child.* Los Angeles: Western Psychological Services.

Beckman, P. (2002). *Strategy instruction.* (ERIC Report No. E638). Retrieved March 3, 2003, from the Council for Exceptional Children's Information Center on Disabilities and Gifted Education: http://www.ericec.org/digests/e638.html

# Asperger Syndrome

Benjamin, A. (2000). *An English teacher's guide to performance tasks and rubrics: High school.* Larchmont, NY: Eye on Education.

Bernstein, D., & Polirstok, S. (Eds.). (2003). *Topics in Language Disorders, 23*(2), 72–74.

Bishop, D. V. M. (1998). Development of the Children's Communication Checklist (CCC): A method for assessing qualitative aspects of communicative impairment in children. *Journal of Child Psychology and Psychiatry, 39,* 879–891.

Bowers, L., Huisingh, R., Barrett, M., Orman, J., & LoGiudice, C. (1994). *The Test of Problem Solving–Elementary, Revised.* East Moline, IL: LinguiSystems.

Bukowski, W. M., & Hoza, B. (1989). Popularity and friendship: Issues in theory, measurement, and outcome. In T. J. Berndt & G. W. Ladd (Eds.), *Peer relationships in child development* (pp. 15–45). New York: Wiley.

Carrow-Woolfolk, E. (1998). *Comprehensive Assessment of Spoken Language (CASL).* Circle Pines, MN: American Guidance Service.

Catts, H., & Kamhi, A. (1999). *Language and reading disabilities.* Needham Heights, MA: Allyn and Bacon.

Church, C., Alisanski, S., & Amanullah, S. (2000). The social, behavioral, and academic experiences of children with Asperger syndrome. *Focus on Autism and Other Developmental Disabilities, 15*(1), 12–21.

Connor, M. (1999). Children on the autistic spectrum: Guidelines for mainstream practice. *Support for Learning, 14*(2), 80–86.

Cowley, G. (2003, September 8). Girls, boys and autism. *Newsweek, CXLII,* 42–50.

Cumine, V., Leach, J., & Stevenson, G. (2001). *Asperger syndrome: A practical guide for teachers.* London, UK: David Fulton Publishers.

Cyr, B. (n.d.). *Applied behavior analysis: A review of the history, theories, methods and techniques.* Retrieved May 30, 2002, from http://www.umm.maine.edu/BEX/students/BarbaraCyr/bcyr450/ent.html

Dewey, M. (1991). Living with Asperger's syndrome. In U. Frith (Ed.), *Autism and Asperger syndrome* (pp. 184–206). Cambridge, England: Cambridge University Press.

Drasgow, E., & Bradley, R. (1999). The IDEA Amendments of 1997: A school-wide model for conducting functional behavioral assessment and developing behavior intervention plans. *Education and Treatment of Children, 22*(3), 244–267.

Dunn, L. M., & Dunn, L. M. (1997). *Peabody Picture Vocabulary Test–III (PPVT–III).* Circle Pines, MN: American Guidance Service.

Dunn, W. (1999). *The Sensory Profile: A Contextual measure of children's responses to sensory experiences in daily life.* San Antonio, TX: The Psychological Corporation.

Education for All Handicapped Children Act (EAHCA), 20 U. S. C. § 1400 *et seq.* (1975).

Ehlers, S., & Gillberg, C. (1993). The epidemiology of Asperger's syndrome—A total population study. *Journal of Child Psychology and Psychiatry, 4,* 1327–1350.

Fling, E. R. (2000). *Eating an artichoke: A mother's perspective on Asperger syndrome.* London, UK: Jessica Kingsley Publishers.

Fridlund, A. J. (1994). *Human facial expression: An evolutionary view.* San Diego, CA: Academic Press.

Frith, U. (1996). Social communication and its disorder in autism and Asperger syndrome. *Journal of Psychopharmacology, 10*(1), 48–53.

Gajewski, N., Hirn, P., & Mayo, P. (1993). *Social star: General interaction skills (Book 1).* Greenville, SC: Super Duper Publications.

Gajewski, N., Hirn, P., & Mayo, P. (1994). *Social star: Peer interaction skills (Book 2).* Greenville, SC: Super Duper Publications.

Gajewski, N., Hirn, P., & Mayo, P. (1996). *Social star: Conflict resolution and community interaction skills (Book 3).* Greenville, SC: Super Duper Publications.

Gajewski, N., Hirn, P., & Mayo, P. (1998a). *Social skill strategies: A social-emotional curriculum for adolescents: Book B* (2nd ed.). Greenville, SC: Super Duper Publications.

Gajewski, N., Hirn, P., & Mayo, P. (1998b). *Social skill strategies: A social-emotional curriculum for adolescents: Book A* (2nd ed.). Greenville, SC: Super Duper Publications.

Garnett, K. (1986). Telling tales: Narratives and learning-disabled children. *Topics in Language Disorders, 6*(2), 44–56.

Garnett, M. S., & Attwood, A. J. (1995). *The Australian Scale for Asperger's Syndrome.* Paper presented at the annual Australian Autism Conference, Brisbane, Australia.

Gartner, A., & Lipsky, D. K. (2002). *Inclusion: A service, not a place. A whole school approach.* Port Chester, NY: Dude Publishing.

Gerland. G. (2001). *Find out about Asperger syndrome, high functioning autism and PDD.* London, UK: Jessica Kingsley Publishers.

Ghaziuddin, M., Tsai, L. Y., & Ghaziuddin, N. (1992). A reappraisal of clumsiness as a diagnostic feature of Asperger syndrome. *Journal of Autism and Developmental Disorders, 22,* 651–656.

Gillberg, C. (1989). Asperger syndrome in 23 Swedish children: A clinical study. *Developmental Medicine and Child Neurology, 31,* 520–531.

Gillberg, C. (1991). Clinical and neurobiological aspects of Asperger syndrome in six family studies. In U. Frith (Ed.), *Autism and Asperger syndrome* (pp. 122–146). Cambridge, MA: Cambridge University Press.

Gillberg, C., & Ehlers, S. (1998). High-functioning people with autism and Asperger syndrome. In E. Schopler, G. Mesibov, & L. Kunce (Eds.), *Asperger's syndrome or high functioning autism?* (pp. 79–106). New York: Plenum Press.

Gillberg, I. C., & Gillberg, C. (1989). Asperger syndrome—Some epidemiological considerations: A research note. *Journal of Child Psychology and Psychiatry, 30,* 631–638.

Gilliam, J. (2001). *Gilliam Asperger's Disorder Scale.* Austin, TX: Pro-Ed.

Goldstein, H., & Morgan, L. (2002). Social interaction and models of friendship development. In H. Goldstein, L. A. Kaczmarek, & K. M. English (Eds.), *Promoting social communication: Children with developmental disabilities from birth to adolescence* (pp. 5–25). Baltimore: Brookes.

Gorman-Gard, K. (1992). *Figurative language: A comprehensive program.* Greenville, SC: Super Duper Publications.

Grandin, T. (1995). *Thinking in pictures and other reports from my life with autism.* New York: Doubleday.

Grandin, T. (2001). *Teaching tips for children and adults with autism.* Retrieved May 23, 2002, from the Center for the Study of Autism: http://www.autism.org/temple/tips.html

Gray, C. (1994). *Comic strip conversations: Colorful, illustrated interactions with students with autism and related disorders.* Jenison, MI: Jenison Public Schools.

Gray, C. (1995). Teaching children with autism to "read" social situations. In K. Quill (Ed.), *Teaching children with autism: Strategies to enhance communication and socialization* (pp. 219–242). New York: Delmar.

Gray, C. (1998). Social stories and comic strip conversations with students with Asperger syndrome and high-functioning autism. In E. Schopler, G. Mesibov, & L. Kunce (Eds.), *Asperger syndrome or high-functioning autism* (pp. 67–168). New York: Plenum Press.

Green, G. (2001). Behavior analytic instruction for learners with autism: Advances in stimulus control technology. *Focus on Autism and Other Developmental Disabilities, 16*(2), 72–86.

Gruenewald, L., & Pollack, S. (1984). *Language interaction in teaching and learning.* Baltimore: University Park Press.

Haas, D. (1993). Inclusion is happening in the classroom. *Children Today, 22*(3), 34–36.

Hagiwara, T., & Myles, B. S. (1999). A multimedia social story intervention: Teaching skills to children with autism. *Focus on Autism and Other Developmental Disabilities, 14*(2), 82–96.

Hallahan, D., & Kauffman, J. (2003). *Exceptional learners: Introduction to special education* (9th ed.). Boston: Allyn and Bacon.

Hamersky, J. (1995). *Cartoon cut-ups: Teaching figurative language and humor.* Greenville, SC: Super Duper Publications.

Harris, K. R., & Graham, S. (1996). *Making the writing process work: Strategies for composition and self-regulation.* Cambridge, MA: Brookline Books.

Heflin, J. L., & Alberto, P. A. (2001). ABA and instruction of students with autism spectrum disorders: Introduction to the special series. *Focus on Autism and Other Developmental Disabilities, 16*(2), 66–68.

Hewetson, A. (2002). *The stolen child: Aspects of autism and Asperger syndrome.* Westport, CT: Bergin and Garvey.

Hodges, E. V., Boivin, M., Vitaro, F., & Bukowski, W. M. (1999). The power of friendship: Protection against an escalating cycle of peer victimization. *Developmental Psychology, 35*, 94–101.

Hodges, E. V., Malone, M. J., & Perry, D. G. (1997). Individual risk and social risk as interacting determinants of victimization in the peer group. *Developmental Psychology, 33*, 1032–1039.

Hutson-Nechkash, P. (2001). *Narrative toolbox: Blueprints for storybuilding.* Greenville, SC: Super Duper Publications.

Individuals with Disabilities Education Act (IDEA), 20 U.S.C. § 1400 *et seq.* (1990).

Individuals with Disabilities Education Act (IDEA) Amendments, 20 U.S.C. § 1400 *et seq.* (1997).

Individuals with Disabilities Education Improvement Act of 2004 (IDEA), 20 U.S.C. § 1400 *et seq.* (2004).

Inspiration Software. (2005a). *Inspiration* [Computer software]. Portland, OR: Author.

Inspiration Software. (2005b). Kidspiration [Computer software]. Portland, OR: Author.

Jackel, S. (1996). *Asperger's syndrome: Educational management issues.* Retrieved May 23, 2002, from http://members.ozemail.com.au/~prussia/asperger/teach.htm

Kadesjo, B., Gillberg, C., & Hagberg, B. (1999). Brief report. Autism and Asperger syndrome in seven year old children: A total population study. *Journal of Autism and Development Disorders, 29*, 327–332.

Kanner, L. (1943). Autistic disturbance of affective contact. *Nervous Child, 2*, 217–250.

Kirk, S., Gallagher, J., & Anastasiow, N. (2000). *Educating exceptional children* (9th ed.). Boston, MA: Houghton Mifflin.

Klin, A., Volkmar, F., Sparrow, S., Cicchette, D. V., & Rourke, B. (1995). Validity and neuropsychological characterization of Asperger syndrome. *Journal of Child Psychology and Psychiatry, 36,* 1127–1140.

Klin, A., & Volkmar, F. (2000). Treatment and intervention guidelines for individuals with Asperger syndrome. In A. Klin, F. Volkmar, & S. Sparrow (Eds.), *Asperger syndrome* (pp. 340–366). New York: The Guilford Press.

Kuttler, S., Myles, B. S., & Carlson, J. K. (1998). The use of social stories to reduce precursors to tantrum behavior in a student with autism. *Focus on Autism and Other Developmental Disabilities, 13,* 166–182.

Ladd, G. W., Kochenderfer, B. J., & Coleman, C. C. (1997). Classroom peer acceptance, friendship, and victimization: Distinct relational systems that contribute uniquely to children's social adjustment. *Child Development, 68,* 1181–1197.

Larson, V. Lord., & McKinley, N. (1987). *Communication assessment and intervention strategies for adolescents.* Eau Claire, WI: Thinking Publications.

Larson, V. Lord., & McKinley, N. (1995). *Language disorders in older students: Preadolescents and adolescents.* Eau Claire, WI: Thinking Publications.

Larson, V. Lord., & McKinley, N. (2003). *Communication solutions for older students: Assessment and intervention strategies.* Greenville, SC: Thinking Publications University.

Leekam, S., Libby, S., Wing, L., Gould, J., & Gillberg, C. (2000). Comparison of ICD–10 and Gillberg's criteria for Asperger syndrome. *Autism: The International Journal of Research and Practice, 4*(1), 11–28.

Luria, A. R. (1996). *The higher cortical functions in man.* New York: Basic Books.

Madden, N., & Slavin, R. (1983). Mainstreaming students with mild handicaps: Academic and social outcomes. *Journal of Education Research, 53,* 519–569.

Manjiviona, J., & Prior, M. (1995). Comparison of Asperger's syndrome and high-functioning autistic children on a test of motor impairment. *Journal of Autism and Developmental Disorders, 25,* 23–39.

Manjiviona, J., & Prior, M. (1999). Neuropsychological profiles of children with Asperger syndrome and autism. *Autism; The International Journal of Research and Practice, 3*(4), 327–356.

Mather, N., & Goldstein, S. (2001). *Learning disabilities and challenging behaviors: A guide to intervention and classroom management.* Baltimore: Brookes.

Mayo, P., & Waldo, P. (1994). *Scripting: Social communication for adolescents* (2nd ed.). Greenville, SC: Super Duper Publications.

McAfee, J. (2002). *Navigating the social world.* Arlington, TX: Future Horizons.

McIntosh, D. N., Miller, L. J., Shyu, V., & Dunn, W. (1999). *The Short Sensory Profile.* San Antonio, TX: The Psychological Corporation.

Meltzoff, A. N., & Gopnick, A. (1993). The role of imitation in understanding persons and developing a theory of mind. In S. Baronn-Cohen, H. Tager-Flusberg, & D. J. Cohen (Eds.), *Understanding other minds: Perspectives from autism* (pp. 335–336). Oxford: Oxford University Press.

Michaels, C. (1994). *Transition strategies for persons with learning disabilities.* San Diego, CA: Singular Publishing.

Miller, L. (2004). *Scripting junior: Social skill role-plays.* Greenville, SC: Super Duper Publications.

Minskoff, E., & Allsopp, D. (2003). *Academic success strategies for adolescents with learning disabilities and ADHD.* Baltimore: Brookes.

Moore-Brown, B. J., & Montgomery, J. K. (2005). Making a difference in the era of accountability: Update on NCLB and IDEA 2004. Greenville, SC: Thinking Publications Univesity.

Moreno, S., & O'Neal, C. (n.d.). *Tips for teaching high functioning people with autism.* Retrieved May 23, 2002, from the Online Asperger Syndrome Information and Support website: http://www.udel.edu/bkirby/asperger/moreno_tips_for_teaching.html

Myles, B. S., & Adreon, D. (2001). *Asperger syndrome and adolescence: Practical solutions for school success.* Shawnee Mission, KS: Autism Asperger Publishing.

Myles, B. S., Bock, S. J., & Simpson, R. L. (2000). *Asperger Syndrome Diagnostic Scale (ASDS).* Austin, TX: Pro-Ed.

Myles, B. S., Cook, K., Miller, N., Rinner, L., & Robbins, L. (2000). *Asperger syndrome and sensory issues: Practical solutions for making sense of the world.* Shawnee Mission, KS: Autism Asperger Publishing.

Myles, B. S., & Southwick, J. (1999). *Asperger syndrome and difficult moments.* Shawnee Mission, KS: Autism Asperger Publishing.

National Joint Committee on Learning Disabilities. (1994). Position paper. *Topics in Language Disorders, 16*(3), 69–73.

National Research Council. (2001). *Educating children with autism.* Washington, DC: National Academy Press.

Newcomb, A. F., & Bagwell, C. L. (1996). The developmental significance of children's friendship relations. In W. M. Bukowski, A. F. Newcomb, and W. W. Hartup (Eds.), *The company they keep: Friendship in childhood and adolescence* (pp. 289–321). New York: Cambridge University Press.

No Child Left Behind Act of 2001, 20 U.S.C., § 6311 *et seq.* (2002).

Ozonoff, S., Dawson, G., & McPartland, J. (2002). *A parent's guide to Asperger syndrome and high-functioning autism.* New York: Guilford Press.

Ozonoff, S., & Griffith, E. M. (2000). Neuropsychological function and the external validity of Asperger syndrome. In A. Klin, F. Volkmar, & S. Sparrow (Eds.), *Asperger syndrome* (pp. 72–96). New York: Guilford Press.

Paul, R. (2003). Enhancing social communication in high functioning individuals with autistic spectrum disorders. *Child and Adolescent Psychiatric Clinics of North America, 12,* 87–106.

Paul, R., & Sutherland, D. (2003). Asperger syndrome: The role of speech-language pathologists in schools. *Perspectives on Language Learning and Education, 10*(4), 9–15.

Paulson, F., Paulson, P., & Meyer, C. (1991). What makes a portfolio a portfolio? *Educational Leadership, 48*(5), 60–63.

Pennington, B. F., & Ozonoff, S. (1996). Executive functions and developmental psychopathologies. *Journal of Child Psychology and Psychiatry, 37,* 51–87.

Phelps-Terasaki, D., & Phelps-Gunn, T. (1992). *Test of Pragmatic Language (TOPL).* Austin, TX: Pro-Ed.

Pierangelo, R. (2003). *The special educator's book of lists.* San Francisco, CA: Jossey-Bass.

Pizzamiglio, M., Bukowski, W., & Hoza, B. (1997, April). Mutual friendship as a mediator of the association between children's popularity and self-reported feelings of competence. In M. Boivin (Chair), *Individual, group, and dyad: Interactions between levels of complexity in peer system.* Paper presented at the biennial meeting of the Society for Research in Child Development, Washington, D.C.

Powers, M., & Poland, J. (2002). *Asperger syndrome and your child: A parent guide.* New York: Skylight Press.

Prutting, C., & Kirchner, D. (1983). Applied pragmatics. In T. Gallagher and C. Prutting (Eds.), *Pragmatic assessment and intervention issues in language* (pp. 29–64). San Diego, CA: College-Hill.

Pyles, L. (2002). *Hitchhiking through Asperger syndrome.* London, UK: Jessica Kingsley Publisher.

Quill, K. A. (Ed.). (1995). *Teaching children with autism: Strategies to enhance communication and socialization.* Albany, NY: Delmar Publishers.

Ramanowski-Bashe, P., & Kirby, B. (2001). *The oasis guide to Asperger syndrome: Advice, support, insights, and inspiration.* New York: Crown Publishers.

Reisman, J., & Hanschu, B. (1992). *Sensory Integration Inventory—Revised for individuals with developmental disabilities: User's guide.* Hugo, MN: PDP Press.

Rimland, B. (1990). Sound sensitivity in autism. *Autism Research Review International, 4,* 1–6.

Rogers, M. F., & Myles, B. S. ( 2001). Using social stories and comic strip conversations to interpret social situations for an adolescent with Asperger syndrome. *Intervention in School and Clinic, 36*(5), 310–314.

Rogers, S. J., & Pennington, B. R. (1991). A theoretical approach to the deficits in infantile autism. *Development and Psychopathology, 3,* 137–162.

Roid, G. H. (2003). *Stanford-Binet Intelligence Scales (SB5;* 5th ed). Itasca, IL: Riverside Publishing.

Safran, S., Safran, J., & Ellis, K. (2003). Intervention ABCs for children with Asperger syndrome. *Topics in Language Disorders, 23*(2), 154–165.

Samovar, L., & Porter, R. (1991). *Communication between cultures.* Belmont, CA: Wadsworth.

Sanderson, J. A., & Siegel, M. (1995). Loneliness and stable friendship in rejected and nonrejected preschoolers. *Journal of Applied Developmental Psychology, 16,* 555–567.

Schopler, E., Mesibov, G., & Kunce, L. (Eds.). (1998). *Asperger's syndrome or high functioning autism?* New York: Plenum Press.

Schreiber, L., & McKinley, N. (1995). *Daily communication: Strategies for adolescents with language disorders* (2nd ed.). Greenville, SC: Super Duper Publications.

Schwartz, D., Dodge, K., Pettit, G., & Bates, J. (2000). Friendship as moderating factor in the pathway between early harsh home environment and later victimization in the peer group. *Developmental Psychology, 36,* 646–662.

Schwartz, D., McFadyen-Ketchum, S., Dodge, K., Pettit, G., & Bates, J. (1999). Early behavior problems as a predictor of later peer group victimization: Moderators and mediators in the pathways of social risk. *Journal of Abnormal Child Psychology, 27,* 191–201.

Schwartz, L., & McKinley, N. (1987). *Make-it-yourself barrier activities: Barrier activities for speakers and listeners.* Eau Claire, WI: Thinking Publications.

Semel, E., Wiig, E., & Secord, W. (2003). *Clinical Evaluation of Language Fundamentals (CELF–4;* 4th ed). San Antonio, TX: The Psychological Corporation.

Shriberg, L. D., Paul, R., McSweeny, J. L., Klin, A., & Cohen, D. J. (2001). Speech and prosody characteristics of adolescents and adults with high functioning autism and Asperger syndrome. *Journal of Speech, Language, and Hearing Research, 44,* 1097–1115.

Simpson, R. L., & Myles, B. S. (1998). Aggression among children and youth who have Asperger's syndrome: A different population requiring different strategies. *Preventing School Failure, 42*(4), 149–154.

Spector, C. C. (1997). *Saying one thing, meaning another: Activities for clarifying ambiguous language.* Greenville, SC: Super Duper Publications.

Spector, C. C. (2002). *As far as words go: Unraveling the complexities of ambiguous language and humor.* Greenville, SC: Super Duper Publications.

Susman, E. (1996, January). How to tell Asperger's from autism. *Brown University Child and Adolescent Behavior Letter, 12*(7), 1–2.

Swaggart, B. L., Gagnon, E., Bock, S. J., Earles, T. L., Quinn, C., Myles, B. S., & Carlson, R. L. (1998). Using social stories to teach social and behavioral skills to children with autism. *Focus on Autistic Behavior, 10*(1), 1–15.

Tantam, D. (1991). Asperger's syndrome in adulthood. In U. Freith (Ed.), *Autism and Asperger's syndrome* (pp. 147–183). Cambridge: Cambridge University Press.

TEACCH staff. (2005). *Structured teaching.* Retrieved February 4, 2005, from the University of North Carolina, Chapel Hill, TEACCH Center Website: http://www.teacch.com/structur.htm

Super Duper Publications. (2003). *Nickel Takes On Teasing* [Computer software]. Greenville, SC: Author.

Super Duper Publications. (2004a). *Nickel Takes On Anger* [Computer software]. Greenville, SC: Author.

Super Duper Publications. (2004b). Nickel Takes On Stealing [Computer software]. Greenville, SC: Author.

Super Duper Publications. (2005). Nickel Takes On Disrespect [Computer software]. Greenville, SC: Author.

Trehin, P. (n.d.). *Some basic information about TEACCH; Behavior problems management.* Retrieved on February 4, 2005, from the University of North Carolina, Chapel Hill, Website: http://www.autismresources.com/papers/TEACCH.htm

Tsai, L. (2002, July). *From autistic disorder to Asperger disorder.* Paper presented at the annual conference of the Autism Society of America, Indianapolis, IN.

Tsatsahis, K. D., Fuerst, D. R., & Rourke, B. P. (1997). Psychosocial dimensions of learning disabilities: External validation and relationship with age and academic functioning. *Journal of Learning Disabilities, 30,* 490–502.

Twachtman, D. (1995). Methods to enhance communication in verbal children. In K. Quill (Ed.), *Teaching children with autism: Strategies to enhance communication and socialization* (pp. 133–162). New York: Delmar Publishers.

Vygotsky, L. (1962). *Thoughts and language.* Cambridge, MA: MIT Press.

Walker, H., Schwarz, I., Nippold, M., Irvin, L., & Noell, J. (1994) Social skills in school-age children and youth: Issues and best practices in assessment and intervention. *Topics in Language Disorders, 10*(2), 63–80.

Wechsler, D. (2003). *Wechsler Intelligence Scale for Children (WISC–IV;* 4th ed). San Antonio, TX: The Psychological Corporation.

Westby, C., & Clauser, D. (1999). The right stuff for writing: Assessing and facilitating written language. In H. Catts and B. Shulman (Eds.), *Language and reading disabilities* (pp. 259–324). Needham Heights, MA: Allyn and Bacon.

Wiig, E., Larson V. L., & Olson, J. (2004). *S-MAPs: Rubrics for curriculum-based assessment and intervention.* Greenville, SC: : Thinking Publications University.

Wiig, E., & Secord, W. (1995). *Test of Language Competence–Expanded Edition (TLC–E).* San Antonio, TX: The Psychological Corporation.

Wiig, E., & Wilson, C. (2001). *Map it out: Visual tools for thinking, organizing, and communicating.* Greenville, SC: Super Duper Publications.

Wiig, E., & Wilson, C. (2002). *The learning ladder: Assessing and teaching text comprehension.* Greenville, SC: Super Duper Publications.

Willey, L. H. (1999). *Pretending to be normal.* London, UK: Jessica Kingsley Publishers.

Williams, K. (1995). Understanding the student with Asperger syndrome: Guidelines for teachers. *Focus on Autistic Behavior, 10*(2), 9–17.

Wing, L. (1981). Asperger's syndrome: A clinical account. *Psychological Medicine, 11,* 115–119.

Wing, L. (1998). The history of Asperger syndrome. In Schopler, E., Mesibov, G., & Kunce, L. (Eds.), *Asperger's syndrome or high functioning autism?* (pp. 11–28). New York: Plenum Press.

Wing, L., & Potter, P. (2002). The epidemiology of autistic spectrum disorders: Is the prevalence rising? *Mental Retardation and Developmental Disabilities Research Review, 8,* 151–161.

Winner, M. (2000). *Inside out: What makes a person with social cognitive deficits tick?* San Jose, CA: Author.

Winner, M. (2002). *Thinking about you: Thinking about me.* San Jose, CA: Author.

Winter, M. (2003). *Asperger syndrome: What teachers need to know.* London, UK: Jessica Kingsley Publishers.

Woodcock, R. W., McGrew, K. S., & Mather, N. (2001). *Woodcock-Johnson Tests of Cognitive Ability (WJ–III).* Itasca, IL: Riverside Publishing.

World Health Organization. (1993). *The ICD–10 classification of mental and behavioural disorders: Diagnostic criteria for research.* Geneva, Switzerland: Author.

Zachman, L., Barrett, M., Huisingh, R., Orman, J., & Blagden, C. (1991). *Test of Problem Solving–Adolescent (TOPS–Adolescent).* East Moline, IL: LinguiSystems.